The Anglo-Norman Gospel Harmony

A translation of the *Estoire de l'Evangile*
(Dublin, Christ Church Cathedral C6.1.1, Liber niger)

by
Brent A. Pitts

FRETS Series Editors
Thelma Fenster and
Jocelyn Wogan-Browne

ARIZONA CENTER FOR MEDIEVAL
ACMRS
AND RENAISSANCE STUDIES

Tempe, Arizona
2014

Published with the assistance of Fordham University.

THE ARIZONA CENTER FOR
MEDIEVAL &
RENAISSANCE
STUDIES

Published by ACMRS (Arizona Center for Medieval and Renaissance Studies)
Tempe, Arizona
© 2014 Arizona Board of Regents for Arizona State University.
All Rights Reserved.

Library of Congress Cataloging-in-Publication Data

[Estoire de l'evangile. English]
The Anglo-Norman gospel harmony : a translation of the Estoire de L'evangile (Dublin, Christ Church Cathedral c6.1.1, Liber niger) / by Brent A. Pitts.
   pages cm. -- (Medieval and Renaissance Texts and Studies ; Volume 453) (The French of England Translation Series (FRETS) ; Volume 6)
  Includes bibliographical references.
  ISBN 978-0-86698-504-8 (alk. paper)
  1. Bible. Gospels--Harmonies, Anglo-Norman. 2. Anglo-Norman dialect--Texts. 3. Anglo-Norman literature--Translations into English. I. Pitts, Brent A., 1950-
   PC2948.E78 2013
   226'.1--dc23

2013044781

Front Cover:
Christ on the Road to Emmaus. British Library, Yates Thompson 13, f. 127v. The caption below in French states that Christ appeared to 'the pilgrims'.
Image is in the public domain. Visit www.bl.uk for this and other illuminated manuscripts.

∞
This book is made to last. It is set in Adobe Caslon Pro,
smyth-sewn and printed on acid-free paper to library specifications.
Printed in the United States of America

The Anglo-Norman Gospel Harmony

A translation of the *Estoire de l'Evangile*
(Dublin, Christ Church Cathedral C6.1.1, Liber niger)

MEDIEVAL AND RENAISSANCE
TEXTS AND STUDIES

VOLUME 453

───────

THE FRENCH OF ENGLAND TRANSLATION SERIES
(FRETS)

VOLUME 7

Table of Contents

Series Editors' Preface — vii
Acknowledgments — ix
List of Abbreviations — xi

Introduction — 1
   1. Title — 2
   2. Interest and Significance — 2
   3. Author and Date — 7
   4. The *Estoire* and Clement of Llanthony's *Concordia quatuor evangelistarum* — 12
   5. The *Estoire* and the Pepysian Gospel Harmony — 14
   6. Manuscript — 18
   7. Audience — 21
   8. Style and Esthetic Considerations — 29

Suggested Further Reading — 41

Translator's Note — 45

The Anglo-Norman Gospel Harmony
   Text — 47
   Notes to the Translation — 139

Appendices
   Biblical Sources of Chapters — 142
   Extracts of Original Text — 144

List of Proper Names — 151

Series Editors' Preface

We are delighted to present as FRETS 7 a translation of the Anglo-Norman gospel harmony by its modern editor, Professor Brent Pitts.

L'Estoire de l'Évangile (literally, "the story of the Gospel") is not a history of the making of the Gospels, but "the Gospel story", in the form of a (perhaps mid-thirteenth century) prose collation and blending of the four Gospel narratives in the French of England. The making of Gospel harmonies has always been an important tradition in the history of Christianity, and this Anglo-Norman version is significant in a number of ways. Shaped as a set of seven meditations on the Life of Christ, it is also of importance in the continuing discussion of medieval laypeoples' access to the scriptures and particularly to the Bible.

In scholarship on the religious and cultural history of medieval England, the biblical translations and theories of the Wycliffites and their opponents in the late fourteenth and fifteenth centuries have garnered most modern attention. But the *Estoire* and other texts witness to a rich tradition of biblical translation and adaptation in the French of England from the twelfth to the fifteenth centuries, in which the politics of translation occupy varying and changing positions, and deserve further exploration than they have yet had. As well as its thirteenth-century significance, the Anglo-Norman Gospel Harmony feeds directly into later medieval biblical translation: Professor Pitts shows that *L'Estoire* is the long suspected but previously unknown French source of the medieval English Pepysian gospel harmony.

Professor Pitts's edition of *L'Estoire de L'Évangile* is published as Medium Ævum Monographs 28 (Oxford: Society for the Study of Medieval Languages and Literature, 2011), and we thank the Society for permission to re-use some of the introductory material from this edition. The FRETS series aims to increase awareness of the extraordinarily rich tradition of French writing in medieval England. Since Gospel Harmonies are of interest to many diverse readerships, we hope Professor Pitts's authoritative translation and illuminating biblical scholarship will both provide new access to this vernacular medieval version for a wide audience and stimulate further interest in French vernacular biblical translation among students and scholars of medieval culture in England and its neighbours.

Thelma Fenster
Jocelyn Wogan-Browne

Acknowledgments

This work is a translation of the Anglo-Norman gospel harmony in the published critical edition of the *Estoire de l'Evangile* (Medium Ævum Monographs, 2011). To study the gospel harmony in Anglo-Norman, then to make it available in modern English, has been a rich and incomparably rewarding experience.

I am indebted to the Meredith College School of Arts and Humanities, and to its dean, first for purchase of a microfilm reproduction of the Liber niger, and later for travel to Dublin to examine that book. Meredith College also defrayed some of my expenses for travel, at Thanksgiving 2010, to places named in the *Estoire*. Dianne Andrews of Carlyle Campbell Library cheerfully and promptly secured many works by interlibrary loan, and Robin Baneth of Technology Services found creative solutions for word-processing problems. I am fortunate to work in a department where research and writing are considered the inseparable companions of good teaching. My research was also advanced by the rich resources of the Walter Royal Davis Library at the University of North Carolina-Chapel Hill and the helpful library staff. The D. H. Hill Library at North Carolina State University very often also had just the book or article required. Nowadays it is often possible to find reliable digital copies of scholarly works online. Several of the bibliographical references in this volume therefore include not only the traditional details of the print publications but also the location of their corresponding online version.

I am grateful to the staff of the Representative Church Body Library, Braemor Park, Churchtown, Dublin, particularly Dr. Raymond Refaussé and Dr. Susan Hood, for their encouragement and especially for making the Liber niger and a new microfilm of same available for consultation. I am thankful also for the kindness of the library staff both during my visit there in December 2005 and in more recent correspondence.

I thank the series editors, Thelma Fenster and Jocelyn Wogan-Browne, for selecting this work for publication in the French of England Translation Series (FRETS). The editorial board of Medium Ævum Monographs had previously offered many helpful suggestions for the improvement of the critical edition of the *Estoire*. Since that publication, I have adapted the Introduction and the Notes to this new setting, preserving much of the substance of the original but also incorporating pertinent new material. I have also taken the opportunity to rectify a few errors in the critical edition; each of the corrections is noted in the

proper place here. All aspects of this volume reflect my continued study of insular gospel harmonies.

During my work on this project I consulted several specialists of medieval languages and literature. I take every opportunity to express my sincere gratitude to the late Ruth J. Dean and to Maureen B. M. Boulton (Notre Dame) for their *Anglo-Norman Literature: A Guide to Texts and Manuscripts*, and want to repeat my thanks here, for without their treasure map I would never have found the *Estoire*. Daron Burrows (Oxford) very helpfully identified an allusion in the prologue of the *Estoire* and responded quickly to questions about AN language. By translating into modern English both the short passages and the longer excerpts from the Pepysian Gospel Harmony, Shearle Furnish (Youngstown State University) has opened yet another grand vista for readers of this work. I am very grateful for his collaboration. Lutz Kube helped with some of the works in German. My medievalist colleague Eloise Grathwohl (Meredith) generously read a late draft of this book and made suggestions for improvement. My Meredith colleague Margarita Suarez helped with some of the descriptions of Hebrew names and observances. I thank these scholars, as well as the anonymous readers for FRETS, for their kind and expert interest in this work. My father, Jesse E. Pitts, who has studied the New Testament since childhood, also read drafts of the translation and offered helpful comments. Any mistakes that may remain in this work are mine alone.

I dedicate this work to my granddaughter, Rhiannon Elizabeth Bell.

Brent A. Pitts, Raleigh, 2012

List of Abbreviations

AN	Anglo-Norman
AND	*Anglo-Norman Dictionary*, ed. Louise W. Stone, William Rothwell, T. B. W. Reid et al. London: Modern Humanities Research Association, 1977-1992.
ANOH	*Anglo-Norman Dictionary*, electronic version, Anglo-Norman On-Line Hub. Aberystwyth University and Swansea University, www.anglo-norman.net/
ANTS	Anglo-Norman Text Society
CCCM	Corpus Christianorum, Continuatio Mediaeualis
Chap.	Chapter
CQE	*Concordia quatuor evangelistarum*, Clement of Llanthony's gospel harmony
Dean	Ruth J. Dean with Maureen B. M. Boulton, *Anglo-Norman Literature: A Guide to Texts and Manuscripts*. ANTS Occasional Publications 3. London: ANTS, 1999.
EETS	Early English Text Society
Estoire	*Estoire de l'Evangile*, ed. Brent A. Pitts. Medium Ævum Monographs 28. Oxford: Society for the Study of Medieval Languages and Literature, 2011.
Goates	*The Pepysian Gospel Harmony*, ed. Margery Goates. EETS o.s. 157. London: H. Milford; Oxford University Press, 1922. www.bookprep.com/read/mdp.39015014775491
Gosman	*La Lettre du Prêtre Jean: les versions en ancien français et en ancien occitan*, ed. Martin Gosman. Groningen: Bouma, 1982.
Gwynn	Aubrey Gwynn, "Some Unpublished Texts from the Black Book of Christ Church, Dublin." *Analecta Biblica* 16 (1946): 281–337.
Hist.evang.	*Historia evangelica*. In Peter Comestor, *Historia scholastica*, PL198.1537–1644. Paris, 1855. www.archive.org
KJV	The Holy Bible, King James Version, www.biblegateway.com
Liber niger	Dublin, Christ Church Cathedral C6.1.1 [Dean §483], source manuscript of the *Estoire* (fols. 34r-63r)
ME	Middle English
MRTS	Medieval and Renaissance Texts and Studies

NIV . . . . . The Holy Bible, New International Version—UK, www.biblegateway.com
NRSV . . . . The Holy Bible, New Revised Standard Version (Grand Rapids: Zondervan, 1989).
Ó Clabaigh . Colmán Ó Clabaigh, "The *Liber niger* of Christ Church Cathedral, Dublin." In *The Medieval Manuscripts of Christ Church Cathedral, Dublin*, ed. Raymond Gillespie and Raymond Refaussé, 60–80. Dublin: Four Courts Press, 2006.
o.s. . . . . . Original series
P . . . . . . Prologue to the *Estoire*
PGH. . . . . Pepysian Gospel Harmony (Cambridge, Magdalene College, MS Pepys 2498)
PL . . . . . . *Patrologiae cursus completus, Series latina*, ed. J.-P. Migne. Paris: Garnier, 1844–1865. www.archive.org
Recognitions . *Recognitions of Clement*, trans. Thomas Smith. In *The Ante-Nicene Fathers*, vol. 8: *Fathers of the Third and Fourth Century*, ed. Alexander Roberts et al., 75–214. New York: Scribners, 1903. http://www.archive.org/details/antenicenefather08robe
Roy. . . . . . BL Royal MS 3.A.x, Clement of Llanthony, *Concordia quatuor evangelistarum*, fols. 2r-20v
V. . . . . . . Vulgate. The principal modern edition consulted is *Biblia Sacra iuxta vulgatam versionem*, ed. R. Gryson, R. Weber et al., 5th ed. (Stuttgart: Deutsche Bibelgesellschaft, 2007), but certain passages have been checked against texts at www.latinvulgate.com.

Introduction

The *Estoire de l'Evangile*, the only known gospel harmony in the French of England, is testimony to medieval England's heightened interest, especially during the late twelfth and thirteenth centuries, in the life, the works, and the Passion of Jesus Christ. As mosaics of the New Testament Gospels of Matthew, Mark, Luke, and John, gospel harmonies competed with the canonical gospels for the attention of medieval Christians. Medieval Latin and vernacular gospel harmonies are sometimes called diatessarons, or lives of Christ in blended, four-in-one format. The harmonist typically removes repetitions, smooths contradictions, and recasts shared episodes, so that a harmony's retelling of a given episode is usually richer and more detailed than any single Evangelist's account. The reader may therefore, in principle, encounter the four, separate canonical gospels in their fullness by moving through the harmony's unified and seamless, chronologically ordered account of Christ's earthly life and ministry, from the Nativity to the Ascension.

In this tradition, the *Estoire de l'Evangile* requires attention and study not only as the sole AN witness to a popular form of medieval biblical text but also as a work whose occasional, curious readings seem to recall much earlier harmonies. While as a rule the *Estoire* is a faithful rendering of the four canonical gospels, the author occasionally departs momentarily from the gospel record to heighten the drama of a scene or to acknowledge discreetly that the work's audience was not restricted to men. The *Estoire* survives in a single manuscript, Dublin, Christ Church Cathedral C6.1.1, Liber niger. This life of Christ recently received its first critical edition,[1] and it is here presented in its first modern English translation. Internal evidence establishes only a broad date of composition, between ca. 1170 and 1294, although it may be possible to place the *Estoire* more specifically in the mid-thirteenth century. The *Estoire*'s single-manuscript status does not mean that the work lacked influence in its day: there is good evidence that the *Estoire de l'Evangile* is the long-sought exemplar of the Pepysian Gospel Harmony (ca. 1400). These texts are compared extensively below (pages 14–18).

---

[1] *Estoire de l'Evangile*, ed. Brent A. Pitts, Medium Ævum Monographs 28 (Oxford: Society for the Study of Medieval Languages and Literature, 2011).

1. Title

The prologue of the *Estoire* refers to the work four times (Liber niger, fol. 34r), first as "the Gospel story of our sweet Lord Jesus Christ" ("[L']estorie des Evangeiles nostre douz Seignur Jhesu Crist"), but abbreviated thereafter as "the Gospel story" ("l'estoire de l'Evangile").[2] To permit ready identification of this distinctive text, the title *Anglo-Norman Gospel Harmony* has been adopted for the present translation. "The *Estoire*" refers to the thirteenth-century AN gospel harmony throughout this work.

2. Interest and Significance

The preponderance of Latin harmony manuscripts are of the end of the twelfth or of the thirteenth century, a period corresponding, as we know, to a great revival of teaching and preaching the Gospels.[3] Some of these harmonies

---

[2] The word *estoire* may be translated "story" or "account" (*ANOH*). See the discussion of *estoire*, including the word's use in medieval chronicles, romances, and epics, in *The History of Saint Edward the King by Matthew Paris*, trans. Thelma S. Fenster and Jocelyn Wogan-Browne, FRETS 1 (Tempe: Arizona Center for Medieval and Renaissance Studies, 2008), 1–3. AN *diatessaron* does not appear in the *Estoire*, although it occurs twice in French, in its musical sense, "the interval of a fourth" (*ANOH*), before 1250. See Glynn Hesketh, "Lexical Innovation in the *Lumere as Lais*," in *De mot en mot: Aspects of Medieval Linguistics*, ed. Stewart Gregory and D. A. Trotter (Cardiff: University of Wales Press, 1997), 53–79, at 59 and n. 13. Unrelated to the *Estoire* is a ME life of Christ called *La estorie del Euangelie* (incipit "Sum-while ich was wiþ sunne i-bounde / And sunne me hath icast to grounde," "Once I was bound to sin / And sin has cast me to the ground [or brought me low]"). According to Celia Millward, ed., *La Estorie del Evangelie*, ME Texts 30 (Heidelberg: C. Winter, 1998), the work "was probably composed in Norfolk in the late thirteenth century" (11). See also James H. Morey, *Book and Verse: A Guide to Middle English Biblical Literature* (Urbana: University of Illinois Press, 2000), 205–8; Carl Horstmann, ed., *The Minor Poems of the Vernon MS*, Part I, EETS o.s. 98 (London: K. Paul, Trench, Trübner, 1892; repr. Millwood, NY: Kraus, 1987), 1–11; Gertrude H. Campbell, "The ME *Evangelie*," *PMLA* 30 (1915): 529–613; Carleton Brown, *A Register of Middle English Religious and Didactic Verse*, vol. 1 (Oxford: Oxford University Press, 1916), §§3938, 30236; vol. 2 (Oxford: Oxford University Press, 1920), §2063; and Thorlac Turville-Petre, "The Relationship of the Vernon and Clopton Manuscripts," in *Studies in the Vernon Manuscript*, ed. Derek Pearsall (Cambridge: Brewer, 1990), 29–44. See also page 24 below for "L'estorie des Evangeiles . . . rimez en romaunz," and footnote 101 below for "j romance book is called ye gospelles" ("One vernacular book is called the gospels"). In the present volume, all quotations of AN text from the *Estoire* refer to the published critical edition, using line numbers from that work.

[3] Daniel Plooij, *A Primitive Text of the Diatessaron: The Liège Manuscript of a Medieval Dutch Translation* (Leiden: A. W. Sijthoff, 1923; www.archive.org), 65–66.

incorporated a commentary on the Gospels, others not. Twelfth-century Europe produced at least seven Latin gospel harmonies, including *De canonibus evangeliorum* of Odo of Cambrai (d. 1113); *In vol. IV evangelistarum commentariorum liber unus* of Rupert of Deutz (d. ca. 1130); and *De concordia et expositione quatuor evangeliorum* of Wazelin II (ca. 1150-ca. 1157).[4] To these we may add the harmonies most commonly found in English libraries, the *In unum ex quatuor* of Zachary of Besançon, and the *Concordia quatuor evangelistarum* (*CQE*) of Clement of Llanthony (d. after 1169);[5] and two more from the university milieu, *Historia evangelica* of Peter Comestor (d. 1178) and *Glossae super Unum ex quattuor* of Peter Cantor (d. 1197).[6]

---

[4] I follow Hubert Silvestre, "Le 'De concordia et expositione quatuor evangeliorum' inédit de Wazelin II, abbé de Saint-Laurent, à Liège (ca 1150-ca 1157)," *Revue bénédictine* 63 (1953): 310–25, at 314.

[5] Clement's work is also known as *Unum ex quatuor* or — in its ME translation — as *Oon of Foure*. See Morey, *Book and Verse*, 333–34. Cherish Ahlgren (Institute for Textual Scholarship and Electronic Editing, University of Birmingham) is preparing the first critical edition of *CQE*: "The Latin Gospel harmony of Clement of Llanthony" is based on Oxford Bodleian MS Hatton 61 (email correspondence, 13 November 2010). For J. Rendel Harris, Clement's is "the original text upon which Wiclif worked" ("Some Notes on the Gospel Harmony of Zacharias Chrysopolitanus," *Journal of Biblical Literature* 43 [1924]: 32–45, at 39). Elsewhere, in his introductory note to Plooij, *A Primitive Text of the Diatessaron*, 3, Harris calls attention to a colophon in a British Library manuscript of a Wycliffite harmony: "Here ends one of four, a book of all four gospel writers gathered concisely into a story by Clement of Llanthony" ("Here endith oon of foure that is a booke of alle foure gospeleris gadered shortli into a storye by Clement of lantony").

[6] Silvestre, "Le 'De concordia'," 314, calls this last work *Concorde des évangiles*. I do not find this gospel harmony, in Latin or otherwise, among Peter Cantor's known works, but Stegmüller lists twenty manuscripts of a *Glossae super Unum ex quattuor* by him. See Friedrich Stegmüller, *Repertorium biblicum medii aevi*, vol. 4: *Commentaria* (Madrid: Consejo Superior de Investigaciones Cientificas, Instituto Francisco Suarez, 1954), 267–69, nos. 6504–6507. Ulrich B. Schmid, "In Search of Tatian's Diatessaron in the West," *Vigiliae Christianae* 57 (2003): 176–99, at 186, reports "at least 25 manuscripts" of Cantor's commentary. Beryl Smalley, "Some Gospel Commentaries of the Early Twelfth Century," *Recherches de Théologie ancienne et médiévale* 45 (1978): 147–80, outlines a new emphasis on the gospels in the schools, first at Laon and later in Paris, in the twelfth and thirteenth centuries. She dates Cantor's gloss 1187–1197 (153). As for Comestor, see Dean's comments on *Hist.evang.* (§483), which effectively rule out this work as a source of the *Estoire*; as Dean indicates, Comestor's work is more commentary than harmony. Ulrich Schmid's essay, "'. . . So that those who read the (Biblical) text and the commentary do not correct one after the other'," in *Paratext and Megatext as Channels of Jewish and Christian Traditions*, ed. A. A. den Hollander, idem, and W. F. Smelik (Leiden and Boston: Brill, 2003), 136–51, focuses on the gospel commentaries by Peter Cantor and Zachary of Besançon.

The tradition of the gospel harmony dates to the early years of the Christian church.[7] Appearing in the second century, Tatian's Diatessaron became the standard gospel harmony text. Several early authors, including Eusebius and Epiphanius in the fourth century, mention the Diatessaron and attribute it to Tatian. The work apparently continued to be read in Christian circles despite charges of Tatian's heretical tendencies by Iraeneus and other church fathers.[8] By the fifth century, reverential use of the Diatessaron was so widespread in Syriac-speaking churches that Bishop Theodoret of Cyrrhus confiscated more than two hundred copies of the work, replacing them with the four separate gospels.[9] Such efforts seem to have effectively suppressed Tatian's Diatessaron. Because no copy of it survives in the original, scholars have long sought patiently to detect fingerprints of the lost work in the early and later medieval harmonies that we possess.[10]

The popularity of the fourfold life of Christ persisted long after Tatian. The oldest witness to the Diatessaron in the West is a Latin manuscript called the Codex Fuldensis.[11] Bishop Victor of Capua commissioned the copy, which he approved in 547. In his preface to the Codex Fuldensis, Victor points to Tatian as the author of the original text,[12] and modern scholars generally endorse the claim that the gospel harmony of the Codex Fuldensis is indeed based on the

---

[7] Stephen J. Patterson, "Gospel Parallels and Harmonies," in *Encyclopedia of Christianity*, vol. 4, ed. Erwin Fahlbusch et al., trans. Geoffrey W. Bromiley (Grand Rapids: W. B. Eerdmans; Leiden: Brill, 2005), 39–42, reviews key harmonies and harmonists from earliest to modern times. For Diatessaronic scholarship since the 1800s, see the helpful account by Ulrich B. Schmid, *Unum ex quattuor: Eine Geschichte der lateinischen Tatianüberlieferung* (Freiburg im Breisgau: Herder, 2005), and the full and useful survey by William L. Petersen, *Tatian's Diatessaron: Its Creation, Dissemination, Significance, and History in Scholarship* (Leiden and New York: Brill, 1994). For further insights, see Etienne Trocmé, *The Passion as Liturgy: A Study in the Origin of the Passion Narratives in the Four Gospels* (London: SCM Press, 1983), esp. chaps. 9 and 10.

[8] See Petersen, *Tatian's Diatessaron*, 76–79.

[9] I follow Schmid, "In Search of Tatian's Diatessaron in the West," 176. For Theodoret's report, see Petersen, *Tatian's Diatessaron*, 41–42.

[10] A scrap of Greek text discovered in 1933 at Dura-Europos was at first believed to be a fragment of Tatian's Diatessaron, but recent scholarship terms the text "non-Tatianic." See Carl H. Kraeling, *A Greek Fragment of Tatian's Diatessaron from Dura*, Studies and Documents 3 (London: Christophers, 1935; www.archive.org); and D. C. Parker, D. G. K. Taylor, and M. S. Goodacre, "The Dura-Europos Gospel Harmony," in *Studies in the Early Text of the Gospels and Acts*, ed. D. G. K. Taylor, SBL Text-Critical Studies 1 (Birmingham: University of Birmingham Press, 1999), 192–228. In a survey of Diatessaronic discoveries since the nineteenth century, Christopher de Hamel, *The Book: A History of the Bible* (London and New York: Phaidon, 2001), 305–7, conveys the importance of Tatian's work for modern New Testament studies.

[11] Fulda, Hessische Landesbibliothek, MS Bonifatius 1. In this paragraph, I follow Petersen, *Tatian's Diatessaron*, 35, 39, 45, 85–86.

[12] For Victor of Capua's preface, see Petersen, *Tatian's Diatessaron*, 45–46.

lost Diatessaron of Tatian.[13] Some believe that the Codex Fuldensis directly influenced several works of the early or central Middle Ages, including the well-known *In unum ex quatuor* by Zachary of Besançon (=Chrysopolitanus, d. ca. 1155?).[14] Moreover, some scholars postulate an "Old Latin version" of Tatian's harmony, one that is earlier even than the Codex Fuldensis and which, in their view, shaped both that copy and several gospel harmonies in medieval vernaculars.[15] In an attempt to reconstruct the lost Diatessaron of Tatian, scholars have therefore sought to discern, through textual analysis, the extent to which "national harmonies"—in departures from the standard text of the Vulgate—share significant agreements either with the sixth-century Codex Fuldensis or with the presumed, earlier "Old Latin" version.[16]

In its account of Christ's ministry, the *Estoire* offers "his life and his teachings, his miracles, his Passion, his Resurrection and his Ascension."[17] Elizabeth Salter establishes five types of medieval English lives of Christ depending on their inclusion of material, whether didactic, homiletic, meditative or lyrical—or some combination of these—that is extraneous to the Gospel narrative proper.[18] As examples of the first type, "Lives consisting of Biblical material only, with little or no homiletic additions," she lists the English translation of Clement

---

[13] Or, in Schmid's words, "Today this judgment is unchallenged in the sense that the harmony extant in Victor's manuscript is understood to derive, ultimately, from Tatian's Diatessaron" (Schmid, "In Search of Tatian's Diatessaron in the West," 177).

[14] Zachary "is representative of the movement, which arose in the twelfth and thirteenth centuries, for the popularisation of Biblical study in general, and of the life of Christ in particular" (Harris, "Some Notes," 40). Earlier works include the Old High German Tatian of the Codex Sangallensis (ca. 830), the Old Saxon *Heliand* (822–840), and Otfrid's *Krist* (ninth c.). See Schmid, *Unum ex quattuor*, 5–6; the dates shown generally follow Petersen.

[15] Schmid, *Unum ex quattuor*, 6.

[16] For a description of this method of reconstruction, see Schmid, *Unum ex quattuor*, 10. Versions in Western vernaculars include—in addition to AN (the *Estoire*) and ME (the Pepysian Gospel Harmony)—harmonies in Old High German, Old Saxon, Middle High German, Middle Italian, and Middle Dutch. See Petersen, *Tatian's Diatessaron*, 463–89. See also Schmid's comments on this "classical" method of reconstruction and his objections to it (Schmid, *Unum ex quattuor*, 27–28). Taking a cue from Schmid, our aim has been to give adequate attention to the search for an "old stratum of Diatessaron readings" ("eines alten Stratums von Diatessaronlesarten") in the *Estoire*, but to focus especially on the contextualization of the *Estoire* as a genuine source, again in Schmid's words, for the exploration of medieval literature or spirituality (Schmid, *Unum ex quattuor*, 10).

[17] P:22–23; "sa vie e sa doctrine, ses miracles, sa Passion, sa Resurection e sa Assencion" (*Estoire*, P:20–21).

[18] Elizabeth Salter, *Nicholas Love's "Myrrour of the Blessed Lyf of Jesu Christ,"* Analecta Cartusiana 10 (Salzburg: Institut für Englische Sprache und Literatur, 1974), 55–56, 114.

of Llanthony's *Concordia quatuor evangelistarum* and the Pepysian Gospel Harmony, about which more later. The *Estoire*, whose author proposes to hew to the letter of the Gospels, "according to the unadorned meaning and the intent of the words,"[19] i.e., without commentary or elaboration of any kind, clearly also is of the first type. In his survey of medieval artistic representations of the Passion, James H. Marrow notes the intensive quest, from the thirteenth to the sixteenth century, "to expand the meager accounts of the four Evangelists, to fill in details of how all these events transpired, to elaborate on the brutality of Christ's torments and the savagery of his tormenters, and indeed to describe actions and events nowhere mentioned in the Gospels."[20] The *Estoire* conservatively shuns such sensational accretions, whether in the Passion section or elsewhere.

Interest in gospel harmonies was sustained into England's Caroline Age and beyond. Christopher de Hamel's survey of the English and American Bible industry tells of the large, illustrated gospel harmony albums produced by Nicholas Ferrar (1592–1637), his family, and members of his religious commune at Little Gidding, in Huntingdonshire.[21] Hand-made with scissors and paste, the albums aroused much curiosity in their day. As many as fifteen Ferrar Bibles survive, among them the de luxe copy presented in 1635 to Charles I, a "splendid volume [with] gilding, coloured inks, abundant illustrations and a handsome binding."[22]

Even in the twenty-first century, we are reminded from time to time of gospel harmonies and their role. The so-called Jefferson Bible, compiled about 1820 by that U.S. president and still noted occasionally in major newspapers, may be the gospel harmony most familiar to modern speakers of English.[23] In today's churches, gospel harmonies often form the basis of Easter cantatas, classes in catechism, and children's Nativity plays. They sometimes also provide the narrative canvas of so-called Jesus films, including Mel Gibson's controversial *The Passion*

---

[19] P:11; "sulunk la sentence e la simple entente de la lettre" (*Estoire*, P:9–10).

[20] James H. Marrow, "Inventing the Passion in the Late Middle Ages," in *The Passion Story: From Visual Representation to Social Drama*, ed. Marcia Kupfer (University Park: Pennsylvania State University Press, 2008), 23–52, at 24.

[21] This sentence and the next follow de Hamel, *The Book*, 250–51, who states, "The Harmonies were made by cutting up printed Bibles into separate verses which were then pasted together to form single consecutive narratives of the Gospel stories, illustrated throughout with cut-out engravings and prints."

[22] Joyce Ransome, "Monotessaron: The Harmonies of Little Gidding," *The Seventeenth Century* 20 (2005): 22–52, at 31.

[23] See, e.g., Louis Sahagun, "A Founding Father's View of God," *Los Angeles Times* (5 July 2008), articles.latimes.com; Jacqueline Trescott, "Smithsonian Undertakes $225,000 Effort to Restore the Jefferson Bible," *Washington Post* (11 March 2011), www.washingtonpost.com; or even Philippe Mora, "Alien Probes Cost a Bundle but Faith is Free," *The [Sydney] Sun Herald* (25 April 2010), www.smh.com.au. Thomas Jefferson's *The Life and Morals of Jesus of Nazareth* may be consulted at etext.lib.virginia.edu.

of the Christ, released during Lent 2004.[24] In making their case, critics like Ched Myers who fault Gibson for perceived liberties taken with the gospel text also sometimes overlook the prolonged success of medieval gospel harmonies. Myers states, "Attempts to 'harmonize' what are four very different versions of the Jesus story have long been discredited because they give the editor such wide license to pick and choose. This effectively creates a 'fifth' Gospel—or in Gibson's case, anti-gospel."[25]

3. Author and Date

Like the *Estoire*'s immediate source, the author of the AN gospel harmony is unknown. Given the work's subject matter, and considering the primacy, for followers of St. Francis, of meditation on the Passion of Christ, it is tempting to speculate that the author was a Franciscan, but this is by no means assured. The harmonist deeply comprehends the Gospels, rendering their substance forcefully, faithfully, and often with admirable dramatic skill. To take only two examples, it is difficult to imagine a more poignant account of "Magdalene at the tomb" (chap. 103) or a more suspenseful retelling of "The road to Emmaus" (108). Although the precise date of the *Estoire* also is uncertain, it is possible to bracket the work using internal and external evidence.

The *Estoire*'s prologue begins, "I find the Gospel story of our sweet Lord Jesus Christ in various French poem-texts."[26] Calling the work a "summary" ("une breve remenbraunce," P:4) of the gospels, the author inserts a catena of allusions to four other works of a religious nature: Clement of Llanthony's *CQE* (P:4–8, 12–13),[27] Aelred of Rievaulx's *De institutione inclusarum* (P:15–16), and a passage in *Recognitiones Clementis*, a "theological novel" attributed to Clement of

---

[24] Mark Goodacre, "The Power of *The Passion*," in *Jesus and Mel Gibson's The Passion of the Christ*, ed. Kathleen E. Corley and Robert L. Webb (London: Continuum, 2004), 28–44, devotes a section (29–34) to the harmonizing tendencies of some Jesus films, including Gibson's. Meanwhile, Andrew Weeks, "Between God and Gibson: German Mystical and Romantic Sources of *The Passion of the Christ*," *German Quarterly* 78 (2005): 421–40, documents Gibson's reliance less on the Gospels than on Emmerich-Brentano's nineteenth-century *Das bittere Leiden unsers Herrn Jesu Christi*.
[25] Goodacre, "The Power of *The Passion*," 30.
[26] P:2; "L'estorie des Evangeiles nostre douz Seignur Jhesu Crist treof jeo diversement rimez en romaunz" (*Estoire*, P:1–2).
[27] All discussion of *CQE* is based on BL Royal MS 3.A.x, fols. 2r-20v, which Richard Sharpe, *A Handlist of the Latin Writers of Great Britain and Ireland Before 1540* (Turnhout: Brepols, 1997), 87, lists among the fourteen Latin manuscripts of Clement's gospel harmony.

Rome (P:16–19).[28] Paraphrasing St. Bernard, finally, and perhaps in the spirit of a renewed interest in the New Testament's first four books, the *Estoire*'s author recommends the study of the Gospels to those who would truly know Christ (P:19–21). As shown below, a strikingly similar passage is found in a sermon by the Franciscan Thomas of Hales. The prologue concludes with a brief outline of the *Estoire*'s contents (P:22–24).

The harmonist's allusions to works by Aelred of Rievaulx and Clement of Llanthony provide guidance in dating the *Estoire*. In addition, the text shared by the *Estoire* and Thomas of Hales's sermon strongly indicates a direct connection between these works.

Aelred of Rievaulx's *De institutione inclusarum* "was probably written between about 1160 and 1162."[29] The specific dates of Clement's birth and death are unknown, as is Clement's life before his installation as the fifth prior of Llanthony.[30] Clement's priorship must have extended from ca. 1150, the date of the resignation of Llanthony's fourth prior, William of Wycombe, to a time before ca. 1174, by which year Roger of Norwich had been installed as Clement's successor.[31] The author of the *Estoire* disconcertingly identifies Clement of Llanthony as archbishop of Canterbury immediately after Becket (d. 1170).[32] Despite

---

[28] This Clement was the fourth pope according to Christian tradition. See *Recognitions of Clement*, trans. Thomas Smith, in *The Ante-Nicene Fathers*, vol. 8: *Fathers of the Third and Fourth Century*, ed. Alexander Roberts et al. (New York, 1903; www.archive.org/details/antenicenefather08robe), 75–214, at 97; and *Die Pseudoklementinen*, vol. 2: *Rekognitionen in Rufins Übersetzung*, ed. Bernhard Rehm (Berlin: Akademie-Verlag, 1965). I am grateful to Daron Burrows (Oxford) for identifying this source (email correspondence, 24 February 2009).

[29] *Aelred of Rievaulx's De institutione inclusarum: Two English Versions*, ed. John Ayto and Alexandra Barratt, EETS 287 (London; New York: Oxford University Press, 1984), xii. See also Aelred of Rievaulx, *De institutione inclusarum*, in *Aelredi Rievallensis Opera Omnia*, ed. A. Hoste and C. H. Talbot, CCCM 1 (Turnhout: Brepols, 1971), 637–82. Aelred (d. 1167), who was an early follower of St. Bernard, was often compared to him.

[30] Numerous contemporary chronicles and charters tell the turbulent story of Llanthony priory, occasionally also offering glimpses of Clement's life and influence. The fullest modern accounts are George Roberts, *Some Account of Llanthony Priory, Monmouthshire* (London: W. Pickering, 1847); and E. W. Lovegrove, "Llanthony Priory," *Archæologia Cambrensis* 97 (1943): 213–29; 99 (1947): 64–77. Also useful are F. G. Cowley, *The Monastic Order in South Wales 1066–1349* (Cardiff: University of Wales Press, 1977), and J. C. Dickinson, *The Origins of the Austin Canons and their Introduction into England* (London: S. P. C. K., 1950). J. Rendel Harris, "The Gospel Harmony of Clement of Llanthony," *Journal of Biblical Literature* 43 (1924): 349–62, describes the medieval harmonist's method.

[31] Petersen places Clement of Llanthony's death ca. 1190 (*Tatian's Diatessaron*, 147). By several accounts, this date is a generation too late.

[32] The passage in question reads, "Clement—the prior of Llanthony who became archbishop of Canterbury immediately after Saint Thomas the martyr" (P:5–7; "Clem-

the error, the statement at issue would surely not have been set down before the martyr's death. Is it reasonable to infer from this blunder that by the time the prologue was written, several generations had passed since Becket's demise?

Another piece of internal evidence bearing on the *Estoire*'s date is a brief text shared with a sermon by Thomas of Hales (fl. ca. 1250).[33] Quoting from a sermon by St. Bernard (d. 1153), the author of the *Estoire* and Thomas of Hales use similar terms to encourage study of the Gospels:

Bernard:
For you can neither love whom you do not know nor possess whom you do not love.

Nec enim potes aut amare quem nescias, aut habere quem non amaveris.[34]

Estoire:
[. . .] for you cannot love our sweet Lord Jesus Christ if you do not know him, nor can you know him well except through the Gospels which impart to us his life and his teachings, his miracles, his Passion, his Resurrection, and his Ascension, and the encouragement he gives his own through the Holy Spirit (P:20–24).

[. . .] vous ne poez amer nostre tresdouz Seignur Jhesu Crist si vous ne le conoissez, ne conoistre ne le poez si bien cum par l'Evangile que nous aprent

---

ent, priour de Lanthony qu'estoyt eslu arceveske de Caunterbires prochein aprés seint Thomas le martir," *Estoire*, P:5–6). Although Clement of Llanthony was a near contemporary of Becket, the prior's rise to the archbishopric, as Dean states, is "not . . . borne out in the usual records of Canterbury" (§483). According to Edward Carpenter and Adrian Hastings, *Cantuar: The Archbishops in their Office*, 3rd ed. (London: Mowbray, 1997), 590, Becket was succeeded by Richard (1174) and Baldwin (1185).

[33] See Ruth J. Dean with Maureen B. M. Boulton, *Anglo-Norman Literature: A Guide to Texts and Manuscripts*, ANTS Occasional Publications 3 (London: ANTS, 1999), §596; and M. Dominica Legge, "The Anglo-Norman Sermon of Thomas of Hales," *Modern Language Review* 30 (1935): 212–18. Only three works — the sermon, a *Vita Mariae*, and a "Love Ron" — can be attributed with certainty to Thomas of Hales (Sarah M. Horrall, "Thomas of Hales, OFM: His Life and Works," *Traditio* 42 [1986]: 287–98, at 287). In *Vita Mariae*, "Thomas is . . . writing almost exactly the same kind of work as the . . . *Meditationes vitae Christi* . . ." (Horrall, "Thomas," 296). Noting Thomas's emphasis on "emotional responses to religious events," Horrall adduces an audience "made up chiefly of women" (296, 297). Thomas's reputation is predominantly English (295). He was in London in the mid-thirteenth century as a high-ranking official in the best Franciscan school of the realm after Oxford (288, 296). Thomas also knew the town of Oxford and Adam Marsh, a close colleague of Grosseteste (288, 295).

[34] Bernardus Claraevallensis, *Sermones in Cantica Canticorum*, Sermo 37, PL183.971B.

sa vie e sa doctrine, ses miracles, sa Passion, sa Resurection e sa Assencion
[. . .] (P:18–21).

Thomas of Hales:
[. . .] no one can love our sweet Lord Jesus Christ if he does not know him,
nor can he receive Christ if he does not love him, nor can he know him except through the Gospels which instruct us about his life and his teachings,
his miracles, his Passion, his Resurrection, and his Ascension.

[. . .] nul hom ne put nostre duz sire ihesu crist amer si nel conust, ne auer
nel put crist si il nel eint, ne conustre nel put nus fors par euangeile ke nus
aprent sa uie e sa doctrine e ses ovres[35] e sa passion e sa resurrecciun e sa
assensiun [. . .].[36]

Thomas continues, "and therefore we must know at least the simple Gospel story
and bear it often in mind."[37]

Thomas's brief sermon is a life of Christ on fast-forward. Thomas implies
that allegiance to saints and even reverence for pagan heroes were more common
in his day than study of the life of Christ.[38] Familiarity with the life of Christ
is required for missionary-like outreach to unbelievers, a sharing of "the life and
teachings of him in whom we believe."[39] Moreover, meditation admits believers
to a private theater in which 'Crist Jesu' may appear: "Come, Lord Jesus. Show
yourself to me."[40] Each of the sermon's ten meditations ("pensers") is likened to
a talent ("besant") in the parable of the Ten Minas,[41] itself an illustration of the
proper use of spiritual gifts. In the fourth "besant," Thomas mentions the "light"

---

[35] Legge, "The Anglo-Norman Sermon," 215, transcribes diplomatically as *oures*,
which might be construed either as "hours" or "works." Thomas later clarifies (216) that
Christ's works (*ovres*) are intended here.

[36] Legge, "The Anglo-Norman Sermon," 215; punctuation modified.

[37] "e pur co auum nus grant mester qe nus suueaunum sachum la simple estoyre del
euangeile mester nus ad qe nus lauum en memorie suuent" (Legge, "The Anglo-Norman
Sermon," 215). Thomas's reference to *estoyre del euangeile* should be understood in its generic sense of "Gospel story," not as a particular recommendation of the source-text of
the present translation.

[38] "and . . . if we strive to know the life of the saints whom we love especially on account of the love of sweet Jesus Christ, how much more should we endeavor to know his
own life" ["e . . . si nus penum de sauer la uie lé seint ke nus amum especiaument pur la
amur duz iheus crist, mult plus nus deuum nos pener sauer la sue vie demeyne" (Legge,
"The Anglo-Norman Sermon," 215; punctuation modified and diacritical mark added)].

[39] "la uie e la ley celi en ki nus creum" (Legge, "The Anglo-Norman Sermon," 216).

[40] "veni domine ihesu manifesta mihi te ipsum" (Legge, "The Anglo-Norman
Sermon," 215).

[41] Lk 19:12–26; cf. Mt 25:14–30.

at Jesus's baptism, in the phrase "the heavenly light and voice."[42] Some sections of the *vita* have numerous sentences beginning with "how," e.g., "how you were shown by the star and worshipped by kings";[43] and the tenth "besant" recalls events from the Acts of the Apostles.

M. Dominica Legge dates the unique manuscript of Thomas's sermon from the latter part of the thirteenth century, possibly as early as 1270 or before.[44] Given the shared theme of the AN passages compared above, their common topic of the benefits of study of the Gospels as a key rationale, their similar phrasing, and—beginning in the third line—their near-identical word-choice, it seems very probable that, although we cannot say definitively which of the texts was earlier, one is quoting the other. On the one hand, it is quite plausible that Thomas, who certainly consulted several other gospel harmonies for his *Vita Mariae*, also knew the *Estoire* and that he quotes it here from memory.[45] This scenario would lead us to date the *Estoire* before Thomas's active period, ca. 1250, but surely no earlier than ca. 1240, on linguistic grounds. If, on the other hand, our author is quoting Thomas's sermon, then the *Estoire* could only have been written in the first decades after 1250. Another possibility: could it be that Thomas wrote both works? In any case, Thomas of Hales, who left writings in AN, ME, and Latin, is eminently qualified to be the author of the *Estoire*.

According to Father Gwynn, the latest of the numerous works in the section of Liber niger containing the *Estoire* was written in 1294.[46] Based on the evidence just reviewed, therefore, we may date the *Estoire* with confidence between about 1170 and 1294. To the extent that the AN expression of a given text is datable, moreover, there is nothing in the language of the *Estoire* to preclude its composition at a time that was also Thomas's most active period, some forty-five or fifty years before 1294. We may therefore very tentatively set the date of the *Estoire* about the middle of the thirteenth century.

---

[42] "la clarté et la uoyz celestiele" (Legge, "The Anglo-Norman Sermon," 216). For this "light," see pages 16–18.

[43] "coment uus esteiez demostré par le esteile e ahoré des rois" (Legge, "The Anglo-Norman Sermon," 216).

[44] Legge, "The Anglo-Norman Sermon," 213–14. She worked from Oxford, St. John's College MS 190.

[45] Thomas consulted the harmonies by Peter Comestor, Zachary of Besançon, Augustine, and Clement of Llanthony in compiling his *Vita Mariae*. See *The Lyf of Oure Lady: The ME Translation of Thomas of Hales' Vita Sancte Marie*, ed. Sarah M. Horrall (Heidelberg: C. Winter, 1985), 12.

[46] Aubrey Gwynn, "Some Unpublished Texts from the Black Book of Christ Church, Dublin," *Analecta Biblica* 16 (1946): 289; see also 297–98, 303. For details, see Manuscript below.

4. The *Estoire* and Clement of Llanthony's *Concordia quatuor evangelistarum*

Our author, who names Clement of Llanthony in his prologue, almost certainly knew the Augustinian prior's noted twelfth-century gospel harmony, the *Concordia quatuor evangelistarum*, and on several points the *Estoire* puts the reader in mind of it. Speaking of the writer of the *Estoire*, Ruth J. Dean states, "it is reasonable to take [him] at his word regarding his reliance on Clement's work."[47] In fact, however, there is little evidence of this reliance in the *Estoire*, for our author follows Clement neither in formal organization nor in details of substance.[48]

Like *CQE*, the *Estoire* arranges the four gospels into a unified, seamless narrative of the life of Christ. To promote easy reference, both authors divide their works first into major sections and again into episodes or chapters. In addition, after the prologue of the *Estoire* and of *CQE*, extensive *capitula*, or chapter titles, which are listed seriatim in table-of-contents format, assist the reader in locating particular episodes.

The differences between the works are too profound, however, for *CQE* to be considered as a direct source of the *Estoire*, or indeed Clement of Llanthony as the *Estoire*'s author. Since our author explicitly describes the *Estoire* as being more succinct (P:12–13) than *CQE*, in comparing the works below we purposely leave aside very numerous examples of *abbreviatio* in the *Estoire*. The remaining divergences may be summarized in seven points:

1) The substance of the prologues is quite different.

In the prologue of *CQE*, Clement speaks in the first person, referring explicitly to Eusebius, Ammonius of Alexandria, and Augustine (Roy. fol. 2r). As noted previously, the author of the *Estoire* names Clement of Llanthony in the third person, alluding also to St. Bernard, Aelred of Rievaulx, and Clement of Rome (P).

2) *CQE* is divided into twelve parts, the *Estoire* into seven "meditations."

3) The *Estoire* very often prefers indirect discourse to the direct discourse of *CQE*.

There are numerous examples of this flattening effect in the *Estoire*, including Mt 1:20b-21, the angel's words to Joseph (Roy. fol. 3v; 2:57–59); Lk 1:60, Elizabeth's rejection of the name Zechariah (Roy. 3v; 2:63–64); the angel's speech to the shepherds (Roy. 3v; 3:12–16); Mt 2:2, 5, 8, the wise men's speeches, the reply of the chief priests, and Herod's charge (Roy. 3v; 3:28–30, 32–33, 35–36); Mt 2:13, the command to flee to Egypt (Roy. 3v; 5:1–3); Mt 3:2, the Baptist's com-

---

[47] Dean §483.

[48] The discussion of *CQE* in this section is based on Roy.; unless noted otherwise, chapter and line numbers refer to the modern English translation of *Estoire* in this volume.

Introduction

mand to repent (Roy. 4r; 7:6–8); Jn 11:11–12, Jesus's conversation with the disciples prior to the raising of Lazarus (Roy. 14v; 80:9–15); and Jn 21:15–19, the "feed my sheep" dialogue (Roy. 20v; 112:18–25).

4) Compared with *CQE*, the substance of the *Estoire* is sometimes amplified.

Examples are: Lk 1:64, in the story of Zechariah, where "And immediately his mouth was opened and his tongue [*sc.* loosed], and he spoke, praising God"[49] becomes "And immediately Zechariah's speech was restored, and—filled with the Holy Spirit—he began praising our Lord God and singing: 'Holy Lord God of Israel'";[50] Lk 2:3, "And all went to register, each in his own city"[51] becomes "that all the earth's inhabitants should be registered in their native cities, and that each should pay a tax to the governor of the land to acknowledge his subjection to the Empire";[52] Jn 6:14, "[when they saw] the sign which he had performed"[53] is expanded to "that Jesus had fed them so abundantly with so little";[54] Jn 6:41, "Therefore the Jews were grumbling about him, because he had said, 'I am the bread that came down from heaven',"[55] becomes "they began to grouse and to ask each other, how he could give his flesh to eat and his blood to drink to those who believed in him?"[56]

5) The *Estoire* sometimes prefers to gloss rather than to translate.

In *CQE*, e.g., Jn 11:9–10 reads "Jesus answered, 'Are there not twelve hours in the day? If anyone walks in the day, he does not stumble, because he sees the light of this world. But if anyone walks in the night, he stumbles, because the light is not in him.'"[57] The *Estoire* explains, rather than relates, the biblical text, as follows: "Then Jesus answered that they should not be afraid to follow him, for he

---

[49] "Apertum est autem illico os eius et lingua eius et loquebatur benedicens Deum" (Roy. fol. 3v).

[50] 2:68–70; cf. "E tantost li estoit sa parole rendue, e il estoit repleni del Seint Esperit e comencea loer nostre Sire Dieu e dist le Benedictus Dominus Deus Israel" (*Estoire*, 2:52–54).

[51] "Et ibant omnes ut profiterentur singuli in suam civitatem" (Roy. 3v).

[52] 3:2–4; "que touz les hommes du munde fuissent escrit en la cité dunt il fuissent, e que chescun portast un dener au seneschal du païs e fuist conoissaunt qu'il fuist souget a l'empire de Roume" (*Estoire*, 3:2–4).

[53] "quod fecerat signum" (Roy. 10v).

[54] 49:25; "que Jhesu les out peu si plentivousement de si pou" (*Estoire*, 49:20–21).

[55] "Murmurabant ergo Iudei de illo quia dixisset ego sum panis qui de celo descendi" (Roy. 10v).

[56] 49:54–56; "comencerent il a groucer e a demaunder entre eus coment il peut sa char e son saunc doner a manger e a beivre a ceus que creroient en li" (*Estoire*, 49:44–46).

[57] "Respondit Iesus nonne .xii. hore sunt diei si quis ambulaverit in die non offendit quia lucem huius mundi videt si autem ambulaverit in nocte offendit quia lux non est in eo" (Roy. 14v).

could always save them. For he was, he said, like the sun whose light keeps man from suffering hurt, at any hour of day."[58]

6) The order of chapters sometimes does not match, particularly after ch. 63.

E.g., as compared with *CQE*, the *Estoire* delays Mk 6:53–56, Jesus heals the infirm of Gennesaret (Roy. fol. 10v; Liber niger fol. 48r); places chaps. 75–77 (Liber niger 53r-v) before the raising of Lazarus, rather than after (Roy. 14v-15r); advances Mt 28:16–17, Jesus's appearance on the mountain in Galilee (Roy. 20v, Liber niger 62r); and delays the substance of Pt XI, Ch. 7 (Roy. 15v), placing it as chap. 92, after the story of the widow's mite (Liber niger 56r).

7) The concluding episode is quite different in the two works.

The final section of *CQE* (Roy. fol. 20v) refers to Mt, Mk, and Lk. The *Estoire*'s final section, on Pentecost, refers to Acts 1:10–11, the appearance of two angels after the Ascension (113:32–35); Acts 1:12–14, the disciples praying in the Upper Room (113:37–39); and Acts 12:1–5, an allusion to the fate of James and Peter ten years after the Ascension (113:43–44). This is a rare instance of the inclusion of texts in the *Estoire* that are lacking in *CQE*.

5. The *Estoire* and the Pepysian Gospel Harmony

Though there is but a single known copy of the *Estoire*, that it was an influential text is further demonstrated by its translation, probably in the fourteenth century, into ME. The *Estoire* is almost certainly the "Old French" exemplar of the Pepysian Gospel Harmony (PGH), which survives in a unique manuscript from ca. 1400, about a century after Liber niger.[59]

---

[58] 80:9–12; "Donc lor dist Jhesu qu'il ne lor covendroit mie qu'il eussent paour pur suire le, quar il les pout toutz tens sauver. Quar il estoit, ce dist, com le solaill par qui clarté homme se puet toutes les oures du jour garder qu'il ne se blesce" (*Estoire*, 80:9–11).

[59] Cambridge, Magdalene College, MS Pepys 2498. For a description of the manuscript, see *Catalogue of the Pepys Library at Magdalene College, Cambridge*, vol. 5: *Manuscripts*, Part i: *Medieval*, comp. Rosamond McKitterick and Richard Beadle (Cambridge: D. S. Brewer, 1992), 86–88. C. William Marx and Jeanne F. Drennan, eds., *The ME Prose Complaint of Our Lady and Gospel of Nicodemus*, ME Texts 19 (Heidelberg: C. Winter, 1987), 10–11, propose a date slightly earlier than ca. 1400. Ralph Hanna, "Augustinian Canons and Middle English Literature," in *The English Medieval Book: Studies in Memory of Jeremy Griffiths*, ed. A. S. G. Edwards, Vincent Gillespie, and idem (London: British Library, 2000), 27–42, at 31, settles on the date, ca. 1375. According to Hanna, Pepys 2498 "may belong linguistically at the site of a major Augustinian house, Waltham (Essex), suburban London" (31). For a general introduction to PGH and its significance in the Diatessaronic tradition, see Petersen, *Tatian's Diatessaron*, 168–70; see also 434, 480–81. According to Petersen, the order of PGH is "different from all other Diatessaronic

For much of the twentieth century, the *Estoire* was a shadow-text whose existence scholars sensed but which they had never seen. Oblivious of the *Estoire*, e.g., ninety years ago Margery Goates brilliantly hypothesized a French source of PGH in a study of the ME work's vocabulary, including mistranslations.[60] She could not, however, establish a direct connection between the *Estoire* and PGH. Reprising Goates's analysis in 1994, Petersen wrote, "If one extends Goates' arguments, then it means that, although no known exemplar exists, the Pepysian Harmony—in addition to being the oldest known English witness to the Diatessaron—proves the existence of an Old French Diatessaron."[61] Very recently, Morey was still calling the French source "nonextant."[62] Meanwhile, despite some differences between PGH and all other Diatessaronic witnesses, Petersen lists five specific readings in which PGH and the Diatessaron agree.[63]

---

witnesses," and PGH itself is "shorter than most witnesses" (170). In his discussion of Goates's hypothesis of a French source, Petersen does not mention the *Estoire* or Liber niger. MS Pepys 2498 contains translations into ME of five AN works: in addition to PGH, these are Robert Gretham's *Mirror*, a prose Apocalypse, a prose Psalter, *Ancrene Wisse*, and Complaint of Our Lady / Gospel of Nicodemus. For the sequence Complaint of Our Lady / Gospel of Nicodemus in MS Pepys 2498, see C. W. Marx, "The *Gospel of Nicodemus* in Old English and Middle English," in *The Medieval* Gospel of Nicodemus: *Texts, Intertexts, and Contexts in Western Europe*, ed. Zbigniew Izydorczyk, MRTS 158 (Tempe, AZ: MRTS, 1997), 207–59, at 221–23; and Jeanne F. Drennan, "The *Complaint of Our Lady* and *Gospel of Nicodemus* of MS Pepys 2498," *Manuscripta* 24 (1980): 164–70. See further Ralph Hanna, *London Literature, 1300–1380* (Cambridge: Cambridge University Press, 2005), 153–63, for the significance of MS Pepys 2498 in English vernacular book-production before 1400 and for discussion of the manuscript's audience. Hanna argues that the various texts of Pepys 2498, including PGH, were developed first in Latin in a monastic milieu, subsequently emerging in AN versions "as staples of a secularised Anglo-Norman book-trade" (157) before translation into ME. Both Hanna, in *London Literature*, and Nicholas Watson, "Lollardy: The Anglo-Norman Heresy?," in *Language and Culture in Medieval Britain: The French of England c. 1100–c. 1500*, ed. Jocelyn Wogan-Browne et al. (Woodbridge, Suffolk, and Rochester, NY: York Medieval Press, 2009), 334–46, at 337, acknowledge that PGH was translated from AN but do not mention the *Estoire* or Liber niger. I am grateful to Jocelyn Wogan-Browne for calling these two works to my attention.

[60] *The Pepysian Gospel Harmony*, ed. Margery Goates, EETS o.s. 157 (London: H. Milford; Oxford University Press, 1922; www.bookprep.com/read/mdp.39015014775491). For extensive discussion of Goates's evidences and comparison with corresponding texts in the *Estoire*, see Appendix I: Analysis of M. Goates' 'Evidence of a French source,' 89–94, in the published critical edition. The present work refers to Goates's edition by page number only.

[61] Petersen, *Tatian's Diatessaron*, 168–69.

[62] Morey, *Book and Verse*, 210.

[63] Petersen, *Tatian's Diatessaron*, 170. For the occurrence of four of the five readings in the *Estoire*, see the notes for 7:35, 100:13–14, 102:6–7, and 103:33. Further stressing

Petersen asserts that PGH represents an early Christian tradition pre-dating even Tatian.⁶⁴ Marie-Emile Boismard agrees that PGH "relies not on Tatian's Diatessaron but, more or less directly, on an older harmony which the apologist Justin already knew and which Tatian presumably took up again, making slight changes to it."⁶⁵ PGH reveals little contact with the Codex Fuldensis (66); the ultimate source of PGH is rather a pre-Tatianic harmony which Boismard calls the "harmonie/Justin."⁶⁶ Justin relied on this "found" harmony, composed in Greek, probably about 140, in drawing up a gospel harmony ca. 150.⁶⁷ Tatian later also based his own Diatessaron on this same "harmonie/Justin." The influence of the "harmonie/Justin" was magnified with the translation of a revised and augmented version of the work into Syriac and Latin. It is this version, called the "Syro-Latin harmony" ("harmonie syro-latine"), that Boismard identifies with a Western harmony tradition "at once close to and different than Tatian's Diatessaron," a tradition whose principal witness is PGH.⁶⁸

Daniel Plooij calls attention to numerous eccentricities of PGH, noting particularly three "all-known test-readings for the Diatessaron."⁶⁹ In these and other samples, as shown below, PGH matches, point for point, the text of the *Estoire*:

1) "Pepys has the Light at the Baptism"

Cf. PGH, "so com þe briȝthnesse of heuene" ("there came the brilliance of the heavens"; Goates, 10); and 7:35: "there came a heavenly brilliance" ("vint la clarté celestiale," *Estoire*, 7:33; see the discussion below).

---

the importance of PGH, Petersen adds, "it is sometimes the *only* Western witness to parallel a given Diatessaronic reading" (*Tatian's Diatessaron*, 170; emphasis Petersen's).

⁶⁴ Petersen, *Tatian's Diatessaron*, 147, 169.

⁶⁵ "[l'harmonie de Pepys] ne dépend pas du Diatessaron de Tatien, mais, plus ou moins directement, d'une harmonie plus ancienne, connue déjà de l'apologiste Justin et que Tatien aurait reprise et quelque peu remaniée" (Marie-Emile Boismard, *Le Diatessaron: De Tatien à Justin*, Etudes bibliques, Nouvelle série 15 [Paris: Lecoffre, Gabalda, 1992], 29).

⁶⁶ Boismard, *Le Diatessaron*, 9.

⁶⁷ I follow Boismard, *Le Diatessaron*, 155–56, in this sentence and the next two.

⁶⁸ [. . .] "à la fois proche et différente du Diatessaron de Tatien" (Boismard, *Le Diatessaron*, 8). While insisting on the originality of PGH (29), Boismard underscores throughout his work the features shared by PGH and other Western witnesses, especially Comestor's *Historia evangelica*, but also the Arabic harmony, the Himmelgarten fragments, a Venetian harmony, and the Liège harmony. Petersen cautions that Boismard's theories "outrun the available evidence" (*Tatian's Diatessaron*, 348), but he also credits Boismard for raising the stature of PGH among Diatessaronic witnesses (356).

⁶⁹ Daniel Plooij, "The Pepysian Harmony," *Bulletin of the Bezan Club* 2 (1926): 14–16, at 14–15.

2) "It has also in the Story of the Young Ruler: 'and Jesus beheld hym amyablelich'" ("and Jesus looked at him fondly"; Goates, 68)
Cf. 74:7: "And Jesus looked at him lovingly" ("E Jhesu li regarda aimablement," *Estoire*, 74:6–7).

3) "and also the descent of Mary from David: 'for þat he was comen of þe kynde of þe kyng David þat was of Bedleem, & his wif also'" ("because he sprang from the lineage of King David, who was of Bethlehem, and with him his wife"; Goates, 5)
Cf. 3:6: "for he and his wife were descendents of King David of Bethlehem" ("quar il estoit du lignage le rey David qu'estoit de Bedleem, e sa espouse ausi," *Estoire*, 3:6).

These and other readings in PGH "suggest some lineal relationship of its Text to the Old-Syro-Latin tradition."[70]

It now appears highly likely that much of what scholars have said about PGH also applies in the first instance to the *Estoire*. Comparison of the *Estoire* and PGH reveals that, although PGH is without prologue, the sequence of 113 chapters and the substance of chapter titles in the two works are otherwise identical.[71] Both works arrange the miracles and teachings of Christ in seven major sections called "meditations." Both omit the same parts of the canonical gospels, e.g., the genealogies of Mt 1:1–17 and Lk 3:23–38. Both have an "abbreviating character," e.g., their references to certain parables by title only or their severe *abbreviatio* of Mt 12:22–37.[72] Both share a tendency to flatten the direct discourse of gospel figures to indirect discourse, and comparison of specific episodes in the *Estoire* and PGH, including "Gifts from the East," "Jesus walks on the water," "Jesus raises Lazarus," "Magdalene at the tomb," and "Pentecost" (see Appendix 2), reveals that word-choice and phrasing in PGH very closely match those in the *Estoire*. To take only two touchstones of Diatessaronic influence, both works

---

[70] Plooij, "The Pepysian Harmony," 15. Plooij gives several other examples of Diatessaronic readings in PGH. Most of these are considered in the Notes section here, alongside equivalent readings in the *Estoire*.

[71] See Appendix II: Sequence of chapters in *Estoire* and PGH, 95–101, in the published critical edition of the *Estoire*. On the importance of the scrutiny of sequences of chapters or pericopes in comparative studies, see Schmid, *Unum ex quattuor*, 26. See Appendix 1 here for the canonical gospel sources of each chapter.

[72] The parables of the Treasure and of the Pearl are named but are not retold. See the *Estoire* and PGH, chap. 45; and Mt 13:44–50. Also in chap. 45, the *Estoire* names the parable of the Net, omitted in PGH. Compare also the thumbnail parables in chaps. 67, 74, 85, and 93. At Mt 12:22–37, Christ's extended response to the Pharisees' accusation that he is an agent of Beelzebub is shortened in both works to "five proofs that it could not be true" (40:10–11).

begin with a chapter based on Jn 1:1–18, and, as previously mentioned, both include the detail—absent in *V*—of the "light" at Jesus's baptism.[73] The accumulated evidence bears out the claim that the *Estoire* and PGH present substantively the same gospel harmony in the prevalent languages of late medieval England.

The foregoing discussion has shown, on the one hand, the dissimilarity of the *Estoire* and *CQE* and, on the other hand, the remarkable likeness—in all but language—of the *Estoire* and PGH. Extended comparison of the *Estoire*'s text with that of other gospel harmonies falls beyond the scope of this work and outside the translator's expertise.[74] J. Neville Birdsall complained in the mid-1970s that, since 1926, PGH had been studied only indirectly, a remark reprised in 1994 by Petersen, who states, "The Pepysian Harmony remains largely unexplored terrain."[75] The connections among the *Estoire*, PGH, and other witnesses are areas that specialists may wish to explore directly in their future researches, perhaps shedding new light on the sources, author, and date of the *Estoire* in the process.[76]

6. Manuscript

The *Estoire* survives in a single manuscript, Dublin, Christ Church Cathedral C6.1.1, Liber niger, fols. 34r-63r. A notation on the recto of the first flyleaf reads "Liber niger Ecclesiae S. Trin. Dublin."[77] The book's owner was Henry La Warr,

---

[73] For Jn 1:1 as "the traditional *incipit* of the Diatessaron," see Petersen, *Tatian's Diatessaron*, 248, and Harris, "Some Notes," 33. For the "light" passage, cf. "vint la clarté celestiale" (*Estoire*, 7:33) and "so com þe briʒthnesse of heuene" ("there came the brilliance of the heavens"; Goates, 10). Louis Leloir, *Le Témoignage d'Ephrem sur le Diatessaron* (Louvain: Secrétariat du CorpusSCO, 1962), 106, quotes the text of PGH and remarks, "This feature is of great significance in the history of the Diatessaron, for it attests to the links between Tatian's work and the apocryphal tradition, and even with heresy" ("Pour l'histoire du Diatessaron, ce trait a une grande importance, car il témoigne des liens de l'œuvre tatianique avec la tradition apocryphe, voire même avec l'hérésie"). See also Petersen, *Tatian's Diatessaron*, 170, and the note for 7:35. PGH recalls two apocryphal traditions: Jesus shared the manger with an ox and an ass, and Judas hanged himself from an elder tree (Goates, 123–24, 132–33). These details are absent in the *Estoire*.

[74] On the linguistic and disciplinary breadth of Diatessaronic studies, see Petersen, *Tatian's Diatessaron*, 5.

[75] J. Neville Birdsall, "The Sources of the Pepysian Harmony and its Links with the Diatessaron," *New Testament Studies* 22 (1975–1976): 215–23, at 217; Petersen, *Tatian's Diatessaron*, 169.

[76] Schmid issues a caveat here: studies of medieval vernacular gospel harmonies should focus not on Tatian's Diatessaron but on the "vast Latin Fuldensis-harmony tradition," including the commentaries by Zachary of Besançon and Peter Cantor ("In Search of Tatian's Diatessaron," 186).

[77] "Black Book, Holy Trinity Church, Dublin."

"an Augustinian canon of Bristol who came to Dublin as prior of Christ Church in the winter of 1300–1301."[78] As shown by Aubrey Gwynn and Colmán Ó Clabaigh, each of the ten sections of Liber niger has its own history, and the compilation of the volume we know today continued from the late thirteenth century to the late fifteenth or early sixteenth. Dean dates the section containing the *Estoire*, XIII[ex].[79]

The codex is bound in sturdy chestnut-colored leather covers measuring 290 x 202 mm. Martin Gosman recognizes the binding's Tudor style and dates it ca. 1500.[80] The front cover is embossed with a diamond pattern set in a rectangle. The leather strap on the book's brass clasp is broken, but cover and clasp are otherwise in good condition.

A very interesting, composite work of 235 sequentially numbered vellum folios, Liber niger contains, in addition to the *Estoire*, a note on the provinces of England; fragments of *Imago Mundi* and of Peter Comestor's *Historia scholastica*; the complete fourth book of Peter Lombard's *Liber Sententiarum*, excerpts from the *Vitae Sanctorum*, a French verse translation of the Letter of Prester John, a chronicle of English history from 1066 to 1291, and other texts.[81] As testimony to their popularity in Augustinian circles, certain texts of the Liber niger recur in volumes that belonged to chapters beyond Dublin.[82] For example, three of the texts included in Liber niger—the *Secretum secretorum*, a treatise on the Tiburtine Sibyl, and Henry of Saltrey's account of St. Patrick's Purgatory—also appear, as Ó Clabaigh notes, "in a volume owned by the Augustinian canons of Leicester."[83] Meanwhile, English Augustinian libraries boasted eight copies of

---

[78] Gwynn, 285. In his description of the contents of the Liber niger, Martin Gosman, ed., *La Lettre du Prêtre Jean: les versions en ancien français et en ancien Occitan* (Groningen: Bouma, 1982), 50–51, calls attention to copies of a safe-conduct form (fol. 3r) and a letter (fol. 172v) by Henry La Warr, who is also named on fol. 204r. The letter is dated May 1307. Henry died sometime between this date and 1317 (Gwynn, 301). Colmán Ó Clabaigh's recent essay, "The *Liber niger* of Christ Church Cathedral, Dublin," in *The Medieval Manuscripts of Christ Church Cathedral, Dublin*, ed. Raymond Gillespie and Raymond Refaussé (Dublin: Four Courts Press, 2006), 60–80, contains black-and-white plates of three pages from other sections of Liber niger. Ó Clabaigh relates the unfortunate circumstances of Henry La Warr's election as prior and tentatively explores his connection to the English family de la Warr ("The *Liber niger*," 62–63). In the volume in which Ó Clabaigh's essay appears, "Holy Trinity" is used interchangeably with the more common name for the Dublin cathedral, "Christ Church."

[79] Dean §483.

[80] Gosman, *La Lettre du Prêtre Jean*, 50.

[81] Gwynn, "Some Unpublished Texts," provides a detailed description. See also Gosman, *La Lettre du Prêtre Jean*, 50–52; and Ó Clabaigh, "The *Liber niger*," 61–62, 64–72.

[82] I follow Ó Clabaigh, "The *Liber niger*," 65, 66, 69, in this sentence and the next two.

[83] Ó Clabaigh, "The *Liber niger*," 65.

Comestor's *Historia scholastica*, and the canons of Leicester possessed several copies, both complete and abridged, of Lombard's *Liber Sententiarum*.

The *Estoire* is written in brown ink by a single hand. This section of Liber niger is devoid of decoration, illustrations, or rubrics, although a one-to-two-line space is regularly left between chapters for the rubricator. Measuring 275 x 184 mm, fol. 34r, the first page of the *Estoire*, has a writing area of 212 x 140 mm. This is arranged in two columns (A, 67 x 212 mm; B, 62 x 212) set inside wide margins and separated by a center gutter 12 mm wide. Column A has 42 lines of text, B 44 lines. As Gwynn notes (284), in the section containing the *Estoire*, the manuscript's pages must have been cut after the scribe completed his work, for in some cases a few words in the chapter titles in the lower margin have been excised.

The *Estoire* begins with the prologue and an abstract of the seven "meditacions." This is followed by a summary of each "meditacion." Next is a table or list of 113 *capitula* in AN, most beginning with "How" ("Coment").[84] These usually correspond closely to the chapter titles inscribed in the lower margin beneath the columns on most folios after fol. 39v. In the *capitula*, meditations 1–3 appear without title or heading (see page 48).

After this prefatory material, the *Estoire* proper begins. As translated and printed here, the work's 113 chapters relate the life of Christ in about 2477 lines, of which 215, or nearly 9%, appear as direct quotations of the words of Christ.[85] Chapters have, on average, 22 lines each. The longest chapter (96) has 87 lines; the shortest chapters (50 and 107), only four. Eight chapters have 50 or more lines; 29, ten or fewer.

The script and sense of the *Estoire* are almost always clear. That one finds scribal slips, e.g., at 2:10–11, 17:8–9, 20:13 etc., and numerous scribal corrections, signals a copy that is nevertheless proximate with the original.

There are three catchwords in the section containing the *Estoire*, in the wide lower margin of fols. 41v ("Jhesu restust e demanda," "Jesus paused to ask"), 49v ("oy dire quil auoyent," "got news of this"), and 57v ("as genuz," "to his knees"). In addition, as Gwynn remarks (289), matching notes in the lower or inner margin of the recto of several folios indicate the proper order of the gatherings, or "fourths," making up this section, i.e., "primus quaternus de ewangeliis" (34r), "secundus quaternus" (42r), "tercius quaternus" (50r), and "quartus quaternus" (58r). These corresponding catchwords and quire labels are not otherwise noted here.

Gwynn states, "Almost the whole of this section [i.e., the third section of Liber niger, fols. 34–65] is filled with the text of a French poem on the Life of Our Lord, with the title (fo. 34): *Estorie des ewangeiles nostre doux seigneur*. The long text is written in a single hand of the thirteenth century, and a *terminus ante*

---

[84] As mentioned previously, the prologue, abstract, summary, and *capitula* of the *Estoire* are absent in PGH, which begins only with the first chapter.

[85] About 79% of Jesus's words are found in "meditacions" 3, 4, and 5, which relate his ministry after the imprisonment of John the Baptist.

quem can be given with fair certainty," i.e., the summer of 1294.[86] Gwynn bases this claim on the circumstances of a short text immediately following the *Estoire*'s final line, namely, a poem commemorating an embassy that summer from Edward I of England to Philip IV of France.[87]

7. Audience

In the prologue, our author calls attention to the *Estoire*'s structure: this is a life of Christ arranged in seven meditations, "so that you may read or meditate on one part each day" (P:14–15; "ke vous pussez chescun jour une partie lire ou penser," P:12–13). Here "penser" means "meditate on," "reflect on," as when *Lumere as lais* urges readers, "Pray to and meditate on the gentle Mary / And she will assist you."[88] From the outset, the author of *Estoire* calls the work, "this meditation."[89] As in other, aforementioned "national harmonies," the *Estoire* proffers the life and Passion of Christ as an organizing principle for a literature aiming at the spiritual formation of a broader cross-section of medieval Christians.[90]

The allusion to Aelred's *De institutione inclusarum* (P:15–16), noted above, sets the *Estoire* more firmly in the rich tradition of insular meditational literature.[91] Aelred addresses the work in the form of a letter to his unnamed sister, a recluse, to encourage and guide her "unceasing rumination" of the Lord's works

---

[86] Gwynn, "Some Unpublished Texts," 289. As will be seen here, the *Estoire* to which Gwynn refers is in fact a prose work, not a poem. Ó Clabaigh also mistakenly calls the *Estoire* a poem ("The *Liber niger*," 66).

[87] Liber niger, fol. 63r-v. Incipit: "Antoine de Beck sent abroad at the king's behest" ("Antoyne de beck dehors tere depar le rey en ueez"). Gwynn prints the poem's first nine verses and gives further details of the embassy, its purpose, and personnel ("Some Unpublished Texts," 289).

[88] "Preez, pensez la duce Marie, / E ele vus serra en aye" (*La Lumere as Lais by Pierre d'Abernon of Fetcham*, ed. Glynn Hesketh, ANTS 54–58, 3 vols. [London: ANTS, 1996–2000], ll. 6193–94). Hesketh dates the work "in (or at the very least by) 1267" (*Lumere*, 3:5).

[89] P:14; "ceste meditacion" (*Estoire*, P:12).

[90] Schmid, *Unum ex quattuor*, 12–13. Schmid suggests, e.g., that "national harmonies," now also including the *Estoire*, were used as an interpretive medium for a comprehensive "christiformitas" or as a systematic guide for the composition of sermon cycles ("sei es als Auslegungsmedium für eine umfassende 'christiformitas', sei es als systematischer Leitfaden für die Gestaltung von Predigtzyklen").

[91] For two ME versions of *De institutione inclusarum*, see *Aelred of Rievaulx's De institutione inclusarum: Two English Versions*, ed. John Ayto and Alexandra Barratt, EETS 287 (London and New York: Oxford University Press, 1984). See also Aelred of Rievaulx, *De institutione inclusarum*, in *Aelredi Rievallensis Opera Omnia*, ed. A. Hoste and C. H. Talbot, CCCM I (Turnhout: Brepols, 1971), 637–82. Mary Carruthers, *The Book of*

in past, present, and future. Evoking more than twenty gospel scenes in succession, the author urges, "Gode sustir, abide here as longe as thou maist and fede thy soule with these delicious meditacions."[92] Aelred's recommended meditative method—that the reader imagine herself as present at the gospel events portrayed—gained great popularity in medieval vernacular devotional literature, its influence extending to *Ancrene Wisse*.[93]

The allusion to *Recognitiones Clementis* (P:16–19) sustains the prologue's theme of private meditation of the words of Christ. The passage in question appears to be our author's recollection of the Clementine passage, in which Peter tells Clement

> when the middle of the night is passed, I awake of my own accord, and sleep does not come to me again. This happens to me for this reason, that I have formed the habit of recalling to memory the words of my Lord, which I heard from Himself; and for the longing I have towards them, I constrain my mind and my thoughts to be roused, that, awaking to them, and recalling and arranging them one by one, I may retain them in my memory.[94]

In the context of the *Estoire*'s earlier references to Clement of Llanthony and Aelred of Rielvaux, this attention to memory-work and its association with the focus of the imagination arising from lost sleep, strongly suggest that—although it is nowhere excluded that the *Estoire* was intended for reading to a community—the author planned the work above all for private or intimate group study and, beyond this—given the *Estoire*'s tendency for *abbreviatio*—especially for readers already familiar with the Gospels.

The format and language of some medieval harmonies suggest that they were used for private devotion or perhaps for reading aloud to a group, but probably not at the altar.[95] A passage on fol. 34r of Liber niger divides the life of Christ into seven readings called "meditacions."[96] Although the length of individual

---

Memory: A Study of Memory in Medieval Culture (Cambridge and New York: Cambridge University Press, 1990), 162–76, discusses the benefits and the motions of meditation.

[92] *Aelred of Rievaulx's De institutione inclusarum: Two English Versions*, 22. The corresponding Latin text is "Hic quamdiu potes, uirgo, morare. Non has delicias tuas somnus interpolet, nullus exterior tumultus impediat" (Aelred of Rievaulx, *De institutione inclusarum*, in *Aelredi Rievallensis Opera Omnia*, 673). For a list of the scenes and their gospel sources, see Morey, *Book and Verse*, 216.

[93] *Aelred of Rievaulx's De institutione inclusarum: Two English Versions*, xiii, xxxviii-ix.

[94] *Recognitions*, 97.

[95] Margaret Deanesly, *The Lollard Bible* (Cambridge: Cambridge University Press, 1920; www.archive.org), 176.

[96] The seven "meditacions" are arranged as follows: I, from the Nativity to Christ's baptism (190 lines); II, thence to the beginning of Christ's public ministry (149); III,

"meditacions" varies, one can imagine that each could be read silently or aloud in a short space of time.[97] Many of the other works in Liber niger are in Latin. The vernacular language of the *Estoire* may indicate, therefore, that the author intended it for a lay, not a learned audience. That the unique manuscript of the *Estoire* belonged to an Augustinian prior ca. 1300 does not rule out the existence of other copies, now lost or unaccounted for, and the circulation of these in communities of believers of both sexes. In this connection, it is worthwhile to note that the *Estoire*'s final chapter intentionally includes women among Christ's disciples, twice specifying "men and women" ("homes e femes") in the closing lines, even though *V* does not mention women in this context.[98] Coming as it does at the end of the *Estoire*, this attention is plausibly an authorial acknowledgement of female listeners or readers of the work. It is perhaps also significant that, in the *Estoire*, Jesus's lengthiest one-on-one dialogue occurs during his encounter with the Samaritan woman at Jacob's well (chap. 13; see below).

Edmund of Abingdon (*d.* 1240) takes up the subject of women's devotional reading in the "Sermon a dames religioses" version of his *Mirour de Seinte Eglyse*:[99]

> Whatever is written can be spoken . . . if you do not know how to understand something written, listen willingly to what is beneficial in what people tell you when you hear anything of holy scripture, whether in public discourse or private conversation.[100]

---

thence to the beheading of John the Baptist and hostile scrutiny of Christ's ministry (665); IV, thence to Christ's triumphal entry into Jerusalem (639); V, thence to the Last Supper (239); VI, an hour-by-hour account of the Passion (350); and VII, the Resurrection and its aftermath, including a brief account of Pentecost and early persecutions in the closing lines (245).

[97] E.g., to read aloud, at moderate speed, the six chapters of the first meditation, requires about ten minutes. On reading in a whisper and in full voice, see Carruthers, *The Book of Memory*, 170.

[98] For "men and women," see 113:14–15 and 113:19; see also "the other disciples and the women" (113:17). Also pertinent here is the author's curiously overstated "this noble woman" (44:7–8; "ceste gentile femme," *Estoire*, 44:6) in the miracle of the stooped woman; PGH "þis gentil woman" ("this noble woman," Goates, 42).

[99] Oxford, St. John's College MS 90, fol. 1b, gives this title for the version, which is addressed to "my dear sister" ("ma treschere suer," fol. 2a). See Alan Wilshere, "The Latin Primacy of St Edmund's 'Mirror of Holy Church'," *Modern Language Review* 71 (1976): 500–12, who states, it "seems very probable [that] the A.N. version was made for nuns" (508); and *Mirour de Seinte Eglyse (St Edmund of Abingdon's Speculum Ecclesiae)*, ed. A. D. Wilshere, ANTS 40 (London: ANTS, 1982; www.anglo-norman.net). My remarks here follow Jocelyn Wogan-Browne, *Saints' Lives and Women's Literary Culture, c. 1150–1300* (Oxford and New York: Oxford University Press, 2001), 38–39. See also note 114 below.

[100] "quantk'est escrit poit estre dit. Si vus ne savez entendre quantk'est escrit, oez volunters le bien ke l'en vus dist, quant vus oez rien de seint' escripture, u en sermon

Thus Edmund's instructions expand the conduct of women's reading from silent and solitary meditation to include small-group or public listening and discussion. In the twelfth- and thirteenth-century hierarchy of literacy in England, it may be that the *Estoire*'s audience consisted not only of high-born laywomen, their children and households who could read and understand French, but also of recluses and anchorites of both sexes who—while proficient readers of French—had entered on their religious vows later in life and were therefore insufficiently skilled in Latin to benefit from a gospel harmony in that language. As Wogan-Browne states in her discussion of *Mirour*, "it is clear that hearing, discussing, and enquiring about texts, rather than solitary reading of them, is the basis of much female devotional learning" (*Saints' Lives*, 39).

As for the reference to a metrical French gospel harmony, "the Gospel story . . . in French poem-texts" (P:2–3; "L'estorie des Evangeiles . . . rimez en romaunz," *Estoire*, P:2), given Hans Robert Jauss's statement that "there is no true translation-adaptation of the Gospels in French verse in the twelfth and thirteenth centuries,"[101] one can only conclude that our author is recalling here a lost biblical poem.

The *Estoire* seems to stand apart from other meditative works of the period by offering as its sole instruction an unadorned life of Christ. No doubt, the author intended that the listener or reader enter a theater of the sacred word in which deft arrangement and vivid images draw the spirit toward a true understanding of the Savior. By means of a focused, personal imagination of the

---

commun, u en privee collaciun" (*Mirour de Seinte Eglyse*, 22; trans. Wogan-Browne, *Saints' Lives*, 39).

[101] "[. . .] il n'y a pas de véritable traduction-adaptation des Evangiles en vers français aux XIIe et XIIIe siècles" (Hans Robert Jauss, *Grundriß der romanischen Literaturen des Mittelalters*, vol. 6: *La littérature didactique, allégorique et satirique* [Heidelberg: C. Winter, 1968–1970], 1: 86). Jauss discusses (52–56) only five "complete" rhymed Bibles in French (ca. 1189 to the early fourteenth c.) that include the New Testament: those by Herman de Valenciennes, the poet of BnF MS fr. 763, Geufroi de Paris, Jehan Malkaraume, and Macé de la Charité. Jean Bonnard, *Les Traductions de la Bible en vers français au moyen âge* (Paris: Imprimerie Nationale, 1884; repr. Geneva: Slatkine, 1967), also states, "We are unaware of any translation, properly so-called, of the Gospels in [French] verse" ("Nous ne connaissons pas de traduction proprement dite des Evangiles en vers"], 194; meanwhile, he gives a general description of, and excerpts from, Robert of Gretham's rhymed Gospels (194–95) and five poems of the Passion (207–14). Contrary to Bonnard's assertion (80), there is no evidence in the unique manuscript of Macé's rhymed *Bible*, BnF MS fr. 401, that the Passion is treated as a separate book. Riddy notes, however, that in 1420 dame Matilda Bowes left "a book of the Gospels in French" ("j romance book is called ye gospelles") to a goddaughter, and that this work may be *La Estorie del Evangelie* in French. See Felicity Riddy, "'Women Talking about the Things of God,'" in *Women and Literature in Britain, 1150–1500*, ed. Carol M. Meale (Cambridge and New York: Cambridge University Press, 1993), 104–27, at 108, 120 n. 24, 122 n. 43.

Life, the meditant, like Aelred's sister, can direct her longing towards the Master's works, teaching, and suffering, and thus "increase her love for the gentle Jesus Christ."[102]

The titles of individual meditations in the *Estoire* strongly suggest that, even though study of the Gospels was encouraged at any season of the liturgical year, the *Estoire* particularly aimed to accentuate, in the context of Christ's teachings and miracles, the events of Holy Week.[103] Of the seven meditations, all but the Palm Sunday devotion are labelled with a specific day of the week. For example, the meditation for Friday bears the heading "Here begins the sixth meditation, for Friday,"[104] Good Friday being the day of Holy Week that this meditation was presumably recommended for reading silently or aloud. The increased length of chapters in the sixth meditation also highlights the events of Good Friday.[105] Moreover, the chronological tags in chaps. 49 and 59 provide good evidence that these passages were read during Lent, for their substance matches liturgical readings for that season.[106] Finally, the abstract of the sixth meditation carries the title, "These are the chapters of the sixth meditation according to the hours of the day";[107] in fact, this devotion lays particular emphasis on the drama of Christ's suffering in an hour-by-canonical-hour account of the Passion.[108] The

---

[102] P:16; "anoiter s'amour vers douz Jhesu Crist" (*Estoire*, P:14–15).

[103] It is tempting to seek some connection between the *Estoire* and the English tradition of the Easter sepulcher, but I have found no evidence of any such link. As described by Pamela Sheingorn, *The Easter Sepulchre in England* (Kalamazoo: Medieval Institute Publications, 1987), the Easter sepulcher was a model or representation of Christ's tomb in Jerusalem that was assembled each year in hundreds of English churches both parish and monastic as they prepared for Holy Week and Easter. Sheingorn documents Easter sepulchers in England from the tenth into the sixteenth centuries, including in her catalogue (77–368) about eighty likely or confirmed examples of Easter sepulchers dating from the thirteenth century. The reproduction of the form of Christ's tomb in English churches was combined with what Sheingorn terms "the commemorative Holy Week and Easter rites" (4).

[104] 95:1; "Ici comence la sime meditacion par venderdi" (*Estoire*, 95:1).

[105] Here one finds the *Estoire*'s two longest chapters, 95 and 96. The average length of chapters in the sixth meditation, at 50 lines, greatly exceeds the average chapter-length in the rest of the *Estoire*.

[106] See the notes for 49:22, 59:20, and 59:53–54.

[107] vi:1: "Ces sunt les chapitres de la sime meditacion solum les houres du jour" (*Estoire*, vi:1–2).

[108] The *Estoire*'s sixth meditation, concerning the Passion, contains seven chapters, 95–101. The colophon of PGH refers to "þe gospels an hundreþ and sex, outenomen þe passioun of Jesu Crist" ("the gospels one hundred and six [parts or chapters], excluding the passion of Jesus Christ"), Goates, 113, 135; cf. Morey, *Book and Verse*, 210, i.e, not including the Passion. The ME colophon has no equivalent in the *Estoire*, but its presence in PGH indicates that the sixth meditation in both works could function, as Morey suggests, as an independent and complete unit.

seventh meditation, for Holy Saturday, then relates the Resurrection and concludes the life of Christ with an account of Pentecost and the Ascension based on the Acts of the Apostles. Through thoughtful study of each "meditacion" in turn, by Holy Saturday the reader was prepared spiritually for Easter mass.[109]

In chap. 108 of the *Estoire*, two pilgrims meet a stranger, then continue unawares with the risen Christ towards Emmaus. Aelred's advice to meditants to imagine themselves as present at gospel events disposes the medieval reader of the *Estoire* to identify here with Cleopas's unnamed companion and to keep pace with the stranger as he walks and explains the Scriptures. But as the attentive meditant strives to grasp and internalize Christ's words and actions in successive scenes of the *Estoire*, does he or she also recreate mentally Jesus's surroundings, imagining the places where the Master walks—Nazareth, Bethany, Cana, Capernaum, Bethsaida, and the Sea of Galilee? Our author does not open the door to imagined pilgrimage or *peregrinatio in stabilitate*, those "interior, meditative practices that allowed monks to make a pilgrimage with their hearts and not their feet."[110] Still, the words of Aelred and the seven-part structure of the *Estoire* do frame a translocative experience in which the meditant at home could both picture Christ in a gospel setting and imagine accompanying him there, for the *Estoire* literally relates the road trip of Jesus and his disciples. The itinerary undergirding the *Estoire* leads the meditant ineluctably through the holy places and towards the Passion and its aftermath, set in and around Jerusalem.[111]

The Passion has been called "the singular focus of the Middle Ages."[112] Enthusiasm in England for meditation on the Passion of Christ may be traced

---

[109] The *Meditaciones Vite Christi* (mid-fourteenth c.) adopted a similar structure. Long attributed to St. Bonaventure, this work is now often ascribed to John of Caulibus, a Franciscan of San Gimignano. See Johannes de Caulibus, *Meditaciones Vite Christi*, ed. M. Stallings-Taney, CCCM 153 (Turnhout: Brepols, 1997), xi, which dates *Meditaciones* between ca. 1346 and ca. 1364; and John of Caulibus, *Meditations on the Life of Christ*, trans. and ed. Francis X. Taney, Anne Miller, and C. Mary Stallings-Taney (Asheville, NC: Pegasus Press, 2000).

[110] Daniel K. Connolly, *The Maps of Matthew Paris: Medieval Journeys through Space, Time and Liturgy* (Woodbridge, Suffolk, and Rochester, NY: Boydell Press, 2009), 40. The early twelfth-century travel account of Abbot Daniel pointedly and repeatedly promises stay-at-home meditants of the holy places the same spiritual rewards received by those who visit the sites in person (36–37). Connolly adds, "The desire to partake vicariously of the holy places motivates imagined pilgrimage, and in the case of medieval pilgrimage guides, is the reason most often cited by their authors for the production of the writing itself" (38). For AN *estorie* denoting a map, see 51.

[111] For processions during Holy Week in Crusader Jerusalem, see Adrian J. Boas, *Jerusalem in the Time of the Crusades* (London and New York: Routledge, 2001), 30–31.

[112] [. . .] "l'unique étude du moyen âge" (E. Mâle quoted by Sandro Sticca, *The Planctus Mariae in the Dramatic Tradition of the Middle Ages*, trans. Joseph R. Berrigan [Athens, GA: University of Georgia Press, 1988], 7).

at least to the late eleventh century.¹¹³ In 1080, the monk Goscelin of Canterbury urges the recluse Eva to focus her meditation exclusively on the sufferings of Christ.¹¹⁴ Similarly, in his *Liber de quadripartite exercitio cellae*, the English Carthusian Adam of Dryburgh (d. 1212) twice recommends meditation on the Passion, pointing out that devotees gain "affection and comfort" ("amor et consolatio") as they combat spiritual inertia. Devotion to the Passion inspired the life and ministry of Aelred's teacher and confrere, St. Bernard. Moving beyond meditation to *imitatio*, as is well known, St. Francis sought to experience Christ's sufferings, and his order adopted as its motto, "May I never boast except in the cross of our Lord."¹¹⁵

The *Estoire*'s arrangement of the Passion section according to the canonical hours adopts an organizing principle endorsed in the above-named Goscelin's *Liber confortatorius*, and the device recurs from the twelfth to the fifteenth century in a broad spectrum of devotional works both literary and pictorial.¹¹⁶ Thus Edmund of Abingdon interpolates in his *Mirour*, mentioned previously, a series of brief meditations on the Passion arranged according to the seven canonical hours.¹¹⁷ Three English books of hours from the 1320s and 1330s present in

---

¹¹³ See Salter, *Nicholas Love's "Myrrour,"* 127 ff. I follow Salter throughout this paragraph.

¹¹⁴ Bella Millett, "Women in No Man's Land: English Recluses and the Development of Vernacular Literature," in *Women and Literature in Britain*, ed. Meale, 86–103, at 88, attributes the *Liber confortatorius* to Goscelin of Saint Bertin. She dates the work ca. 1082–1083 and identifies Goscelin's addressee as Eve of Wilton (88). For AN narratives and meditations of the Passion, see Dean §§958–64; for meditations of the Cross, §§966–80. See also the versions of the Gospel of Nicodemus, §§497–501.

¹¹⁵ Gal 6:14, "Mihi absit gloriari nisi in cruce Domini." See Sticca, *The* Planctus Mariae, 11; for the *Liber de Passione Christi et doloribus et planctibus Matris eius*, which is generally attributed to Bernard, see 103 ff. The circuit of the Via Dolorosa was not plotted until the thirteenth century, after St. Francis's disciples had made a spiritual exercise of the experience of Christ's sufferings (Maurice Halbwachs, *La Topographie légendaire des Evangiles en Terre sainte*, 2ⁿᵈ ed. [Paris: Presses Universitaires de France, 1971], 30, 83–84).

¹¹⁶ Connolly, *The Maps of Matthew Paris*, 44, follows Jean Leclercq in attributing to an anonymous monk of the twelfth century, probably a Cistercian, the device of a weekly schedule of meditations keyed to a seven-part biography of Christ.

¹¹⁷ Edmund states in his preface, "you should know that for each hour of the day there are two meditations, one on the Passion, the other on another theme" ("devez saver ke chescun hore del jur a duble meditacion, une de la passion, une autre de autre sesun": *Mirour de Seinte Eglyse*, 58). For the Terce of the Passion, e.g., he links the Flagellation of Christ and Pentecost (62–64). For the original Latin text of St. Edmund's work and a Latin translation from AN, see *Edmund of Abingdon, Speculum religiosorum and Speculum ecclesiae*, ed. Helen P. Forshaw, Auctores Britannici Medii Aevi 3 (London: Oxford University Press, 1973); for the Passion section, see 82–96. Forshaw judges that "the treatise must almost certainly have been written before Edmund became archbishop in 1234,"

turn, and again in hour-by-hour fashion, framed full-page miniatures of the Passion, the Hours of the Passion, and a mixed Hours of the Virgin and Hours of the Passion.[118] Later works incorporating the device include the *Vita Christi* of Ludolphus the Carthusian (*d.* 1377), John of Caulibus's *Meditaciones Vite Christi* (mid-fourteenth c.), and *De Meditatione Passionis Christi per septem diei horas libellus* (fourteenth c.).[119] Nicholas Love's translation of *Meditaciones*, the *Myrrour of the Blessed Lyf of Jesu Christ*, appeared in the early fifteenth century. As Salter states in her discussion of the *De Meditatione Passionis Christi*, "The Hours of the Passion have, by this time, become firmly established as a devotion."[120]

The *Estoire*'s author concludes the prologue with a recommendation, "Thus I entreat you to read or meditate on the Gospel story."[121] There are no further, explicit guidelines, other than the aforementioned three chronological tags, regarding the proper use of the work.[122] Perhaps the author, in placing the *Estoire* under the aegis of Bernard and Aelred, considered such information unnecessary.

---

possibly even before the 1220s (16). Thomas H. Bestul, *Texts of the Passion: Latin Devotional Literature and Medieval Society* (Philadelphia: University of Pennsylvania Press, 1996), 42, discusses the Passion by Edmund and that by Stephen of Sawley (d. 1252), which is also organized around the canonical hours. M. Mary Philomena, "St. Edmund of Abingdon's Meditations before the Canonical Hours," *Ephemerides liturgicæ* 78 (1964): 33–57, retraces the practice of meditation of certain events and mysteries of the Passion at a specific canonical hour, with special emphasis on Edmund.

[118] Kathryn A. Smith, *Art, Identity and Devotion in Fourteenth-Century England* (London: British Library; Toronto: University of Toronto Press, 2003), 299–300 (De Lisle Hours, fols. 19r-86r), 303 (De Bois Hours, fols. 72r-89v), 321 (Neville of Hornby Hours, fols. 53r-101v). In the Neville of Hornby Hours, moreover, an AN *Complaint of Our Lady* and *Gospel of Nicodemus* (fols. 131r-189v) is accompanied by 36 historiated initials of which two-thirds depict the events of the Passion (322–23).

[119] In this sentence and the next, I follow Salter, *Nicholas Love's "Myrrour,"* 42, 114, 155. In his brief treatment of Pepys 2498, Ralph Hanna describes the manuscript's gospel harmony as "a unique diatessaron (in part fusing the ps.-Bonaventuran *Meditations* with a more conventional text)" ("Augustinian Canons and Middle English Literature," 31). According to Salter, Bestul, and others, however, and dating the *Estoire* mid-thirteenth c. and the *Meditations* mid-fourteenth c., the latter appeared five generations too late to inspire or shape the *Estoire*.

[120] Salter, *Nicholas Love's "Myrrour,"* 156; Bestul calls the device "conventional" by the time of the *Meditaciones* (*Texts of the Passion*, 48). See also Marion Glasscoe, "Time of Passion: Latent Relationships between Liturgy and Meditation in Two ME Mystics," in *Langland, the Mystics and the Medieval English Religious Tradition*, ed. Helen Phillips (Cambridge: D. S. Brewer; Rochester, NY: Boydell & Brewer, 1990), 141–60, at 141–42; and Smith, *Art, Identity and Devotion*, 58.

[121] P:19–20; "Dount vous lou jeo que vous lisez ou pensez l'estoire de l'Evangile" (*Estoire*, P:17–18).

[122] For the chronological tags, see 49:22, 59:20, and 59:53–54, and the corresponding notes.

One can imagine, however, that the instructions, if they existed, might be similar to the user's manual included in the *Meditaciones*:

> Divide the meditations [into daily readings]. Follow this schedule every week of the year, so that you familiarize yourself with those meditations. And the more often you do so the more easily and the more joyfully they will reoccur to you. Be glad to have personal conversation with your Lord Jesus, and . . . strive to fix firmly in your heart, like Good News, that holy life of his.[123]

8. Style and Esthetic Considerations

No plausible, immediate sources of the *Estoire* have been proposed to date. Still, we may wonder whether the author composed the work directly in AN, or whether the *Estoire* is not rather a translation or paraphrase of an earlier harmony, most likely a Latin one. It seems reasonable to assume that the ultimate source of the *Estoire* was the New Testament Gospels of the Vulgate, and that from these flow not only the substance but also, demonstrably, a good measure of the AN harmony's expressiveness and energy. While no doubt inspired by the New Testament Gospels, meanwhile, the *Estoire*'s direct style and purposeful pace vivify the gospel narrative, successfully focusing the reader's attention.

To whom or to which specific, earlier source should we attribute the stylistic traits of the *Estoire*? In the Sermon on the Mount, e.g., is the anaphora of Christ's message—eight blessings beginning "Blessed are" ("Beneurez sount," chap. 24)—a reflection of our author's style or is it rather the style of a model, the Beatitudes? To whom do we credit the epiplexis of Jesus's words at Gethsemane, "Friend, why have you come? Are you betraying me, Judas, with a kiss?";[124] or the Master's intensive use of paradox, riddles, exempla, and parables in his teachings?[125] Are the metaphors and similes not the familiar biblical ones trans-

---

[123] John of Caulibus, *Meditations on the Life of Christ*, 332–33. Thus, according to Denise Despres, *Ghostly Sights* (Norman, OK: Pilgrim Books, 1989), the reader of *Meditaciones* "witnessed Christ's life weekly, inextricably meshing her life with the gospel in an internal rhythm like that of the liturgical year but even more personal" (48). The Latin reads "Meditaciones uero sic diuide . . . Et sic per singulas ebdomadas facias ut ipsas meditaciones tibi reddas familiares quod quanto magis facies tanto facilius tibi concurrent, et iucundius. Libenter conuerseris cum Domino Iesu, et uitam ipsius tanquam Euangelium . . . in corde studeas inseparabiliter collocare" (Johannes de Caulibus, *Meditaciones Vite Christi*, 350).

[124] 96:33; "'Amis, a quei este vous venu? Me traissez vous, Judas, par baiser?'" (*Estoire*, 96:30).

[125] For paradoxes, see, e.g., "whoever exalts himself will be humbled, and whoever humbles himself will be raised up" (Lk 14:11) (71:24–25; *Estoire*, 71:18–19); "those who

ferred to AN by our author?[126] Absent knowledge of the *Estoire*'s direct medieval models, the best approach is to analyze the chief stylistic traits of the AN harmony as we know it, and these are discussed briefly under seven headings below.

Brevity

The style of the *Estoire* is generally spare and economical. In the prologue, our author states clearly that the *Estoire* is intended as a "summary," and thereafter we find relatively few digressions from the gospel account of the Vulgate. Direct discourse in *V* is frequently transposed to indirect discourse, a clerkly technique favoring summaries of speeches over a verbatim record of what was said. Sentences are usually crisp and straightforward, often series of subject-verb clauses linked by conjunctions "and" or "neither," e.g., with adverbs "because" or "then," or by relative pronouns "who" or "that," but with little complexity overall.

Allied with *brevitas* in the *Estoire* is the author's use of *abbreviatio*. For example, the harmonist gives the titles of four canticles and of the Lord's Prayer, but withholds their respective texts—perhaps assuming that the audience knew them by heart.[127] In addition, on a few occasions the author mentions Jesus's parables by name only, as if the parables—perhaps like the canticles and the Pater noster just mentioned—were so familiar to the harmony's audience that writing them out or telling them in full was judged unnecessary. Thus near the end of chap. 45, we find Jesus conversing telegraphically with the apostles:

> And then he told them a parable of a treasure hidden in a field, another of the fine pearl, and a third of the net. And he asked them if they understood, and they said yes.[128]

---

appear as last will be the very first, and those who seem first will be the very last" (Mt 19:30, Mk 10:31, Lk 13:30) (74:23–24; *Estoire*, 74:18–19); and "the eldest [...] would be as the youngest, and the sovereign a servant" (Lk 22:26) (95:21–22; *Estoire*, 95:18).

[126] Among the *Estoire*'s similes: "like sheep lying and waiting along the roads" and "as crafty as serpents and as innocent as doves" (Mt 10:16) (28:3, 15; *Estoire*, 28:3, 16); "like a reed stirred by the wind" (Mt 11:7, Lk 7:24) (30:14; *Estoire*, 30:11–12) and "as the hen gathers her chicks under her wings" (Mt 23:37) (90:14; *Estoire*, 90:12).

[127] For the canticles, see "My soul magnifies the Lord" (2:52; *Estoire*, 2:40–41), "Holy Lord God of Israel" (2:70; *Estoire*, 2:54), "Glory to God in the highest" (3:19; *Estoire*, 3:16), and "Now thou dost dismiss thy servant, O Lord" (4:12; *Estoire*, 4:9); the Our Father is mentioned at 36:4.

[128] 45:14–15; "E pus lour dist il une parable du tresor muscé en chaump, e une autre de la preciouse margarite, e la tierce de la seine. E lour demaunda si il entendirent, e il disoient que oyl" (*Estoire*, 45:13–15).

Elsewhere in chap. 45, our author alludes to the parables of Mt 13:44–50 but does not spell them out.[129] Later, in a disputation with the Pharisees, Jesus defeats his adversaries' arguments with five proofs, but readers are not told which proofs these are.[130] Chap. 47 ends cryptically with the statement, "Then Jesus made them a long speech to show that he could very well do such things on the Sabbath."[131] Does *abbreviatio* also explain the absence, in chap. 11, of the well-known question in Nicodemus's private conversation with Jesus, "How can a man be born when he is old? Surely he cannot enter a second time into his mother's womb to be born" (Jn 3:4). In any case, the author omits this passage and other portions of Nicodemus's interview with Jesus.

Exempla

Two kinds of short narrative are mentioned repeatedly in the *Estoire*, the "ensaumple," or exemplum, and its subset, the "parable."[132] Their prominence may be explained by the author's habitually reductionist approach. Parables and exempla are short, self-contained narratives inserted into a broader discourse to illustrate a teaching point or to bolster an argument.[133] Specific parables in the *Estoire* often receive summary treatment, as indicated above; "ensaumples," on the other hand, are usually related in some detail, over several lines of text. In every case, it is Jesus who tells the stories to listeners. Despite the fundamental, illustrative purpose of exempla, in the *Estoire* as in the New Testament Gospels, paradoxically, the disciples sometimes do not grasp their meaning and must request clarification.[134]

---

[129] For thumbnail accounts of "The Lost Sheep" (Lk 15:3–7), "The Lost Coin" (Lk 15:8–10), and "The Prodigal Son" (Lk 15:11–32), see 67:4–9 (*Estoire*, 67:3–9).

[130] "And then Jesus [. . .] demolished their accusation with five proofs that it could not be true" (40:10–11; *Estoire*, 40:8–9), a severe pruning of Mt 12:25–37, Mk 3:23–29.

[131] 47:18–19; "Dount lour fist Jhesu un long sermoun e monstra qu'il poeit bien fere teus choses en sabat" (*Estoire*, 47:15–16). See Jn 5:15–47.

[132] In the translation, "ensaumple" appears as "example" or "story." According to J.-Th. Welter, *L'Exemplum dans la littérature religieuse et didactique du Moyen Age* (Paris: Occitania, 1927; repr. New York: AMS Press, 1973), the parable is the most common of three types of gospel exemplum, along with comparisons drawn from nature (10 n. 1). Claude Bremond, Jacques Le Goff, and Jean-Claude Schmitt, *L'Exemplum*, Typologie des sources du moyen âge 40 (Turnhout: Brepols, 1982), view parables, allegory, and animal fables, among other story-types, as subsets of the "metaphorical exemplum" (117).

[133] For the five *ensaumples*, see 42:10, 68:3, 68:5, 71:11, and 71:7, but there are other, unlabeled exempla at 40:23–27 and 66:4–7; Jesus tells one or more parables on eleven occasions, at 34:7, 43:11, 45:3, 45:14, 63:35, 65:14, 67:4, 74:25, 77:14, 85:2, and 93:24, for a total of 25 parables either told or named in the *Estoire*. These tallies omit references to the *Estoire*'s prefatory material and chapter titles.

[134] See 45:11–12 and 62:4–6.

Artful Dialogue

Though the *Estoire*'s author frequently replaces the direct, back-and-forth dialogues of the New Testament Gospels with indirect discourse, even the reshaped exchanges can be lively and skillfully conducted.

The longest sustained dialogue in the *Estoire* is Jesus's conversation with the Samaritan woman at Jacob's well. There are six exchanges in this encounter, all of them indirect quotations except two direct quotations of the woman's words. In comparison with Jn 4:1–42, its principal source, the dialogue in chap. 13 of the *Estoire* reveals no further, significant authorial modifications. At first, the conversation concerns water and the well. We sense that Jesus is toying with the foreign woman; enigmatic and clear by turns, he challenges her about her husband and finally reveals himself to her as the Christ. The dialogue depicts the woman as a good sparring partner until she is deflated by Jesus's challenge. She is cheeky and prone to banter; her quips invite a witty response. She sometimes appears to mock the thirsty stranger with her repartee. She seems to look at Jesus from the corners of her half-closed eyes, as if anticipating his reaction to her remarks. Having come to the well, she never draws water or gives Jesus a drink, as Martha of Bethany might do.

In chap. 103, Jesus's post-resurrection conversation with the Magdalene in the garden is as moving and lachrymose as the dialogue by the well is sardonic. Separated for a time from the other women, as she nears the sepulcher, Mary Magdalene knows only that Jesus's body has vanished from the tomb, not that he has risen from the dead. She arrives tearfully for one exchange with the angels at the tomb and two more with the risen Christ; of the six speeches, half are direct quotations. The author insists on Mary's troubled state, as both the angels and Jesus ask her the same question in identical words, "why was she crying?" The Magdalene answers both questions, "her Lord had been carried away," stammeringly repeating the verb "emporté" ("carried away"), as if in her distress she could not, at that moment, find a synonym. Thus her answer to the gardener / Christ:

> My lord, you have taken him away. Tell me where you have put him, and I will take him and carry him away! (103:28–29).

> Sire, vous l'avez emporté. Dites moi ou vous l'avez mis, e je le prendrai e l'emporterai! (*Estoire*, 103:23–24)

Troubled by unanswered questions, the Magdalene is alone, without her sisters, in the presence of the supernatural, the uncanny, and the unexplained.

Meanwhile, the author is patently complicit in the drama of this chapter, for on two occasions the characters' actions are stage-managed by additions not found in *V*. The chief biblical source of these encounters in the garden is Jn 20:11–17. Independently of *V*, our author adds the lines

> Behold, the angels rose to greet Jesus who had come to stand behind the Magdalene (103:24–25);
>
> Este vous leverent les angles countre Jhesu qui vint e estuit derere la Magdaleyne (*Estoire*, 103:20–21);[135]

and

> With that, she turned again towards the angels as though to seek solace (103:30);
>
> A ce se turna ele vers les angles ausi com queraunt confort (*Estoire*, 103:24).

Both of the added observations in the Hortulanus scene focus on the Magdalene's movements. Like stage directions, the lines emphasize Mary's distress as she turns away from the angels to see the gardener, then looks back to the angels for reassurance. Once Mary has recognized Jesus, the brevity of their dialogue adds to the scene's poignancy:

> And Jesus called her, saying:
> "Mary!"
> And she, recognizing his voice, turned and fell at his feet, saying:
> "Ah, fair Teacher!" (103:31–34)
>
> E Jhesu l'apela e dist: 'Marie'. E ele conuyst sa voiz e se returna e chei a ses piez e dist: 'A, beau Mestre!' (*Estoire*, 103:24–26)

Redundancy and Repetition

Despite its tendency toward economy of style, the *Estoire* also frequently uses redundancy and repetition. Even in a gospel harmony, we would expect to find certain repetitions, e.g., in Jesus's thrice-repeated question to Peter in the "feed my sheep" dialogue; in fact, the *Estoire* gives a full account of this (chap. 112). Still other repetitions in *Estoire* have almost surely also been taken over by the author from an earlier source. In this practice, the *Estoire* usually conforms closely to the language of the familiar New Testament account: the harmonist repeats key phrases to highlight Christ's power, to underscore his rejection or to foreshadow his Passion, a technique befitting a work intended for small-group or public listening.

A prominent form of repetition in the *Estoire* involves a command followed by a report, in nearly identical terms, of the execution of the command, often as

---

[135] In *V*, immediately after her reply to the angels' question, it is Mary, not the angels, who turns and sees the "gardener": "haec cum dixisset conversa est retrorsum et videt Iesum stantem" (Jn 20:14).

the prelude to a miracle of Jesus and the subsequent amazement of witnesses. In the story of the miracle at Cana, e.g.,

> And Jesus told them to fill the pitchers with water, and they filled them to the rim. Then he told them to take them up and carry them to the wedding-steward, and they brought them to him (10:7–9).

> E Jhesu lour dist qu'il les emplissent d'ewe, e il les emplirent toutes pleines. Donc lour dist il qu'il empreissent e portasent au cheveteyn des hostes, e il li porterent (*Estoire*, 10:6–8)

Likewise, in the account of Jesus's healing of the paralytic:

> Then Jesus commanded him to get up and carry his bed to his house; and at once he was healed, and he rose up and carried his bed home (47:10–12).

> Dount li dist Jhesu q'il levast sus e portast a l'ostel son lit. E il fu tantost gari e leva sus e porta son lit vers l'ostel (*Estoire*, 47:9–10).

There are still other instances of this type of repetition in the *Estoire*.[136] In each case, the statement of the execution of a command in language and sequence identical to those of the order serve to confirm the miracle-worker's authority and power.

Repetition in the *Estoire* may simply be redundant, however, as when Christ calls the disciples three times (chaps. 15, 17, 24), when he twice clears the Temple of vendors (11 and 82), when he preaches three times from a ship (15, 39, and 45), when he issues similar instructions to the Twelve and the Seventy-Two (28 and 32) or twice compares changes in weather to the signs of his coming (42 and 55). When Jesus heals blind men both in entering and in exiting Jericho (76 and 78), the author relates the events in similar language. After the crucifixion, likewise, the women twice buy balm to anoint Jesus's body (101 and 102).

Repetition becomes refrain in chaps. 13, 16, 23, and 46, where Jesus or the narrator states, "A prophet is nowhere without honor except in his own country." Indeed, the short chapters 23 and 46 are very similar in substance. Twice in the series of chapters about Jesus's miracles, the infirm awaiting Jesus's arrival and touch are compared to sheep lying patiently along the roads (28 and 49). This refrain kindles the reader's or listener's feeling of compassion for the helpless sick while also effectively conveying the love and power of Jesus, depicted here as a figure of health and hope. The same refrain reminds the reader of miracles in other, adjacent chapters—e.g., the paralytic lying by the water (47), the man

---

[136] See, e.g., the expulsion of a demon (18:6–7; *Estoire*, 18:5–6), the raising of the widow's son (29:6–7; *Estoire*, 29:6–7), and Jesus's command to Zacchaeus (77:6–8; *Estoire*, 77:5–6).

blind from birth (59), or, again, the blind men sitting by the road near Jericho (76 and 78) — for in each case the infirm or troubled wait expectantly for Christ and are subsequently healed.

Repetition may be used to foreshadow future events, particularly in the chapters on the Passion and its aftermath. In chaps. 95 and 96, e.g., Jesus foretells that the apostles will desert him, and the prophecy is fulfilled with Peter's third denial (96:65). Twice in chap. 95, Jesus tells Peter that the cock will not crow before the apostle has denied him three times; this betrayal also comes to pass in chap. 96. Again, the disciples are told on three occasions to go ahead of Jesus into Galilee, and that "after he was raised from the dead," he would meet them there (chaps. 96, 104, and 111). Jesus keeps this appointment in the final scenes (111, 112).

Regarding the lexis of the *Estoire*, finally, the repetition of deictic *este vous*, "behold" or "lo," which occurs nearly sixty times, further dramatizes events, as it were magnifying them before the listener's eyes.

Stenographic Character

As suggested above, the *Estoire* is very much a "reported" gospel: verbs of communication — "say," "reply," "ask," "bid," etc. — punctuate and quicken the narrative; and adverbs "when," "then," "as (soon as)," "later," and others lend immediacy and clarity of sequence to the unfolding story. In this, the *Estoire*'s narrator simply borrows a technique of the four Gospel narrators, who report the words and deeds of Christ and of others who interact with him, often specifying the order of events as well.

Riddles and Judgment

Bread tastes saltier when the baker reduces even slightly the amount of water and flour in the dough. Likewise, certain aspects of the well-known gospel account stand out more prominently in the *Estoire*'s unified, streamlined narrative. It is as though, in pruning out many redundancies, in skimming over parables, and in judiciously concentrating thematically related chapters and pericopes, the *Estoire*'s author brings familiar Gospel situations into sharper focus.

Riddles in the *Estoire* are a specialized form of dialogue. In the New Testament Gospels, the scribes' and Pharisees' antagonism towards Jesus is often expressed very aggressively in the pointed questions they put to him. In his teaching or argumentation, meanwhile, Jesus frequently also puts riddles to others; similarly, characters outside the Jewish elite may question him.[137] Both a test and a trap, the riddle commonly takes the form of a dilemma in which either answer offered by the riddler can potentially damn, humiliate, or further embroil the

---

[137] For riddles put to Jesus by characters not belonging to the elite, see, e.g., the Samaritan woman's question opposing Mount Gerizim and Jerusalem (chap. 13) and the disciples' question about the man blind from birth (59).

unwary respondent. Such is the situation when Jesus's adversaries bring him the riddle of the tribute to Caesar:

> And right away they began flattering him, saying that they were well aware that he spoke the truth to all men, and asking him to state whether they should pay tribute to Caesar, or not. And Jesus, knowing their intent immediately, told them to produce the coin required for the tribute; and they showed him a penny. And he asked whose likeness it was, and whose inscription; and they said, Caesar's. And he told them to render unto Caesar what was his, and to God what was his. And they went away confounded (86:6–12).

> [. . .] e le comencerent primes a losenger e li disoient qu'il savoient bien qu'il dist verité a touz, e li prierent qu'il lor deist si il dussent doner le truage a Cesar ou noun. E Jhesu savoit tantost lor entente e lor dist qu'il li moustrasent la monoie que um lor demaunda, e il li moustrerent un dener. E il lor demaunda a qui estoit l'ome e la superscripcion, e il disoient a Cesar. E il lor dist qu'il rendisent a Cesar ce que suen estoit e a Dieu ceo que suen estoit. E il s'en alerent confus (*Estoire*, 86:5–11).

Earlier in the chapter, Jesus's detractors had devised a strategy to entrap him in their riddle:

> Then the Pharisees went and plotted with Herod's soldiers to arrest Jesus as a felon and a traitor if he said not to pay tribute to the Romans. And if he said to pay it, they would denounce him and embroil him with the people.[138]

> Donques alerent les phariseus e se conseillerent as chivalers Herodes que eus prendroient Jhesu com feloun e treitre si il deist que um ne dust[139] doner truage as Romains. E si il deist qe om le devoit doner, il l'escrieroit e le melleroit au people (*Estoire*, 86:1–4).

The process of riddling may lead to a judgment or determination. Thus the author of the *Estoire* sometimes uses the words "judge" or "judgment" in cases where a riddle is satisfactorily resolved.[140] Elsewhere, a determination is made,

---

[138] 86:2–4 (see also the notes for this passage); chap. 86 is based primarily on Mt 22:15–22, and secondarily on Mk 12:13–17 and Lk 20:20–26. Mt 22:15 has only, "Tunc abeuntes Pharisaei consilium inierunt [. . .]." None of the three passages in *V* gives details of the Pharisees' deliberation prior to their putting the riddle about the tribute.

[139] See the note for 86:2.

[140] E.g., Jesus poses a riddle that is successfully answered in the parable of the creditor with two debtors (chap. 31). Likewise, after the parable of the Good Samaritan, Jesus asks, "Which of the three was the wounded man's neighbor, the priest, the deacon, or the Samaritan?" (34:15–16; *Estoire*, 34:13–14).

and the language of this passage particularly evokes a medieval law-court or lecture hall:

> And Jesus asked them whether one should do good or evil on the Sabbath, and they fell silent. And Jesus told them that none of them would hesitate to haul out his sheep on the Sabbath if it fell into a ditch, and surely one should more readily help a man than a sheep.
> "Thus I determine," said he, "that it is lawful to do good on the Sabbath" (38:6–10).

> E Jhesu lour demaunda si home deust fere bien ou mal en sabat, e il se teurent. E Jhesu lour dist qu'il n'i out cil d'eus qui ne levast sa berbiz en sabat si ele fust chue en une fosse, e mout plus tost dust home socoure a un home que a une owaille. 'Donc je di', dist il, 'qu'il lest fere bien au sabat' (*Estoire*, 38:5–8).

Amplification

Although the style of the *Estoire* trends toward economy, the author also occasionally augments the New Testament story. Instances of amplification have already been noted above, e.g., the author's elucidation of the Pharisees' riddling strategy and the staging of the Magdalene's movements in the garden. Among other significant examples of elaboration of the New Testament account in the *Estoire* are:

• The details of Pilate's massacre of the Galileans

> [. . .] Pilate had slain many Galileans who had gone up Mount Gerizim with a false prophet. And they had made their offerings there, and he promised to ascend to heaven before them; but Pilate arrived and killed them along with the prophet (43:2–5).

> [. . .] Pilate out occis une masse des Galileis qui estoient alez o un faus prophete en le mount de Garizin. E li offrirent la lour offrendes, e il lour promist qu'il mounteroit au ciel devaunt eus. E sourvint Pilate e lé occist ensemblement o li (*Estoire*, 43:2–5).

The biblical source is Lk 13:1–9. Lk 13:1 mentions only "Galilaeis quorum sanguinem Pilatus miscuit cum sacrificiis eorum," giving no further details.
The corresponding text of PGH is more detailed than the *Estoire*'s, adding, e.g., that the offerings were being made to Jesus, "and offreden to Jesu her offrandes" ("and offering to Jesus their offerings," Goates, 41).

• The rationale of the scribes and Pharisees who asked Jesus about punishment for the woman taken in adultery

And they did this so that if Jesus said to stone her, they could discredit him for harshness, and the people who thought him so compassionate would love him less; and if he said to release her, they could accuse him of transgressing God's law (59:36–39).

E ce firent il pur ce que si il deist: 'Lapidez la!', il l'eussent escrié com cruel, e le people que le tynt si pitous l'ust moyns amé; e si il deist: 'Lessez la quite!', il l'eussent pris com celi que eust fet contre la lei Dieu (*Estoire*, 59:30–33).

The biblical source is Jn 8:1–11. In *V*, the scribes and Pharisees are not said to deliberate before bringing the accused woman before Jesus. Jn 8:3 has only, "adducunt autem scribae et Pharisaei mulierem in adulterio deprehensam."
PGH substantially matches the *Estoire* here (Goates, 55).

• The apostle Thomas's opinion that, in returning to Bethany, Jesus was defying his enemies and risking death

For, as Thomas saw it, Jesus was going deliberately among his mortal enemies (80:19–20).

Quar Jhesu, ce li fui vis, ala de gré entre ses morteaus enemis (*Estoire*, 80:15–16)

The biblical source is Jn 11:7–16. Yet, *V* records only Thomas's words, "eamus et nos ut moriamur cum eo" (Jn 11:16b), not his rationale.
In PGH, the rationale is incorporated in Thomas's speech: "Goo we now and dye wiþ oure maister: for why, he were his frende þat ȝede wiþ hym wiþ his owene good wille aȝein his enemyes" ("Go we now to die with our master: because one would be his friend who would go with him with his own good will to meet his enemies"; Goates, 73).

• Jesus's unsuccessful bid for lodging

And then he looked around for anyone who would offer him lodging; and when no one volunteered, he retired with his apostles to Lazarus's house in Bethany and taught them about the Christian faith (82:17–19).

E donqes regarda il entour luy si nul le vousist prier a herberger. E quant nul ne le fist, donqes s'en parti il ové ses apostres en Betaigne chief Lazere e lor aprist la crestienté (*Estoire*, 82:15–17).

The biblical sources are Mt 21:14–17 and Mk 11:11. Only Mk 11:11 hints at the authorial reinterpretation in the *Estoire*: "Et introivit Hierosolyma in templum et circumspectis omnibus cum iam vespera esset hora exivit in Bethania cum

duodecim." Thus, in explaining Jesus's retreat to Bethany, our author adds to the late hour the inhospitality of Jesus's listeners at the Temple.

Again, the text of PGH substantially matches the *Estoire* here (Goates, 77–78).

- The gathering of the disciples before the Ascension

> Then Jesus told them to gather all the followers dwelling in the houses round about, men and women alike, and to go out to meet him on the Mount of Olives. For the eleven apostles were staying in the same spacious upper room where Jesus had given the Last Supper, and the other disciples and the women lived in houses nearby, in a district of the city called Mount Sion (113:13–18).

> Donc lor dist Jhesu qu'il assemblassent touz les deciples qe mistrent as hosteaus environ, homes e femes, e alassent countre li eu mount d'Olivete. Quar les xi. apostres mistrent en cel graunt soler—la ou Jhesu out fet sa Cene—e les autres deciples e les femes mistrent en les hosteaus decoste en cele partie de la cité qu'estoit apelé mount Sion (*Estoire*, 113:12–16).

This passage, which has no direct biblical source, appears to be another example of imaginative stage-setting by the author of the *Estoire* (see pages 32 and 33).[141] It is a dramatization of the assembly of Jesus's followers that was necessary if the disciples were to witness the Ascension on the Mount of Olives. The author thrice mentions the women among Jesus's followers in these lines. The pertinent biblical passages are Luke 24:50–53, which has Jesus leading the disciples to the Mount of Olives, and Acts 1:4–12.

PGH's reading very closely corresponds to the account in the *Estoire* (Goates, 111–12).

---

[141] See the note to 113:15 for a twelfth-century description of this site.

Suggested Further Reading

Primary Sources of Special Interest

Aelred of Rievaulx, *De institutione inclusarum*. In *Aelredi Rievallensis Opera Omnia*, ed. A. Hoste and C. H. Talbot. CCCM 1. Turnhout: Brepols, 1971.

Aelred of Rievaulx's De institutione inclusarum: Two English Versions, ed. John Ayto and Alexandra Barratt. EETS 287. London and New York: Oxford University Press, 1984.

Estoire de l'Evangile, ed. Brent A. Pitts. Medium Ævum Monographs 28. Oxford: Society for the Study of Medieval Languages and Literature, 2011.

Itinéraires à Jerusalem et Descriptions de la Terre sainte rédigés en français aux XIe, XIIe et XIIIe siècles, ed. Henri Michelant and Gaston Raynaud. Geneva: Imprimerie Jules-Guillaume Fick, 1882; www.archive.org.

Johannes de Caulibus, *Meditaciones Vite Christi*, ed. M. Stallings-Taney. CCCM 153. Turnhout: Brepols, 1997.

John of Caulibus, *Meditations on the Life of Christ*, trans. and ed. Francis X. Taney, Anne Miller, and Mary Stallings-Taney. Asheville, NC: Pegasus Press, 2000.

The Lyf of Oure Lady: The ME Translation of Thomas of Hales' Vita Sancte Marie, ed. Sarah M. Horrall. Heidelberg: C. Winter, 1985.

Mirour de Seinte Eglyse (St Edmund of Abingdon's Speculum Ecclesiae), ed. A. D. Wilshere. ANTS 40. London: ANTS, 1982; www.anglo-norman.net.

The Pepysian Harmony, ed. Margery Goates. EETS o.s. 157. London: H. Milford, Oxford University Press, 1922; www.hathitrust.org.

The Sarum Missal, trans. A. Harford Pearson. 2nd ed. London: Church Printing Company, 1884; www.archive.org.

Secondary Sources

(I) Medieval Religious Practice

Bestul, Thomas H. *Texts of the Passion: Latin Devotional Literature and Medieval Society*. Philadelphia: University of Pennsylvania Press, 1996.

Connolly, Daniel K. *The Maps of Matthew Paris: Medieval Journeys through Space, Time and Liturgy*. Woodbridge, Suffolk, and Rochester, NY: Boydell Press, 2009.
de Hamel, Christopher. *The Book: A History of the Bible*. London and New York: Phaidon, 2001.
Despres, Denise. *Ghostly Sights*. Norman, OK: Pilgrim Books, 1989.
Gameson, Richard, ed. *The Early Medieval Bible*. Cambridge: Cambridge University Press, 1994.
Halbwachs, Maurice. *La Topographie légendaire des Evangiles en Terre sainte: Etude de mémoire collective*. 2nd ed. Paris: Presses Universitaires de France, 1971.
Hanna, Ralph. "Augustinian Canons and Middle English Literature." In *The English Medieval Book: Studies in Memory of Jeremy Griffiths*, ed. A. S. G. Edwards, Vincent Gillespie, and idem, 27–42. London: British Library, 2000.
Horrall, Sarah M. "Thomas of Hales, OFM: His Life and Works." *Traditio* 42 (1986): 287–98.
Jansen, Katherine L. *The Making of the Magdalen: Preaching and Popular Devotion in the Later Middle Ages*. Princeton: Princeton University Press, 2000.
Kupfer, Marcia, ed. *The Passion Story: From Visual Representation to Social Drama*. University Park: Pennsylvania State University Press, 2008.
Legge, M. Dominica. "The Anglo-Norman Sermon of Thomas of Hales." *Modern Language Review* 30 (1935): 212–18.
Meale, Carol M., ed. *Women and Literature in Britain, 1150–1500*. Cambridge and New York: Cambridge University Press, 1993.
Morey, James H. *Book and Verse: A Guide to Middle English Biblical Literature*. Urbana: University of Illinois Press, 2000.
Pringle, Denys. *The Churches of the Crusader Kingdom of Jerusalem: A Corpus*. 4 vols. Cambridge: Cambridge University Press, 1993–2009.
Salter, Elizabeth. *Nicholas Love's "Myrrour of the Blessed Lyf of Jesu Christ."* Analecta Cartusiana 10. Salzburg: Institut für Englische Sprache und Literatur, 1974.
Smalley, Beryl. "Some Gospel Commentaries of the Early Twelfth Century." *Recherches de Théologie ancienne et médiévale* 45 (1978): 147–80.
Smith, Kathryn A. *Art, Identity and Devotion in Fourteenth-Century England*. London: British Library; Toronto: University of Toronto Press, 2003.
Sticca, Sandro. *The* Planctus Mariae *in the Dramatic Tradition of the Middle Ages*, trans. Joseph R. Berrigan. Athens, GA: University of Georgia Press, 1988.
Wilkinson, John, with Joyce Hill and W. F. Ryan. *Jerusalem Pilgrimage 1099–1185*. London: Hakluyt Society, 1988.

(II) Gospel Harmonies and Diatessaronic Studies

Birdsall, J. Neville. "The Sources of the Pepysian Harmony and its Links with the Diatessaron." *New Testament Studies* 22 (1975–1976): 215–23.
Boismard, Marie-Emile. *Le Diatessaron: De Tatien à Justin*. Etudes bibliques, Nouvelle série 15. Paris: Lecoffre, Gabalda, 1992.
Harris, J. Rendel. "The Gospel Harmony of Clement of Llanthony." *Journal of Biblical Literature* 43 (1924): 349–62.
———. "Some Notes on the Gospel-Harmony of Zacharias Chrysopolitanus." *Journal of Biblical Literature* 43 (1924): 32–45.
Patterson, Stephen J. "Gospel Parallels and Harmonies." In *Encyclopedia of Christianity*, ed. Erwin Fahlbusch et al., trans. Geoffrey W. Bromiley, 4:39–42. Grand Rapids: W. B. Eerdmans; Leiden: Brill, 2005.
Petersen, William L. *Tatian's Diatessaron: Its Creation, Dissemination, Significance, and History in Scholarship*. Leiden: Brill, 1994.
———. "Diatessaron." In *The Anchor Bible Dictionary*, ed. David Noel Freedman et al., 2:189–90. New York; London: Doubleday, 1992.
Plooij, Daniel. *A Primitive Text of the Diatessaron: The Liège Manuscript of a Medieval Dutch Translation*. Leyden: A.W. Sijthoff, 1923; www.archive.org.
———. "The Pepysian Harmony." *Bulletin of the Bezan Club* 2 (1926): 14–16.
Schmid, Ulrich B. "In Search of Tatian's Diatessaron in the West." *Vigiliae Christianae* 57 (2003): 176–99.
———. "'. . . So that those who read the (Biblical) text and the commentary do not correct one after the other'." In *Paratext and Megatext as Channels of Jewish and Christian Traditions*, ed. A. A. den Hollander, idem, and W. F. Smelik, 136–51. Leiden and Boston: Brill, 2003.
———. *Unum ex quattuor: Eine Geschichte der lateinischen Tatianüberlieferung*. Freiburg im Breisgau: Herder, 2005.

(III) The French of England: Language and Literature

Crane, Susan. "Anglo-Norman Cultures in England, 1066–1460." In *The Cambridge History of Medieval English Literature*, ed. David Wallace, 35–60. Cambridge: Cambridge University Press, 1999.
Dean, Ruth J., with Maureen B. M. Boulton. *Anglo-Norman Literature: A Guide to Texts and Manuscripts*. ANTS Occasional Publications 3. London: ANTS, 1999.
Legge, M. Dominica. *Anglo-Norman Literature and its Background*. Oxford: Clarendon Press, 1963.
Meale, Carol M., ed. *Women and Literature in Britain, 1150–1500*. Cambridge and New York: Cambridge University Press, 1993.

Rothwell, William. "The 'Faus français d'Angleterre': Later Anglo-Norman." In *Anglo-Norman Anniversary Essays*, ed. Ian Short, 309–26. ANTS Occasional Publications 2. London: ANTS, 1993.

———. "The Role of French in Thirteenth-Century England." *Bulletin of the John Rylands University Library of Manchester* 58 (1976): 445–66.

Short, Ian. *Manual of Anglo-Norman*. ANTS Occasional Publications 7. London: ANTS, 2007.

———. "On Bilingualism in Anglo-Norman England." *Romance Philology* 33 (1980): 467–79.

———. "*Tam Angli quam Franci*: Self-Definition in Anglo-Norman England." *Anglo-Norman Studies* 18 (1995): 153–75.

Wogan-Browne, J. et al., ed. *Language and Culture: The French of England c. 1000–c.1500*. Woodbridge: York Medieval Press with Boydell and Brewer, 2009.

Translator's Note

The translation seeks above all to convey clearly and faithfully, in modern English, the sense of the *Estoire*. For variety of sentence structure, syntax is sometimes altered slightly, e.g., by substituting a present participle for a past-tense verb. Repetitive "and" is occasionally omitted, and *tut le poeple* ("all the people") is often translated "the people" or "the multitude." The harmonist repeatedly inserts "he said" to signal a direct or indirect quotation. To avoid repetition of such tags in a single sentence or series of sentences, an acceptable synonym is often substituted when authorized by the context.

For clarity, I sometimes substitute the corresponding proper noun for a subject pronoun whose antecedent is left vague. I also occasionally add a brief explanatory tag, translating, e.g., *pur qu'il* (read *qui il*) *estoit descenduz*, "for whom he had come down the mountain" (iii), since "the mountain" is clearly assumed by the *Estoire*'s text. In translating *la femme que out eu set freres a baruns* as "the woman who had married seven brothers," *a baruns* ("as husbands") being redundant, is dropped.

In the section of Liber niger containing the *Estoire*, the titles in the *capitula* very often match those found in the lower margin, but discrepancies do occur. For example, the marginal titles are often shorter, as when (in the *capitula*) "Jesus exonerates his disciples for eating corn on the Sabbath" becomes "Jesus defends his disciples" in the marginal title.

A few recurring words call for brief comment. AN *mestre* is "scribe," occasionally "lawyer"; but *mestres* is "rulers" at 98:15. Sometimes called *mestres de la ley* (*Estoire*, 6:6), scribes were indeed experts, teachers or doctors of the Law (Greek *grammateis, nomodidaskaloi*).[1] AN *eveskes, princes* (*des prestres*), *archeprestres*, and *les plus hauz prestres* are alternately "chief priests" or "high priests." *Prestres* is "chief priests" at 97:24 and 108:13; *princes* is "chief rulers" at 92:25 and "rulers" at 99:23 and 108:13. For *chevaler*, *ANOH* gives "horseman," "knight," "(mounted) soldier." As the first two meanings are historically inappropriate for a life of Christ, "soldier" is favored throughout this translation, e.g. in the episode of the healing of the centurion's servant (chap. 27) and in the scene of Christ's arrest in

---

[1] D. A. Hagner, "Scribes," in *The International Standard Bible Encyclopedia*, ed. Geoffrey W. Bromiley, vol. 4 (Grand Rapids, MI: W. B. Eerdmans, 1988), 359–61, at 361.

Gethsemane (96). *Seneschal* (*ANOH* "steward [of the king's household]") is alternately "governor" (3:3) and "steward" (113:22).

After a prologue (abbreviation P), an abstract of the seven meditations (A), and a list of the *capitula* for each meditation (indicated here by lower-case Roman numerals, i-vii), the *Anglo-Norman Gospel Harmony* recounts the life of Christ in 113 chapters. Though unnumbered in the Liber niger, chapters are numbered here for convenience of reference. Line numbering restarts with each new chapter and includes chapter titles and section headings. Rejected readings are folded into the Notes section.

Chapter numbers in this translation match those in the published critical edition of the *Estoire*. The line numbers take chapter or section titles into account where these exist. Because of typographical differences with the critical edition, however, line numbers given in connection with the *Anglo-Norman Gospel Harmony* are peculiar to this translation.

The scribe of the *Estoire*, who consistently notes the beginning of each new chapter, never once marks breaks within a chapter. The present translation respects scribal practice except in the case of direct quotations, each of which, following modern convention, is set off here in a separate paragraph.

In preparing this work, I have frequently consulted three modern English translations of the Bible: King James (KJV), New International—United Kingdom version (NIV), and the New Jerusalem Bible (NJB), occasionally also checking the New Revised Standard Version (NRSV) and the Douai-Rheims. In the Notes section, these are collectively termed the "modern English Bibles." For capitalization and the specific form of toponyms and personal names, unless otherwise indicated, I generally follow KJV.

The Anglo-Norman Gospel Harmony

These are the seven meditations of Jesus concerning the . . .[1]

P. I find the Gospel story of our sweet Lord Jesus Christ in various French poem-texts. It seems to me that certain things in these works are stated otherwise than in the text of the Gospels, simply to preserve the rhyme. Thus I am making here for your benefit a prose summary of the Gospel story in the same way that Clement — the prior of Llanthony[2] who became archbishop of Canterbury immediately after Saint Thomas the martyr[3] — arranged his book, which he extracted from the four gospels. But know this one thing: that our sweet Jesus says a number of things in the Gospels either figuratively or in parables, and in such cases we should credit less the words than the intent. Thus I present these selections according to the unadorned meaning and the intent of the words, not according to a higher interpretation. And I shall also follow, albeit more briefly, Clement's division of his work into chapters so as to make the story clearer. First, I divide this meditation into seven parts, so that you may read or meditate on one part each day. For abbot Aelred instructs his sister especially to peruse the Gospel story to increase her love for the gentle Jesus Christ. And Saint Peter remarked to Saint Clement[4] that the words and miracles of his gentle master Jesus seemed so sweet to him, that each night he lay awake to meditate on the Gospels, nor could he preach anything else, albeit without rhyme. Thus I entreat you to read

---

[1] P:1 **concerning the . . .** *de 1 . . .*: the title is incomplete in the manuscript.

[2] P:5–6 **Clement — the prior of Llanthony** *Clement, priour de Lanthony*: Clement of Llanthony was the head of that Augustinian priory in Wales and the author of a Latin gospel harmony that circulated widely in England, the *Concordia quatuor evangelistarum*. For biographical details, see Introduction, pages 8–9.

[3] P:7 **Saint Thomas the martyr** *seint Thomas le martir*: Thomas Becket, the best-known saint of England, was appointed chancellor (1155), then archbishop of Canterbury (1162) by Henry II. In 1170, after a protracted and acrimonious dispute with the king over royal and ecclesiastical rights, Thomas was murdered in Canterbury Cathedral by four of Henry II's household knights (Sally N. Vaughan, "Becket, Thomas (1120–1170)," in *Key Figures in Medieval Europe: An Encyclopedia*, ed. Richard K. Emmerson [New York and Abingdon, Oxfordshire: Routledge, 2006], 59–60).

[4] P:17 **Saint Clement** *seint clement*: Clement, bishop of Rome (ca. 88–ca. 97). See Introduction, page 8, n. 28.

or meditate on the Gospel story, for you cannot love our sweet Lord Jesus Christ if you do not know him, nor can you know him well except through the Gospels which impart to us his life and his teachings, his miracles, his Passion, his Resurrection, and his Ascension, and the encouragement he gives his own through the Holy Spirit. (1–24)

A. The first meditation contains the life of our sweet Lord Jesus Christ until his baptism. The second meditation contains his life from the time of his baptism by Saint John[5] until he began his public ministry, when Saint John was in prison. The third contains his life during his public ministry until the beheading of Saint John and the surveillance of Jesus. The fourth contains his life from the time of Saint John's beheading and the rejection of Jesus until he came openly to Jerusalem to show that he was the Christ and their rightful king, and to suffer his Passion. The fifth contains his life from the entry into Jerusalem until the Last Supper. The sixth contains his Passion. The seventh contains his Resurrection. (1–9)

i. On the divinity of our sweet Lord Jesus Christ. On his Conception and its signs. On his Nativity and its signs. On his Presentation and its signs. On his flight and its signs. On his childhood and its signs. (1–3)

ii. On the baptism of our sweet Lord Jesus Christ. On his fasting and his temptation. On his first disciples. How he turned water into wine. How Jesus first appeared at the Passover in Jerusalem. How Saint John the Baptist recommended our sweet Lord Jesus Christ to his disciples. (1–4)

iii. How our sweet Lord Jesus Christ left Judea and went into Galilee as soon as Saint John the Baptist was imprisoned. How he healed the son of the royal official at Cana. How he preached in Saint Peter's ship. How he read at Nazareth. How he called Saint Peter and his companions. How he healed a man possessed by demons, the mother of Saint Peter's wife,[6] and many others in Capernaum. How he passed over the Sea of Tiberias, discouraged a scribe who wished to follow him, calmed the storm, and drove out the legion. How, on returning to Capernaum, he healed the palsied man and called Saint Matthew. How he revived Jairus's daughter and cured the woman who for twelve years had been afflicted with bleeding.[7] How he healed two blind men and a mute. How he was despised in his own country. How he chose the twelve disciples and taught them

---

[5] A:3 **Saint John** *seint Johan*: the reference here and in the lines following is to John the Baptist.

[6] iii:5 **the mother of St Peter's wife** *la mere [d]e la femme seint Pierre*

[7] iii:9–10 **the woman who for twelve years had been afflicted with bleeding** *la feme que avoit seigue* [read *la feme que avoit eu flux de sanck*]: that the woman's condition involves bleeding is made clear in chap. 21. *V* "sanguinis fluxum" (Mt 9:20).

on Mount Tabor. How he healed all those who approached him on the plain, repeating his sermon[8] to the multitude of people for whom he had come down the mountain. How he healed the leper at the entrance to Capernaum. How he healed the centurion's servant at Capernaum. How he sent the twelve apostles to preach, what power he gave them, and how he taught them. How he revived the widow's son. How Saint John the Baptist, from prison, sent him two of his disciples, and Jesus's response. How he converted the Magdalene and how she and the other women followed him. How he sent out ahead the seventy-two[9] disciples and rebuked those who rejected his teaching. How he received the seventy-two[10] disciples who, on their return, told him of the wonders they had performed in his name. How he answered the lawyer who asked what was the Law's greatest commandment and who was his neighbor. How Saint Martha lodged him. How he taught his disciples to pray. How he exonerated his disciples for collecting ears of corn on the Sabbath. How he healed a palsied hand on the Sabbath and answered the Pharisees who reproached him. How he fled and hid himself, healing those who followed. How he healed a man become blind and mute and replied to the scribes concerning Beelzebub and Jonah and the queen of Sheba,[11] and how his sweet mother needed to speak to him but could not on account of the crowd. How he answered the Pharisee who reproached him as if for sinning because he did not wash his hands before eating. How he taught his disciples to shun avarice and to be charitable by reason of two brothers who quarreled over their inheritance. How he admonished the people to repent by reason of the Galileans slain by Pilate. How he healed the woman who had been stooped for eighteen years. How he preached parables while sitting in the ship. How he came again to preach in his country, and the people insulted him. How the Jews persecuted him for healing on a Sabbath[12] the paralytic who had lain by the pool for thirty-eight years, and Jesus's response. (1–38)

---

[8] iii:13 **repeating his sermon** *e recorda sun sermon*: Jesus had earlier given his Sermon on the Mount (Mt 5). Having come down the mountain (Lk 6:17), in the harmonist's scheme, Jesus summarizes the sermon for those on the plain. See chap. 25 and the note for 25:4–5.

[9] iii:19 **seventy-two** *cinquante douzze* [read *settante deus*]

[10] iii:20 **seventy-two** *cinquante douzze* [read *settante deus*]

[11] iii:28 **Beelzebub and Jonah and the queen of Sheba** *de Belzebub e de Jona e de la reigne de Saba*: Beelzebub or Beelzebul is another name for Satan. Jonah's three days and three nights in the belly of a fish (Jonah 2:1) prefigure Christ's burial and resurrection. The modern English Bibles have "queen of the south" (Mt 12:39–40, 42; see 1 Kings 10:1, 2 Chron. 9); *V* "regina austri." The queen of the South (Sheba) "came from the ends of the earth to hear Solomon" (*Eerdmans Commentary on the Bible*, ed. James D. G. Dunn and John W. Rogerson [Grand Rapids: W. B. Eerdmans, 2003], 1029). See 40:20–21 and Mt 12:22–42.

[12] iii:37 **Sabbath** *samadi*

These are the chapters of the fourth meditation

iv. How sweet Jesus went privately into the wilderness after he got word of Saint John's beheading. How he fed five thousand men, calmed the storm, and taught followers in Capernaum about his body and his blood, and how many of his disciples went away. How he healed all those who drew near him in the land of Gennesaret. How he answered the scribes who criticized his disciples for not washing their hands before a meal. How he healed the Canaanite woman's daughter.[13] How he healed the deaf-mute and many others on the mountain at the Sea of Galilee. How he fed four thousand men with seven loaves. How he answered the Pharisees in Magadan when they asked him for a sign from heaven. How he encouraged his disciples when they forgot to take bread with them into the wilderness. How he healed a blind man in Bethsaida by spitting on his eyes. How Herod became afraid when he heard of Jesus's works and miracles. How Jesus fared when he went in secret to the feast of tabernacles in Jerusalem, where he freed the woman taken in adultery and gave sight to a blind man with mud made from his spittle. How for the first time he privately forewarned his apostles of his Passion. How he was transfigured on the mountain and, on descending, healed the lunatic. How he again warned his disciples of his Passion. How in Capernaum he paid the temple tax for himself and Saint Peter and taught his disciples about meekness and charity. How the Samaritans refused him lodging, how he said that few would be saved, and how the Pharisees warned him against Herod. How he healed a man afflicted with dropsy and preached at mealtime about meekness, charity, and contempt for this world. How on the way he preached against worldly inclination. How he answered those who grumbled when he entertained sinners. How he taught his disciples to be compassionate and reproved the Pharisees who sneered at him. How he taught his disciples to avoid scandal and to have faith and humility. How he healed the ten lepers. How he answered[14] the Pharisees who asked when the Messiah would come, and how he taught his disciples to prepare for the Judgment, particularly through prayer and humility. How he answered the Pharisees who asked if a man might leave his wife for any reason. How he blessed and embraced the children. How he answered the rich man[15] who asked how he might be saved, and[16] his reply to Saint Peter. How for the third time he forewarned his disciples of his Passion, and how he answered Saint James and corrected the other disciples. How he healed a blind man on entering Jericho. How he turned aside to Zacchaeus's house where he told the parable of the ten talents. How he healed two blind men on leaving Jericho. How he

---

[13] iv:7–8 **the Canaanite woman's daughter** *[l]a fille la Chananee*

[14] iv:27 **he answered** *il respundirent* [read *il respundi*]: see 71:1–2 and Lk 17:20.

[15] iv:31–32 **rich man** *riche homme* here, but *prince* ("ruler") in the marginal title (Mt 19:20; see chap. 74).

[16] iv:32 **saved, and** *sauf [e]*

answered the Jews at the feast of the dedication of the Temple and then slipped away. How he revived Lazarus and how, for this, the chief priests and the Pharisees plotted against him. (1–39)

These are the chapters of the fifth meditation

v. How he came through Bethany to Jerusalem and was given a triumphal entry. How he fared that day in the Temple and how he answered the chief priests and scribes who challenged him about the children.[17] How he cursed the fig tree on returning to Jerusalem[18] the next day. How he sat observing the Temple and answered those who questioned his authority. How he confounded the scribes and the Pharisees with three parables sanctioned by the Psalms. How he answered the Pharisees and the Herodians about the tribute. How he answered the Sadducees about the woman who had married seven brothers. How he answered the lawyer about the greatest commandment. How he asked the Pharisees whose son Christ was. How he taught the multitude and his disciples about the hypocrisy of the Pharisees. How Jesus praised the poor widow's offering. How Jesus answered when pagans[19] asked to speak with him, and about the voice from heaven. How he warned his disciples privately of the destruction of the Temple and taught them in four parables how to prepare for the Judgment. How Judas plotted his betrayal before the council. (1–16)

These are the chapters of the sixth meditation according to the hours of the day[20]

vi. Of sweet Jesus in his Passion, from compline until matins. Of sweet Jesus from matins until prime. Of sweet Jesus from prime until the third hour. Of sweet Jesus from the third hour until midday. Of sweet Jesus from midday until

---

[17] v:4 **who challenged him about the children** *qi le purposerent* [read *opposerent*] *des enfaunz*: see chap. 82 and Mt 21:15.

[18] v:5 **returning to Jerusalem** *il returna [vers] Jerusalem*

[19] v:13 **pagans** *paens*: the modern English Bibles have "Greeks"; *V* "gentiles." See Jn 12:20.

[20] vi:2 **the hours of the day** *les houres du jour*: The canonical hours began with matins in the third quarter of the night, continuing with *prima* (*hora*) at sunrise, *tertia* at midmorning, *sexta* at midday, *nona* at mid-afternoon, *vesperae* in late afternoon, and *completa* at the end of the day. For discussion of the hours in relation to medieval monastic practice, see *Ancrene Riwle: Introduction and Part I*, ed. and trans. Robert W. Ackerman and Roger Dahood, MRTS 31 (Binghamton: MRTS, 1984), 29–38. See also William Rothwell, "The Hours of the Day in Medieval French," *French Studies* 13 (1959), 240–51; and

the ninth hour. Of sweet Jesus from the ninth hour until vespers. How sweet Jesus was taken away after his death. (1–7)

These are the chapters of the seventh meditation

vii. How our sweet Lord Jesus Christ rose from the dead and revived several other saints. How he appeared to the Magdalene. How he appeared to the other women. How the soldiers were bribed. How the women announced sweet Jesus's resurrection to the apostles. How sweet Jesus appeared to Saint Peter.[21] How sweet Jesus appeared to Cleopas and his companion. How sweet Jesus appeared to ten apostles at vespers on his resurrection day. How sweet Jesus appeared to Saint Thomas and to the others on the eighth day. How sweet Jesus appeared on the mountain in Galilee. How Jesus appeared at the Sea of Tiberias.[22] How Jesus twice appeared on the day he ascended to heaven. (1–10)

1. On the divinity of sweet Jesus. In accordance with his divinity, our sweet Lord Jesus Christ had being before the Creation, for through him God created all that exists. For his is the power and the knowledge of God his Father, and—without altering his divinity—he became a true man and gave life, light, and grace to humankind that it might know God. And by the Law and the prophets, he was promised to all who believed in God his Father. But when he came, many[23] rejected him; but on those who received him he bestowed divine favor to make them children of God; for all who believed in him received grace from his abundance of grace. No one ever beheld God with his own eyes, wherefore the Son of God became a man to teach humankind how he might be seen in the spirit. Thus he became a man of the lineage of saints David and Abraham, for he had been promised especially to them. (1–12)

---

idem, "A Further Note on *Nonne*," *French Studies* 20 (1966): 223–25. Rothwell cites a late thirteenth-century text showing that, in some places, *"midi* and *nonne* were roughly synonymous" ("The Hours of the Day," 241, 245).

[21] vii:5 **How sweet Jesus appeared to Saint Peter** *Coment douz Jhesu apparust a seint Pere*: here the *Estoire* interverts this chapter title and the next (Cleopas). Compare the corresponding chapters (107 and 108), where Christ appears first to Peter. The interversion is not noted in the published critical edition. See the note for 107:1.

[22] vii:9 **How Jesus appeared at the Sea of Tiberias** *Coment Jhesu apparust a la mer de Thabayre*: The chapter title lacks in the *capitula*, an omission that is not noted in the published critical edition.

[23] 1:6 **many** *plusours*: the modern English Bibles have "the world"; *V* "mundus." See Jn 1:10.

2. On the Conception of sweet Jesus. In the time of Herod, a pagan king who enslaved God's people and reigned in Jerusalem, there was an honorable priest, Zechariah, and his wife Elizabeth, of Aaron's line. And she was barren and advanced in years, and Zechariah too was old, and therefore they had begotten no children. Now a very important feast arrived as Zechariah offered incense at the high altar of the Temple. All the people were in prayer outside; and Zechariah, alone inside the Temple, entreated God to save them. Then an angel appeared to him, standing at the right of the altar; and Zechariah was startled and petrified with fear. But the angel reassured him, saying that Zechariah's prayer for his people had been heard and that his wife would conceive and bear a son who would be called John,[24] for whose birth Zechariah and the people would rejoice.[25] And the angel told him that the child—in the spirit and power of the prophet Elijah—would appear before the One who would save the people, for he would be filled with the Holy Spirit in his mother's womb and would forego earthly delights.[26] And he would turn many to God and to the true faith[27] of the patriarchs and prophets and would prepare them as a people loyal to the Lord.[28] Then Zechariah asked how this could be[29] since he was old, he said, and his wife, old and barren. And the angel answered that he was the angel Gabriel who stood before God and had been sent to Zechariah to proclaim this good news. And the angel told Zechariah that because he had not believed him as he should have, he would be unable to speak until these things had come to pass. The people were waiting outside for Zechariah, and they marvelled that he tarried so long in the Temple. But when, on coming out, he could not speak to them, they gathered that he had had some sort of vision in the Temple; and he made signs to them and returned dumb to his home. After this, Elizabeth conceived; and for five months she secluded herself until she knew she was pregnant and that God had bestowed such honor on her. In the sixth month after the conception of Saint John, the angel Gabriel was sent to a city of Galilee called Nazareth, to a virgin[30] pledged to

---

[24] 2:10–11 **would conceive and bear a son [. . .] called John** *conceiueroit un fiz i enfauntereyt que aueroit a noun Johan* [read *conceiveroit e enfauntereyt un fiz que averoit a noun Johan*]: the emendation follows a similar line in the account of the angel's visit to Mary (see 2:33–34).

[25] 2:11–12 **would rejoice** *aver[oi]t graunt joye*

[26] 2:14–15 **and would forego earthly delights** *e ceo descendroit dé delices de cest secle*: paraphrase of Lk 1:15. The modern English Bibles have variants of "he must drink no wine, no strong drink" (NJB); *V* "et vinum et sicera non bibet."

[27] 2:15 **he would turn [. . .] to God and to the true faith** *tor[n]eroit a dieu [e] a la droite creaunce*: see Lk 1:16–17.

[28] 2:16 **prophets and would prepare them [. . .] to the Lord** *prophetes [e] appara[i]lereit a dieu*: see Lk 1:16–17.

[29] 2:17 **this could be** *ceo p[o]e[i]t estre*

[30] 2:28 **Nazareth, to a virgin** *Nazareth [a] une pucele*: for the reports of medieval pilgrims regarding Nazareth's church of the Annunciation, see Denys Pringle, *The Churches*

a man named Joseph. The virgin's name was Mary. And the angel went in to her, greeted her, and told her that she was full of grace, that God was with her, and that she was blessed above all women. And when she heard these words, Mary was taken aback, pondering how the angel could address such a greeting to her. But the angel reassured her, saying that she had found favor with God and would conceive and bring forth a son who would be named Jesus, and that he would be called the Son of God and would rule forever as king of Israel.

Then Mary replied:

"How will this happen, since I intend never to have relations with a man?"

And the angel answered:

"The Holy Spirit will come upon you, and the power of almighty God overshadow you, and consequently the child born of you will be called the Son of God. Know that your cousin Elizabeth has conceived a son in her old age and is now in her sixth month; wherefore God can do whatever is pleasing to him."

Then Mary replied:

"Behold the handmaid of God, may it be with me as you have said."[31]

And immediately the Son of God, a man perfect in body and soul and the true God, was conceived in the virgin; and the angel departed. And Mary immediately went out of Galilee in Judea and, entering Zechariah's house, greeted Elizabeth.[32] And when Elizabeth heard Mary's voice, the child in her womb rejoiced, and she was filled with the Holy Spirit. And she began to shout, praising Mary above all women, and her child, and telling what had befallen her.

Then Mary answered, praising God and singing:

"My soul magnifies the Lord."[33]

Mary then stayed with her for about three months, returning home afterwards to Nazareth. And upon her return, before Joseph had taken her in

---

of the Crusader Kingdom of Jerusalem, 2: *L–Z (excluding Tyre)* (Cambridge: Cambridge University Press, 1998), 116–40. According to Abbot Daniel (1106–1108), the holy cave on this site was the locus of the Annunciation, Jesus's childhood, and Joseph's burial.

[31] 2:44 **Behold the handmaid [. . .] as you have said** *Veez moi ci la auncele Dieu, ensi me pusse avenir cum vous avez dist*: antiphon for the Feast of the Annunciation (Lk 1:38). In the ME *Estorie,* the impregnation of Mary is compared with the sun penetrating glass. See Celia Millward, ed., *La Estorie del Evangelie,* ME Texts 30 (Heidelberg: C. Winter, 1998), 25, 103.

[32] 2:47–48 **entering Zechariah's house, greeted Elizabeth** *entra en la meson Zacarie e salua Elizabeth*: some thirteenth-century texts locate the Visitation not in Jerusalem but in the vicinity of Nazareth. See Pringle, *Churches* 2:144–45. *Estoire* suggests here that Mary had travelled a good distance, however. As early as the sixth century, 'Ain Karim near Jerusalem was identified as the home of Elizabeth and Zechariah, the site of the Visitation, the birthplace of John the Baptist, and the refuge of Elizabeth and her baby during the Slaughter of the Innocents (see *Churches,* 1:30–47, at 30–31, 39).

[33] 2:52 **My soul magnifies the Lord** *Magnificat anima mea Dominum*: canticle of Mary (Lk 1:46–55)

marriage, he perceived that she was great with child. And he thought to break it off with her quietly, for he was a just man, hesitant to partake of sin.[34] Behold, as he was pondering these things, the angel of God appeared to him in a vision and told him not to fear, for Mary had conceived by the Holy Spirit and would bear a son who would be called Jesus because he would save his people from their sins. And Joseph awoke and did as the angel commanded. And when the time came for Elizabeth to give birth, she brought forth a son; and all who heard this news rejoiced. And on the eighth day, their kinsmen arrived to circumcise the child, and they named him Zechariah for his father; whereupon his mother answered that he should be called John instead. And they said that no man among Zechariah's kindred had such a name; and they made signs to Zechariah to inform them which name he wished the child to have. And Zechariah asked for a tablet and wrote that the child was already named John, and all marveled at this.

And immediately Zechariah's speech was restored, and — filled with the Holy Spirit — he began praising our Lord God and singing:

"Holy Lord God of Israel."[35]

And throughout Judea, whoever heard of this miracle believed that when he came of age, the child would be wondrous and mighty before God. And the child grew and thrived, strengthened by the Holy Spirit. And when he came of age, he went into the wilderness, sojourning there until the Holy Spirit directed him to preach the advent of Jesus Christ. (1–75)

3. On his Nativity and its signs. In those days the Roman emperor Caesar Augustus decreed that all the earth's inhabitants should be registered in their native cities, and that each should pay a tax to the governor of the land[36] to acknowledge his subjection to the Empire. For that reason Joseph with his wife Mary, who was great with child, travelled from Nazareth to Bethlehem to make recognizance in his city, for he and his wife were descendents of King David of Bethlehem. Behold, while they were staying there, Mary's time came, and she brought forth her firstborn, a son. And she wrapped him in cloths and laid him in a manger where livestock were wont to eat, for there was no place in their lodging where she could more fittingly put him.[37] And shepherds were keeping watch in the countryside,

---

[34] 2:56 **to partake of sin** *parti[r] del peché*

[35] 2:70 **Holy Lord God of Israel** *Benedictus Dominus Deus Israel*: canticle of Zechariah (Lk 1:68–79).

[36] 3:3 **to the governor of the land** *au seneschal du païs*: "governor of Syria" (NJB); *V* "praeside Syriae" (see Lk 2:1–3). For *seneschal*, see page 46 and the note for 113:22.

[37] 3:9–10 **where she could more fittingly put him** *ou ele le pust plus covenablement mettre*: Abbot Daniel's pilgrimage narrative (1106–1108) gives a detailed description: "The cave and the manger where Christ's nativity took place are beneath the great altar like a great cavern, beautifully made . . . These places, the Nativity and the manger, are close together, only three fathoms apart; the two places are in the same cave, and this cave

tending their sheep. And an angel appeared with the glory of heaven and stood by them, and they were overcome with terror. But the angel reassured them, saying that he was bringing them tidings that Christ, who would save[38] the people, was born in Bethlehem,[39] for which they and all mankind should greatly rejoice. And he said that, as a sign, they would find a child wrapped in swaddling clothes and laid in a manger.

Behold, a multitude of angels suddenly appeared with him, praising God and singing:

"Glory to God in the highest."

And when the angels had ascended to heaven, the shepherds conferred and, hurrying to Bethlehem, found Mary and Joseph and—lying in a manger—the babe. And, understanding that this was the child of whom the angel had spoken, they told others what they had seen that night; and all marvelled. And Mary stored up all these things in her heart. And the shepherds returned, praising God who had shown them such a great wonder. On the eighth day the child was circumcised and given the name Jesus, just as the angel had called him before his conception. Behold, on the twelfth day, three wise men from the East arrived at Jerusalem. They were seeking the King of the Jews who had been born and whose star they had seen in the East; and they said they had come to worship him. King Herod was disturbed when he heard this, and all Jerusalem with him. And he convened all the chief priests and scribes and asked where the Christ was to be born. And they answered, in Bethlehem, for so had God promised through his prophet. Then Herod summoned the wise men privately and inquired when they had first seen the star. And he sent them on to Bethlehem, instructing them to inquire diligently after the child, and when they had found him, to alert Herod, and he would come to worship him. And when they had heard the king, the wise men departed for Bethlehem. Behold, the star they had seen in the East appeared, leading them onward until it arrived and hovered above the place where the child was. And, overjoyed at seeing the star, they went

---

is decorated with mosaic and beautifully paved" (Wilkinson, *Jerusalem Pilgrimage*, 143–44). For a detailed description of the medieval church of St Mary (or the Holy Nativity), see Denys Pringle, *The Churches of the Crusader Kingdom of Jerusalem*, 1: *A–K (excluding Acre and Jerusalem)*, 137–56. For the cave of the Nativity, see further Pringle, *Churches*, 1:137–57, at 137, 138, 146–48.

[38] 3:13 **Christ, who would save** *Crist [qe] sauveroit*

[39] 3:13–14 **Christ [. . .] was born in Bethlehem** *Crist [. . .] estoit né en Bedleem*: the pilgrimage account called the Seventh Guide (ca. 1160) notes several nearby points of interest: "In Bethlehem Christ was born, and there is the Tomb of Saint Jerome, and the Well in which the star fell, and there is a painting of the Table on which Mary [ate with] the Three Kings. In this area are the Tombs of the Innocents. In the crypt of the Blessed Virgin is the altar where she gave birth. And not far from Bethlehem is the Church where the angel appeared to the Shepherds. And there is the church where Saint Mary rested when she carried the Lord" (Wilkinson, *Jerusalem Pilgrimage*, 236).

into the house and found the child with his mother. And they fell down to worship the child and—opening their treasure-chests—offered him gold, incense, and myrrh. And just as they were considering going again to Herod, an angel appeared to them in a dream, telling them not to return through him; and they went back to their country by another way. (1–44)

4. On his Oblation and its signs. Behold, as Herod awaited the wise men's return, there came Mary's day of purification in the Temple, the day when—according to the Law of Moses—she should give her child to God and redeem him from the priests.[40] And so Mary arrived at Jerusalem with Joseph, bringing her son and the offering required of the poor. And there was a just and devout man in Jerusalem named Simeon who longed for the Messiah's coming in his lifetime. And the Holy Spirit dwelling in him had promised Simeon that he would not die before seeing the Messiah; and immediately the Holy Spirit led Simeon into the Temple.

And as Joseph and Mary arrived to present Jesus and their offering there, Simeon came and—taking Jesus in his arms—praised God, singing:

"Now thou dost dismiss thy servant, O Lord."[41]

Now another old person, a widow named Anna, was also present; she never departed from the Temple, but served God night and day in fasting and prayer. And Anna appeared in that instant before them, praising God and manifesting that the child was the Messiah. Now Joseph and Mary marveled at the things they were saying of the child.

And Simeon came and said to Mary:

"Behold, woman, this child has come that the hearts of many may be revealed; and many will fall, and many rise, on account of him. And he is also like a standard-bearer whom man will deny.[42] And though you love his life as your own, he will experience death and suffering."[43]

---

[40] 4:3–4 **redeem him from the priests** *rechater le des prestres*: KJV and NIV have "offer a sacrifice," NJB and NRSV "present him to the Lord"; *V* "ut sisterent eum Domino" (Lk 2:22).

[41] 4:12 **Now thou dost dismiss thy servant, O Lord** *Nunc dimittis servum tuum Domine*: canticle of Simeon (Lk 2:28).

[42] 4:19–21 **this child has come [. . .] like a standard-bearer whom man will deny** *cest enfaunt est venu pur moustrer les corages des plusors de cest poeple; e pluisors cherrunt par encheson de ly, e plusors releverent par li. E il est ausi cum banere a qui home countredirra*: see Lk 2:34–35.

[43] 4:21–22 **And though you love his life as your own, he will experience death and suffering** *E la soue vie que vos amez cum la vostre soffra mort e passion*: less vivid paraphrase of Lk 2:35, e.g., NRSV "a sword will pierce your own soul too"; *V* "tuam ipsius animam pertransiet gladius."

And when Joseph and Mary had fulfilled their obligations in the Temple, they returned to Nazareth. (1–24)

5. On his flight and its signs. Behold, the angel appeared to Joseph in a dream and told him to take the child and his mother and flee to Egypt,[44] staying there until he notified him, for Herod would seek to kill the child. And Joseph immediately arose by night and, taking the child and his mother, departed into Egypt where he remained until Herod's death. And Herod was furious when he perceived that the kings had duped him and returned to their country. And he sent his men to slay all the children of Bethlehem and of the country round about who were under two years of age, according to the time of the star's first appearance, as he had ascertained from the kings. Now immediately upon Herod's death, the angel appeared to Joseph in Egypt, instructing him to return, because those who had sought the child were dead. But Joseph was afraid to go back to Bethlehem on account of Herod's son, who was reigning in Judea in his father's stead. But on the angel's advice, Joseph took the child and his mother back to Galilee and dwelt in Nazareth. And the child grew and thrived and was filled with the grace of God.[45] (1–15)

---

[44] 5:2 **and flee to Egypt** e *fuist en Egipte*: several apocryphal stories of the Holy Family's exile in Egypt were circulating at this time, including the tales of the Balsam Grove, the Fruit Tree, and the Fountain or Well in which Mary washed the child Jesus's clothes. According to the Ethiopic Synaxarium, the grove of balsam trees was planted by the child Jesus during the Holy Family's sojourn in Matariyah. It was believed that balsam trees could not survive without water from this particular well (Otto F. A. Meinardus, *The Holy Family in Egypt* [Cairo: American University in Cairo Press, 1986], 38–39). For the Miracle of the Fruit Tree, see Maureen B. M. Boulton, ed., *The Old French Evangile de l'Enfance* (Toronto: Pontifical Institute of Medieval Studies, 1984), 8, 32–36, a passage based on the Gospel of Pseudo-Matthew, chaps. 20–21. In this Continental French version, the tree supplies both fruit and water for the Holy Family (ll. 345–408). Boulton dates the work from the late thirteenth century or earlier (16). The Itinerary from London to Jerusalem by Matthew Paris (ca. 1244) summarizes the Miracle of the Fruit Tree (see Henri Michelant and Gaston Raynaud, *Itinéraires à Jérusalem et descriptions de la Terre Sainte* [Geneva: Fick, 1882; repr. Osnabrück: Otto Zeller, 1966; gallica.bnf.fr], 133–34).

[45] 5:14–15 **filled with the grace of God** *plein de la grace de Dieu*: "filled with wisdom, and the grace of God was upon him" (NIV); *V* "plenus sapientia et gratia Dei erat in illo" (Lk 2:40). Abbot Daniel's pilgrimage narrative (1106–1108) gives a detailed account of Nazareth and local events related to the life of Christ (Wilkinson, *Jerusalem Pilgrimage*, 163–64). Pringle, *Churches*, 2:141–44, describes Nazareth's church of St Gabriel and its fountain or spring. According to Saewulf (1102–1103) and others, here the boy Jesus drew water for his mother.

6. Jesus's childhood. And after Jesus's twelfth birthday, when the feast of the Passover came, Joseph and Mary departed for Jerusalem—as was their custom each year—and Jesus accompanied them. And as they returned home after the feast, the child stayed behind in the city, unbeknownst to them. They had journeyed a full day, supposing Jesus to be on the way. But because they could not find him after inquiring among all their friends, they turned back to Jerusalem to look for him. And on the third day they found him sitting among the teachers of the Law, listening to them and asking questions; and all who saw and heard him were dumbfounded by his understanding and argumentation.

Then his mother asked:

"Son, why have you done this to us? We have been looking for you with heavy hearts!"

And Jesus answered:

"Why were you so sorrowful? Didn't you know I must be busy with my Father's work?"

But they did not understand his meaning, for he was speaking of his heavenly Father. And he went down from the Temple and accompanied them to Nazareth and was obedient to them. And his mother kept all these things in her heart. And thenceforth Jesus showed day by day his wisdom and refinement, finding favor with God and man. (1–20)

Here begins the second meditation, for Monday

7. On the baptism of Jesus Christ. When Saint John the Baptist had dwelt in the wilderness until his thirtieth year, and after the Romans had quartered the kingdom of Jerusalem, the Holy Spirit came, commanding John to preach to the people and to tell them to prepare to receive the Messiah whose coming was at hand. Thus he went off throughout the countryside along the River Jordan, exhorting the people to confess their sins and be baptized in the name of the One who would follow him. And John's food was locusts and wild honey, and his clothing camels' skins and a hide girding his loins. Now then the Pharisees, the religious of that time,[46] came to him for baptism. And he told them to do meritorious penance without relying on their forebears who had once found such favor with God; for God could also make worthy men of hopeless wretches,[47] and he

---

[46] 7:9–10 **the Pharisees, the religious of that time** *la gent de religion de cel tens qui estoient apelez phariseus*: the modern English Bibles have "publicans" or "tax collectors"; *V* "publicani" (Lk 3:12; see Mt 3:7, Jn 1:19, 24).

[47] 7:12 **God could also make worthy men of hopeless wretches** *Dieu purr[oit] fere ausi prodeshomes de ceus de qui nule esperaunce ne fu*: the metaphor of the stones raised as children to Abraham, found in *V* and in the modern English Bibles, is lost in the paraphrase (Mt 3:9).

would not be slow to treat each as he deserved. Now then the people asked what they should do to be saved; and John answered, to be charitable to the poor in God's name. The publicans—Jews who served the pagan rulers[48]—also asked what they should do; and he answered: wrong no one. Some soldiers also asked what they should do; and he told them to harass no one, nor wrongly accuse, but to make do with their wages. Behold, the people supposed that John himself was the Christ; and from Jerusalem the Jews sent Pharisees, priests, and deacons[49] to him to inquire who he was. And he answered that he was neither the Christ nor Elijah nor a prophet. And they begged him for an answer, that they might satisfy those who had sent them. And then he told them that he was the one whom the prophet Isaiah had said must come before Christ to prepare his way. And they asked why he was baptizing since he was neither the Christ nor Elijah nor another prophet. And he answered, saying:

"I am he who washes you with water by way of penance, but another among you—whom you know not, and who is incomparably worthier than I—will baptize you with the Holy Spirit. And he will judge each one as he finds him, rewarding each eternally, according to his merit."

Then came Jesus of Nazareth to the River Jordan to be baptized by Saint John;[50] but John forbade it, saying that it was more fitting that he be baptized by Jesus than Jesus by him. And Jesus answered that John should comply because it behooved them to set an example of all righteousness, and especially of humility. And so John baptized Jesus. And when he had been baptized and was praying for those who would receive baptism in his name, there came a heavenly brilliance;[51] and the Holy Spirit descended upon him in the form of a dove and rested on him. And from heaven came the voice of God the Father, saying to him:

"You are my beloved Son, with whom I am well pleased."

And Jesus, who was then entering his thirtieth year, was still thought of as Joseph's son. (1–40)

---

[48] 7:15 **The publicans—Jews who served the pagan rulers** *les Gyus que furent serjaunz au bailifs payens que estoient apelez pupplicans*: see Lk 3:12.

[49] 7:19 **the Christ; and [. . .] the Jews sent Pharisees, priests, and deacons** *Crist, [e] envoierent les Gyus [. . .] phariseus, prestres e diaknes*: the modern English Bibles have "priests and Levites"; *V* "sacerdotes et Levitas" (Jn 1:19). See also the note for 34:9.

[50] 7:30–31 **to be baptized by Saint John** *pur estre baptizé de seint Johan:* for discussion of the place of Christ's Baptism, see Pringle, *Churches*, 1:108–9 [chapel (of Christ's Baptism)] and 2:241–44 (church of St John the Baptist).

[51] 7:35 **there came a heavenly brilliance** *vint la clarté celestiale*: of the corresponding reading in PGH (Goates, 10), Petersen points out that PGH "is the sole Western harmonized witness to mention the 'light' at Jesus's baptism" (*Tatian's Diatessaron*, 170). See also *Hist.evang.*, "inæstimabilis splendor factus est circa eum" (col. 1555), and pages 16, 17, and 18.

8. On the fast of Jesus. As soon as the Holy Trinity had collectively borne witness to Jesus at his baptism, the Holy Spirit that filled him led him into the wilderness to be tempted by the Devil.[52] And after he had been among the wild beasts and had fasted for forty days and forty nights, he became hungry. And then the Devil came to him, saying that if he was the Son of God, he should make bread of the stones simply by commanding it. And Jesus answered that man does not live only on physical bread, but that God can sustain him by his word alone. Then the Devil took him, leading him[53] onto a very high mountain and showing him in a moment's time all the world's kingdoms and their splendor. And the Devil offered him all he had seen if he would fall down and worship him.[54] Then Jesus said:

"Away with you, Satan! For it is written that man must worship and serve God alone."

Then, taking him, the Devil conducted him[55] to Jerusalem and set him on the pinnacle of the Temple. And he told him that if he were the Son of God, he should cast himself down; for God had promised him through the prophet David that his angels would bear him up in all things, lest he be harmed.[56] And Jesus answered that the Father forbids man to tempt God to save him; rather, man

---

[52] 8:3 **to be tempted by the Devil** *pur estre tempté du Diable*: the Work on Geography (1128–1137) places the Temptation of Christ at "the second milestone south of Jericho [. . .], a place now called Quarentena." From a high mountain two miles from Quarentena, "the Devil showed Jesus all the kingdoms of the world" (Wilkinson, *Jerusalem Pilgrimage*, 205). Belard of Ascoli (ca. 1155) adds, "Half way up this mountain, but not at the top, is a cave dug out in the rock, in which Christ fasted. It is reached by a narrow path which hangs in mid-air" (Wilkinson, *Jerusalem Pilgrimage*, 230). For Quarentena, see further the discussion of several medieval pilgrims' accounts by Pringle, *Churches*, 1:252–58 (Jabal Quruntul). Theodoric's report (ca. 1175) describes in detail the tortuous ascent of the high mountain, through gates and up multiple switchbacks and stairs, before reaching the place where Jesus had fasted (1:253). Later, in a text titled *Fragments relatifs à la Galilee* (ca. 1231), Ernoul relates that the mountain of Jesus's temptation towers above the cliff near Nazareth called the Precipice or the Fall ("le Saut"), from which, as in chap. 16, Jesus's persecutors wished to cast him down (*Itinéraires à Jérusalem*, 61). See also 16:17 and the note. Pringle, *Churches*, 2:45–48 (Mount of Precipitation), considers medieval pilgrims' accounts of this site and provides a description of its ruined chapel.

[53] 8:8 **took him, leading him** *le prist [. . .] e l'amena*: Plooij lists PGH's phrase "toke & ledd" ("took and led"; Goates, 10) among his "test-readings for the Diatessaron" (Plooij, "The Pepysian Harmony," 15). See the notes for 8:14 and 53:3.

[54] 8:10–11 **and worship him** *e [l]e aorast*

[55] 8:14 **taking him, [. . .] conducted him** *li prist [. . .], si l'amena*: Plooij includes PGH's "tok & brou3th" ("took and brought"; Goates, 10) among his "test-readings for the Diatessaron" (Plooij, "The Pepysian Harmony," 15). See the notes for 8:8 and 53:3.

[56] 8:17 **lest he be harmed** *qu'il ne se blessast*: Ps 91:11–12.

must rely on himself as best he can. Then the Devil left him a while, and angels came and cared for him. (1–20)

9. On Jesus's first disciples. After sweet Jesus had left the wilderness, he returned to Saint John the Baptist. And, on seeing him, John said:
"Behold the Lamb of God who takes away the sins of the world! This is he of whom I said that a man would follow me who was before me; and to magnify him I came baptizing the people. And I saw the Holy Spirit settle upon him in the shape of a dove, and the Holy Spirit gave me this sign for recognizing Christ when it sent me baptizing. Thus I say, this is the Son of God."

Later, John was standing with two of his followers and, observing Jesus as he walked, he said:
"Behold the Lamb of God!"

And the followers approached Jesus to ask where he was staying; and he led them to his house and—since it was mid-afternoon—he lodged them there overnight. And one of the two was Andrew, Simon's brother. And he went looking for his brother Simon and told him that he had found the Christ; and he led him to Jesus. And as soon as Jesus saw him, he told him he was Simon, son of John,[57] and that he would be called Peter. And the next day Jesus called Philip, their neighbor in Bethsaida. And then Philip found Nathanael and told him that he had found the Christ; and he led him to Jesus. And when he saw him, Jesus said:
"You are a true Jew in whom there is no deceit."

Then Nathanael asked how he had known him, and Jesus answered that he had seen him under a fig tree before Philip had called him. Then Nathanael replied:
"Teacher, you are the Son of God, the King of Israel."

And Jesus answered:
"Do you believe because I said I had seen you beneath the fig tree? You will see much more than that: you will see heaven open and the angels of God ascending and descending upon me." (1–28)

10. How Jesus turned water into wine. On the third day, Jesus came into Galilee and was invited[58] with his disciples to a wedding where his mother also was.[59]

---

[57] 9:15–16 **son of John** *le fiz Johan*: the critical edition overzealously emends *Johan* to *Johné*, "Jonah." PGH "Johannes" (Goates, 11); *V* "tu es Simon filius Iohanna" (Jn 1:42). See *Hist. evang.*, col. 1581.

[58] 10:2 **was invited** *estoit con[vi]é*

[59] 10:2 **where his mother also was** *la ou sa mere estoit*: this place is later identified as Cana (see chap. 14). In a pilgrim guide called *Les sains pelerinages* (ca. 1231), the groom is named Archedeclin and the place, Quane Galilée (*Itinéraires à Jérusalem*, 104–104¹). See Pringle, *Churches*, 1:285–6 (Kafr Kanna) and 2:162–4 (Khirbat Qana). According to

And the wine happened to run low, and his mother told him that they had no more wine. And Jesus replied that the time to show his power had not yet come; then his mother instructed the servants to do whatever he told them. Now they had six pitchers there, each holding two or three measures, which the hosts used for bathing-water. And Jesus told them to fill the pitchers with water, and they filled them to the rim. Then he told them to take them up and carry them to the wedding-steward, and they brought them to him. And when he had tasted it, the wedding-steward called for the groom and told him:

"The wise man pours the best wine first, and when people are drunk, he serves the inferior wine; but you have reserved the best wine until now."

This was Jesus's first miracle, whereby his disciples believed in him. (1–13)

11. On Jesus's first appearance at the Passover in Jerusalem. Then Jesus, with his mother and his disciples, went to Capernaum and stayed there a while. And presently, at Passover-time, he went to Jerusalem. And he came into the temple-close and found them selling oxen, sheep, and doves for sacrifice; and he saw money changers sitting to change money. And he made a scourge of thin cords and drove them all from the Temple[60] with their beasts, and he scattered the money-changers' coins and overturned their tables. And he told the sellers of doves to remove them lest they make a bazaar of his Father's house. And his disciples recalled the scripture:

"Zeal for God's house will devour the heart of Christ."[61]

And, on witnessing these acts, the Jews asked Jesus for a sign, that they might believe he had the authority to perform them. And he answered that they would destroy the Temple, and he would raise it again in three days. And they replied that to build the Temple had taken forty-six years[62] and that they doubted he could rebuild it so soon; but Jesus was referring to his body and they to the physical Temple. And while Jesus was at the Passover feast, many believed in him for the miracles he performed; but he—knowing their hearts and their inclination—placed no trust in them. Now a ruler of the Jews, a Pharisee named Nicodemus, came to Jesus by night and told him that they knew well that he was sent by God, for no one could perform such miracles if God were not with him. And Jesus answered that he should believe even more, because none could enter the kingdom of God without baptism by water and rebirth through the Holy

---

Belard of Ascoli (1112–1160), Khirbat Qana's cave of the Wedding Feast could accomodate a party of fifty people (Pringle, *Churches*, 2:163).

[60] 11:5–6 **and drove them all from the Temple** *e [les] chasa hors trestouz*

[61] 11:10 **"Zeal for God's house [. . .] the heart of Christ"** *la gelousie de la maison Dieu mangeroit le quer Crist*: Ps 69:9 (an antiphon for Tenebrae, modified).

[62] 11:14 **to build the Temple had taken forty-six years** *le temple estoit edefié [en] quaraunte e sis aunz*

Spirit. And just as Moses raised up the serpent[63] in the wilderness to deliver the people, so too would he be lifted on a cross, that all who believed in him might be saved. He said:

"For God so loved the world that he gave his Son, that everyone who believes in him might have everlasting life. For God sent not his Son into the world to condemn it, but to save it. Whosoever believes in him will never be condemned; but whosoever believes not in him, he is already judged for believing not in the Son of God. And here is the rationale of the judgment: God sent light into the world, but men loved darkness more than light, for their deeds were wicked. And evildoers prefer darkness to light, lest they be reproved; but the righteous come boldly to the light, that their actions may appear godly." (1–33)

12. How John the Baptist recommended Jesus. Later, Jesus and his disciples came into Judea, baptizing the people; meanwhile, John the Baptist was baptizing elsewhere. Behold, Jews approached John's disciples, saying that baptism by Jesus was preferable to theirs. And they came to John and told him that the One to whom he had borne witness by the River Jordan was baptizing in Judea, and that the people were abandoning John's baptisms to go to Jesus's. And John answered, saying they knew well—as he had often told them—that he was not the Christ but his forerunner. And he said that Jesus was like the bridegroom and he the bridegroom's friend, and that he was delighted that Jesus was more renowned than he. For it was fitting that Jesus increase, and he decrease; for as far as heaven was from earth, so was it between them. For, said John, Jesus's Father God had given him the Holy Spirit, and abundantly, committing all things to him; and because he believed in him, he would have life everlasting. And whosoever believed not in him would never see the joy of eternal life, rather God would rage forever against him. (1–15)

Here begins the third meditation, for Tuesday

13. How Jesus left Judea and went into Galilee. Afterwards John the Baptist came to reproach King Herod for all his evil deeds, and especially for taking his brother's wife in marriage. And Herod seized and bound him and threw him in prison. And though he heard John gladly and saw to his needs, he would have killed him but for his fear of the people. And his wife[64] especially kept an eye on John, thinking to kill him, but she never did because Herod was guarding John as if he feared him. For he knew well that John was a holy, worthy man, and a true prophet. And when Jesus learned of John's imprisonment and heard that the

---

[63] 11:23 **Moses raised up the serpent** *Moises eschaunta* [read *eschauça*] *la serpente* (Num 21:6–9)

[64] 13:6 **his wife** *[s]a feme*

Pharisees were grumbling about his baptism of the multitudes, he left Judea and went into Galilee. Now he had to pass through a people called Samaritans who were part Jewish and part pagan; and he arrived near a city called Sychar and sat beside a well.[65] His disciples went into the city to buy food, for it was already noontime. And as Jesus sat[66] wearily by the well, a Samaritan woman came to fetch water; and he asked her for a drink. And she inquired how he could ask her for a drink since he was a Jew and she a Samaritan, because Jews neither ate nor drank with them. And Jesus said that if she knew who he was, she would ask him for living water and he would supply it. And the woman replied that the well was deep and he had nothing with which to draw out the water. And she asked him where he would get the living water, because he was no worthier than Jacob the patriarch who had dug the well, drunk from the water, and watered his beasts there.[67] And Jesus answered, whoever drank of that water would thirst again, but whoever drank of the water he gave would never be thirsty. And the woman said jokingly:

"My lord, give me of your water lest I thirst again or have to return here to fetch water."

Then Jesus told her to go get her husband and come back, and she answered that she had no husband. And Jesus said, indeed, she had had five spouses, and the one keeping her then was not her husband. And immediately she changed the subject, saying:

"My lord, clearly, you are a prophet. Now tell me which is better, to pray here on Mount Gerizim as our forebears did, or in Jerusalem?"

And Jesus answered that the hour was appointed when people would not concern themselves about one or the other; rather, sincere worshippers would pray to God in spirit everywhere. Then the woman said that she knew well that the Christ would soon come to teach them what they should do; and Jesus told her, he was the Christ. Then, on returning from the city, his disciples were amazed

---

[65] 13:12–13 **he arrived [. . .] and sat beside a well** *vint coste une cité que out noun Sichar e s'asist coste une funtaigne*: the pilgrimage account called the Second Guide (ca. 1170) calls this place "Neapolis, where the well is on which the Lord sat when he was in conversation with the woman from Samaria" (Wilkinson, *Jerusalem Pilgrimage*, 238). According to Pierre Maraval, *Lieux saints et pèlerinages d'Orient: Histoire et géographie des origines à la conquête arabe* (Paris: Cerf, 1985), 289, Sychar is a southeastern suburb of Neapolis. For other medieval pilgrim accounts of Jacob's Well and a description of the site, see Pringle, *Churches*, 1:258–64; for Neapolis, 2:94–115 (Nablus).

[66] 13:14 **Jesus sat** *il [s]ist*

[67] 13:21–22 **and watered his beasts there** *e enbevera ent ses bestes*: the pilgrimage narrative of John Phocas (1185) locates Sychar between two mountains. "The slopes on the right belong to the mountain on which the Samaritans say that Abraham spoke with God, and intended to sacrifice Isaac . . . At the foot of this mountain is the place which Jacob gave to his son Joseph, and it contains the Well of this very Jacob" (Wilkinson, *Jerusalem Pilgrimage*, 322–23).

to find him speaking with the Samaritan woman, yet none inquired what he was seeking from her. And she left her water-jar there and, going back into the city, reported finding a man who told her everything she had done in secret; and she asked the people to ascertain if he was the Christ. Meanwhile, the disciples reminded Jesus to eat, and he replied that he had food to eat of which they knew nothing. And they asked among themselves if someone else had given food to Jesus. Then he told them that his food was submission to the will of God who had sent him to earth. Then the Samaritans approached Jesus, and many believed in him on account of the woman's testimony; and they invited him into the city. And he went into the city and stayed two days with them, and many more believed in him because of his teaching. And they told the woman:

"Now we do not believe because of your word, for we ourselves have heard and we know that this is the true Savior of the world."

On the third day, Jesus went out of the city and came into Galilee; and he affirmed that a prophet is honored less in his own country than elsewhere. And nevertheless, because they had seen the wonders he had performed at the Passover in Jerusalem, the people of that country received him. (1–54)

14. How Jesus healed the royal official's son. After this Jesus came into Cana in Galilee, where he had turned water into wine, and the son of a royal official lay ill at Capernaum. And the official, when he heard that Jesus had come from Judea, approached him and asked him to go to Capernaum to heal his son. And Jesus reproached him that they would not believe in him without public miracles. And the official begged Jesus to come quickly, before his son died. And Jesus told him to go away, that his son was already healed; and he believed Jesus's words and went away. And as he neared Capernaum, his servants met him, saying that his son was healed. And he asked at what time the sickness had left him. And they answered:

"The fever broke yesterday at noon."[68]

Then he realized that this was the very hour at which Jesus had said his son was healed, and thereafter he and his whole household believed in Jesus. (1–13)

15. How Jesus preached in Saint Peter's ship. Then Jesus arrived at the Sea of Tiberias, and a great throng followed him to hear his teachings. Behold, two ships were standing offshore, the fishermen having disembarked to wash their nets. And Jesus boarded the ship belonging to Simon Peter and asked him to put out a little distance from shore; and thus he sat in the ship and taught the people. And when he had finished speaking, he asked Simon to take the ship out to the depths and to cast their nets there. And Simon answered that they had worked all night and caught nothing, but nevertheless he would lower his net as Jesus asked. And

---

[68] 14:11 **at noon** *a houre de haute midi*: some modern English Bibles have "at the seventh hour," but NRSV "at one in the afternoon"; *V* "hora septima" (Jn 4:52).

having let down nets, they caught so many fish that their net broke. And Jesus told James and John—the sons of Zebedee and Simon's shipmates—to come and help them; and they came and filled both ships so full, they nearly sank. When Simon saw this, he fell down at Jesus's knees and asked him to leave the ship, for—as Simon said—he was a sinner. And all were astonished at the catch of fish. And Jesus told Simon not to be afraid, for thenceforth he would fish for men. And they all immediately brought their ships to shore and, leaving everything there, followed him a while. And then they resumed fishing until Jesus called them again.[69] (1–17)

16. How Jesus read at Nazareth. Then Jesus came to Nazareth where he had grown up. And he went up to the synagogue on a Saturday and read a passage from the prophet Isaiah about the goodness of Christ, saying that it was he of whom the prophet spoke. And they bore him witness, observing attentively his noble bearing[70] and marvelling at his gentle words. And they said among themselves:

"Isn't this Joseph's son?"

And Jesus said that they might well direct him to perform in his home city such marvels as he had worked elsewhere; but he did not intend to do this, he said, for no prophet is as honored in his own country as abroad. And therefore the prophets of old granted to foreigners what they denied their own people: for when the famine persisted for three and a half years, the prophet Elijah was sent not to a widow in Israel but to a widow dwelling among pagans in the region of Sarepta, that she might be fed[71] by him. Nor did the prophet Elisha cure lepers in Israel, but Naaman, a pagan in Syria. And when they heard this, they were enraged; and they rose up and drove him out of the city. And they led him to the slope of the mountain, intending to cast him down;[72] but he passed through their midst and went away. (1–18)

---

[69] 15:16–17 **until Jesus called them again** *jusques il les apelast un' autre foiz*: noting that in PGH, Peter, Andrew, and John are called twice—here and in chap. 17—Plooij includes this peculiarity among his "test-readings for the Diatessaron" (Plooij, "The Pepysian Harmony," 14, 15). PGH "euer til Jesus hem cleped anoþer tyme" ("until Jesus called them another time"; Goates, 18). See also *Hist.evang.*, cols. 1557, 1561, 1562, for Comestor's chapters on the first, second, and third calling of the Twelve.

[70] 16:4–5 **observing attentively his noble bearing** *e agarderent ententivement sa bele porture*: this phrase is absent in the modern English Bibles (Lk 4:22).

[71] 16:14 **that she might be fed** *q'ele peut est[re] puwe*. Cf. Lk. 4:26–27.

[72] 16:17 **intending to cast him down** *le voleient tresbocher vers val*: the Work on Geography (1128–1137) specifies, "A mile south of Nazareth is the place called 'The Fall'. It is the summit of a mountain, from which the relatives of Jesus wished to throw him, but he disappeared from them" (Wilkinson, *Jerusalem Pilgrimage*, 193). In *Fragments relatifs à la Galilee* (ca. 1231), Ernoul describes "le Saut" as a cliff from which convicts from nearby Nazareth were cast down to their deaths. After Jesus disappeared from the midst

17. How Jesus called Saint Peter and his companions. Then Jesus left the city of Nazareth and went to dwell in Capernaum. And he began to preach repentance, saying that for those who accepted the coming of Christ, the kingdom of God was near. Then as he came walking by the Sea of Tiberias, he saw Simon Peter and his brother Andrew fishing offshore; and he called to them, saying to follow him[73] and he would make them fishers of men. And they left their nets immediately and followed him. Then he went a bit farther along and saw James, his brother John, and their father Zebedee mending their nets in a ship; and they left their father[74] on the ship with his servants and followed Jesus. (1–9)

18. How Jesus healed the demoniac. Then Jesus went with them into Capernaum, and on the Saturday he entered the synagogue and began preaching in such a way that all marvelled. Now there was in the synagogue a man possessed by a demon. And he began to cry out, asking if Jesus had come to drive him and the others from the earth before their time,[75] and saying that he knew well that Jesus was the Christ. And Jesus commanded him to be quiet and to come forth. And immediately he came forth, and all who saw it were amazed; and this news spread throughout the country. And, going out of the synagogue, Jesus entered Saint Peter's house with Saints James and John. And the mother of Saint Peter's wife was then in bed with a high fever; and they entreated Jesus on her behalf, and he took her by the hand and raised her up. And immediately she stood, completely healed; and she moved about, serving them. And after sundown, the sick, the demon-possessed, and the city's entire population converged at his house; and he touched and healed every one. And the devils he had expelled cried out, saying that he was the Son of God; and he hushed them, forbidding them to reveal him. And very early in the morning, he slipped away into the wilderness to pray. And Saint Peter with the others went searching for him, saying that everyone was looking for him; and so they took him back to the people. And when the people had found him, they sought to restrain him lest he leave them; but he

---

of his tormentors, according to Ernoul, he sat on a stone which could still be seen there (*Itinéraires à Jerusalem*, 61). See also *Hist. evang.*, col. 1574 (*De saltu Domini*), and the note for 8:3.

[73] 17:5–6 **and he called to them, saying to follow him** *e les apela e lour dist qu'il le venisent suyre*: second calling of the Apostles. See the note for 15:16–17. PGH "And Jesus hem cleped to hym and seide hem þat hij comen & foloweden hym" ("And Jesus called them and charged them to come and follow him"; Goates, 19). Jesus again calls, then appoints the Twelve in chap. 24.

[74] 17:8–9 **and they left their father** *e [lesserent] lour piere*

[75] 18:4–5 **to drive him and the others from the earth before their time** *pur enchacer le e les autres hors de terre avaunt qe lour tens venist*: the modern English Bibles have simply "to destroy us"; *V* "perdere nos" (Mk 1:24, Lk 4:34).

The Anglo-Norman Gospel Harmony

explained that he must preach in other cities also. And he went away preaching and expelling demons in synagogues throughout Galilee. (1–21)

19. How he passed over the Sea of Tiberias and drove out the legion. Then, when Jesus saw such a throng of people following him, he commanded his disciples to cross over the Sea of Tiberias, steering toward Galilee in Gergesa. And as he went toward the ship, a scribe told him that he would follow him anywhere. And Jesus answered that he had no home of his own to go to:

"For birds have their nests and foxes their lairs, but I have no place to lay my head."

And when Jesus bade another to follow him, he begged Jesus to let him go bury his father first. And Jesus told him to let the dead bury their dead, but that he should go preaching the kingdom of God. And another told Jesus that he would follow him, but that he first needed to tend to some affairs at home. And Jesus answered:

"Whoever puts hand to the plow and looks back is ill suited for the kingdom of God."

And when he and his disciples reached the ship, evening had already fallen; and his ship and some others transited the sea. And there came such a storm that the ship was entirely awash; and Jesus was sleeping abaft, resting his head on a pillow. And they awakened him, begging him to save them, for they were about to perish. And he asked where their faith was, and why were they afraid. And he commanded the wind to be quiet and the sea calm, and immediately they were still; and everyone was amazed that the wind and the sea should obey him. And as soon as Jesus went ashore, two demoniacs came out from some tombs.[76] These two madmen were so violent that no one ever dared pass that way, nor could chains restrain them; they were always among the tombs crying out, wailing, and dashing themselves against the rocks. And when they saw Jesus, they ran to meet him, fell down, and worshipped him, entreating him for God's sake not to drive them from that country. And the devils begged him not to order them into the abyss[77]—for he commanded them to come forth—and they begged him not to torture them. And he asked how many they were, and they answered, a legion, that is, six thousand six hundred sixty-six.[78] And they begged him, for

---

[76] 19:22 **two demoniacs came out from some tombs** *vindrent deus dymoniacs hors de sepulcres*: the *Estoire* conflates Mt 8:28–34, about two demon-possessed men, and Mk 5:1–17 and Lk 8:26–36, about one called Legion. In *Fragments relatifs à la Galilee* (ca. 1231), Ernoul locates the story of Legion close by the Sea of Galilee in the countryside near Nain, where Jesus raised the widow's son (*Itinéraires à Jérusalem*, 59–60). See chap. 29.

[77] 19:27–28 **to order them into the abyss** *les comaundast aler en abyme*: Lk 8:31.

[78] 19:30 **six thousand six hundred sixty-six** *sis mile sis cenz e seisaunte six*: in the Gospel account, the Gadarene demoniac says only, "My name is Legion: for we are many"

charity's sake, to allow them to go into the swine feeding on the mountain. And he consented at once, and they went into the swine—well nigh two thousand head were drowned in the sea. And when the swineherds saw what had happened to the demoniacs and the swine, they flew to the cities and towns to report it. And the people came to Jesus and found one of the demoniacs clothed, entirely healed, and sitting at his feet; and all were amazed and so terrified, that they asked him to leave the country. And as he returned to the ship, the demoniac he had healed asked to follow him, but Jesus told him to stay and tell his country-men of his deliverance from the legion of demons; and he went throughout the land telling how Jesus had healed him. And when Jesus came back into Galilee, the people sought him, for they had much desired his return. (1–41)

20. How he healed the palsied man and called Saint Matthew. And Jesus came to Capernaum and preached in a house; and such a throng of people, including scribes and Pharisees, gathered around him that no one else could reach him. Behold, four men came bearing a paralytic on a litter, seeking to carry him inside and set him down before Jesus. And seeing the entrances blocked by the multitude, they climbed to the roof and opened it, lowering him to Jesus between the roof-laths. And when he saw their faith, Jesus told the paralytic that his sins were forgiven. And the scribes thought Jesus had blasphemed by taking upon himself the forgiveness of sins, which God alone can do. And Jesus knew their thoughts immediately and, questioning their adverseness, declared he could just as easily forgive the man's sins as heal his body.

"But nevertheless," he said, "so that you know I have power on earth to forgive sins, rise, paralytic, take up your bed, and carry it[79] home."

And immediately the man stood before them, took up his bed, and carried it to his house. And he and all the people praised God for giving such power to Jesus. And then Jesus went out to walk beside the sea; and the multitude followed him, and he preached to them. And on his return, as he was passing through the town, he saw a publican named Matthew Levy sitting and collecting tax. And Jesus bade him to follow, and at once he dropped everything, following him and making a great celebration in his house; and many other publicans and sinners came and ate with Jesus and his disciples. And the scribes and Pharisees grumbled, asking Jesus's disciples why he ate with such people. And Jesus answered that he had come to call not the righteous to repentance, but sinners; for the healthy have no need of a doctor, but the sick do, and God favors mercy and

---

(Mk 5:9; see also Lk 8:30). "Legion" is the name both of the demoniac and of the devils possessing him, but the word also reminds the reader or listener of the Roman legion, which in some configurations counted six thousand men. Here the harmonist conflates this figure with the number of the beast (Apoc 13:18). PGH "sex þousande and sex hundreþ and sexti and sex" (Goates, 22).

[79] 20:13 **paralytic, take up your bed, and carry it** *paraletik [pernez vostre lit] e portez le*

compassion over punishment or revenge. Then came the followers of Saint John the Baptist; and the Pharisees, who were fasting, asked him[80] why his disciples did not fast as they did. And he answered that it would not befit a bridegroom's friends to fast while the wedding celebration lasted; but the time would come when the bridegroom would be taken from them, and then they would fast. Moreover, he said:

"A wise man mends not old fabric with new cloth, for the new would tear the old, making it less useful. Nor does the wise man put new wine in old wine-bushels, for both would be spoiled. Nor does a man who has drunk mature wine presently want the new, for he prefers the old." (1–34)

21. How Jesus raised the girl and healed the woman. And as Jesus was answering them, a ruler named Jairus arrived. And he fell at Jesus's feet, worshipped him, and begged him to come and lay hands on his daughter, who was already near death, saying he had only her. And Jesus rose up at once and accompanied him, with his disciples and a great throng of people in tow. And a woman who for twelve years had been prone to bleeding, who by the Old Law dared not enter a city nor approach any man, and who had spent all she had on doctors but had only fared worse for it—this woman entered the throng and touched Jesus's garment,[81] for she believed that if she could only touch the hem of his cloak, she would be healed. And immediately the blood was staunched, and she sensed that she was healed. And Jesus paused to ask who had touched him, and all denied it. And Saint Peter remarked, it was amazing that—with a multitude crowding about and vexing him—he should ask who had touched him. And Jesus said that he was certain that someone had touched him, for he had felt power surging from him to cure someone; and he stood, looking to see who it might be. And realizing that she could not hide,[82] the woman came forth tremblingly, fell at his feet, and related what had happened before all the people. And Jesus told her to depart in peace, for her faith had healed her. And as he stood there, the ruler's servants arrived; and they told him that his daughter was dead and that he should trouble Jesus no more. And on hearing this, Jesus told him not to fear but only believe that he could save her, and she would be saved. And on arriving at the ruler's house, Jesus found pipers playing and people weeping and wailing. And he told

---

[80] 20:26 **who were fasting, asked him** *que junerent e li demaunderent* [read *que junerent li demaunderent*]

[81] 21:8–9 **touched Jesus's garment** *e toucha les dras Jhesu*: Saewulf's pilgrimage account (1101–03) locates this event in Jerusalem close by Bethsaida (also called Bethesda) and the Church of Saint Anne (Wilkinson, *Jerusalem Pilgrimage*, 105–6). For Bethsaida (Bethesda) and the Sheep Pool, see Pringle, *The Churches of the Crusader Kingdom of Jerusalem*, 3: *The City of Jerusalem* (Cambridge: Cambridge University Press, 2007), 389–97; for the Abbey Church of St Anne, 142–56. See also the note for 47:2–3.

[82] 21:16 **she could not hide** *ele ne [se] poeit tapir*

them not to weep, for she was not dead, but sleeping; and they scoffed at him, and he drove them all outside. And taking with him the girl's father and mother, Saints Peter and John and John's brother Saint James, he entered where the girl was lying. And he took her by the hand and said in a loud voice:

"Child, rise up!"

And she stood at once and walked about. And he ordered that she be given something to eat, for she was twelve years old. And he forbade them to tell anyone about these things, but nevertheless the report[83] went throughout the country. (1–31)

22. How Jesus healed two blind men and a mute. And as Jesus was leaving there, two blind men approached, crying out as if to Christ for compassion. And when he reached his house, they appeared before him. And Jesus asked if they believed he could heal them. And they answered yes. And Jesus told them that just as they believed, so would it be; and immediately they regained their sight. And Jesus expressly forbade them to tell anyone of this, but they went and reported it throughout the country. And immediately as they left, a mute demoniac appeared; and as soon as Jesus had expelled the demon, the mute spoke. And all were amazed, saying that never had such a thing been seen in Israel. But the Pharisees said he drove out devils by authority of their master, Beelzebub. (1–10)

23. How he was despised in his country.[84] Then Jesus went with his disciples into his country, towards Nazareth, and preached in the synagogues. And the people, amazed by his wisdom and his works, began to talk about him, saying:

"Isn't this Jesus the carpenter, Mary's son? And the men and women of his family, aren't they here among us?"

And thus they despised him among themselves. And Jesus told them:

"A prophet is nowhere without honor except in his own country and among his kinsmen and friends."

But they were so unbelieving, he could do only a little healing thereabout, by a laying on of hands; and he appeared to marvel at this. (1–10)

24. How he chose the twelve apostles. Then Jesus went preaching throughout Galilee, but such multitudes from the lands round about followed him, and so many brought him their sick, they could not all reach him. And he went to

---

[83] 21:30 **the report** *la femme* [read *la fame*]: the modern English Bibles have "fame," "news," "report"; likewise, *V* "fama" (Mt 9:26). The published edition of the *Estoire* needlessly corrects to *la novele*. See also the note for 29:9.

[84] 23:1 **How he was despised in his country** *Coment il estoit despit en son pays*: much of the substance of this chapter is repeated in chap. 46.

Mount Tabor to pray, remaining in prayer all that night.[85] And the next day he called his followers to him there and chose the twelve apostles.[86] And he gave Saints James and John the name "Boanerges," meaning "Sons of Thunder." And when he had chosen the twelve and appointed them as apostles, he conveyed to them the commandments of the New Law, not out of meanness but as a promise. And he said:

"Blessed are the spiritually poor, for theirs is the kingdom of heaven. Blessed are the meek, for they will possess the earth. Blessed are those who weep, for they will be comforted. Blessed are those who seek righteousness as their food or drink, for they will be satisfied. Blessed are the merciful, for they will obtain mercy. Blessed are the pure of heart, for they will see God. Blessed are the peaceful, for they will be called sons of God. Blessed are those who suffer persecution for righteousness' sake, for theirs is the kingdom of God."[87]

Then he turned his remarks to the apostles, teaching them how to live. And he told them that they must be more righteous than the scribes and Pharisees of the Old Law, for they were the light of the world who were to guide and lead everyone else. And when he had taught them to perform righteous works, to demonstrate pure-heartedness in their actions, and to avoid the false prophets who would come to spy on them, Jesus went down with them to a plain where the people were waiting for him. (1–23)

---

[85] 24:4 **remaining in prayer all that night** *e tote nuyt i demora en oreison*: Abbot Daniel's pilgrimage account (1106–1108) provides a detailed description of Mount Tabor, also reporting the difficulties of its ascent (Wilkinson, *Jerusalem Pilgrimage*, 161–62). In the prelude to the Fifth Crusade, the sultan al-Adil reluctantly agreed to the construction of a fortress on Mount Tabor by his son al-Muazzam, in violation of a truce then in force. The outrage was underscored by Innocent III in his appeal for a new crusade. Completed in June 1211, the fortress was attacked in late November 1217 by an expedition led by John of Brienne, who failed to capture it. Al-Muazzam dismantled the fortress probably after November 1219, but perhaps earlier. See James M. Powell, *Anatomy of a Crusade, 1213–1221* (Philadelphia: University of Pennsylvania Press, 1986), 19; and Jean Richard, *The Latin Kingdom of Jerusalem*, trans. Janet Shirley (Amsterdam: North-Holland, 1979), 1:217, 219. In medieval pilgrim accounts, Mount Tabor was associated primarily with the Transfiguration. According to John Phocas (1185), there was a monastery at the summit of the mountain where the Transfiguration had occurred: "And at the place where the Lord's feet were set one sees a white boss, in the middle of which is engraved the Holy Cross" (Pringle, *Churches*, 2:63–85, at 66).

[86] 24:4–5 **he called his followers to him there and chose the twelve apostles** *apela iluques meimes a soi ses deciples e esleust les douzze apostres*: third calling of the Twelve. See the notes for 15:16–17 and 17:5–6.

[87] 24:16 **for theirs is the kingdom of God** *car lour est le regne Dieu*: In the late fourth century, the pilgrim Etheria located the Sermon on the Mount at At-Tabgha (Gr. *Heptapegon*, Seven Springs), along with the Feeding of the Five Thousand and Christ's post-Resurrection breakfast of fish with the disciples (see Pringle, *Churches*, 2:334–39).

25. How, in going back down the mountain, he healed all those on the plain. And when Jesus reached the people, they all pressed in on him to hear him and to be cured of their infirmities; for a power issuing from him healed all who touched him. And then he began to summarize his commandments and the sermon he had made to his apostles.[88] And he told them, they would have to be more righteous than those under the Old Law, to love their enemies and be patient in all things, and to treat others as they wished to be treated. And he told them especially that, in every respect, they should avoid setting a bad example for unbelievers, and that they should demonstrate their Christian faith by their works, not in words only. Finally, he said, those who obeyed his teachings would never be vanquished, no more than a house with a good foundation collapses on account of wind or flood. But a house with a faulty foundation cannot withstand storms, thus it falls apart with a great crash. (1–13)

26. How he healed the leper. When Jesus had finished speaking, he went down and accompanied the people, heading for Capernaum. Behold, a leper came and, falling to the ground before him to worship him,[89] said:

"My lord, if you are willing, you can cleanse me."

And Jesus touched him, saying:

"I am willing, be clean."

And at once the leper was completely healed. And Jesus forbade him to tell anyone that he had cured him, but that he give to the priest the offering required by the Law so that his healing and cleansing might be made known. But he went away and reported throughout the land that Jesus had healed him. As a result, so many people came to Jesus that, on account of the throngs, he could no longer enter publicly into a city; rather, he had to stay outside in the desert. And even so, they came to him from all sides; but he often withdrew from them, retiring into the wilderness to pray. (1–14)

27. How he healed the centurion's servant. Once Jesus had entered Capernaum, there came the pagan chief of a hundred soldiers whose servant was paralyzed. And he entreated the city's most honorable Jews to ask Jesus to heal his servant, for he was very attached to him. And they came to Jesus and earnestly begged him to come and heal his servant, saying that the centurion deserved Jesus's favor, for he loved the Jews and had built them a synagogue. And Jesus said that

---

[88] 25:4–5 **then he began to summarize [. . .] the sermon he had made to his apostles** *il comensa donc a recorder ses comaundemenz e le sermon q'il out fet a ses apostres brevement*: see the note for iii:13.

[89] 26:3 **falling to the ground before him to worship him** *e l'aorra e chei a terre devant li* [read *e chei a terre devant li e l'aorra*]: *V* "veniens adorabat eum" (Mt 8:2) and "videns Iesum et procidens in faciem" (Lk 5:12); see also Mk 1:40. Clarity requires the correction, which is missed in the published critical edition of the *Estoire*.

he would gladly do it; and he willingly accompanied them there. And as Jesus approached the house, the centurion sent word to him by his friends that Jesus should not trouble himself to come there, for he was not worthy to receive Jesus in his house nor even to talk with him, requesting rather that Jesus only command that his servant be healed. For he had soldiers under him, he said, and they all followed his orders, and his servants, too; and he believed that, in the same way, the sickness would retreat and good health return if Jesus commanded it. And Jesus, on hearing this, turned and said to his followers:

"I have not found such faith among the Jews as in this pagan. And I tell you, many pagans will come from afar to the kingdom of God and will repose with the patriarchs, but the Jews will be cast out into eternal punishment."

Then Jesus sent word back to the centurion through these messengers that it was as he had believed, and they returned and found the servant healed. (1–19)

28. How Jesus sent the twelve apostles to preach. Then Jesus went into all the towns and villages, preaching and healing the sick. And so many people followed him, they were like sheep lying and waiting along the roads.[90] Then he called his twelve apostles and empowered them to expel demons and cure all illnesses; and he sent them everywhere in twos. And he told them to go only among the Jews, preaching that Christ was near and healing all the sick without reward. And he told them to take neither gold nor silver nor any money, and to carry neither bread nor scrip nor two coats nor shoes nor staff, except only sandals on their feet and a rod in their hand. But when they came to a town or village, they should inquire who was worthy to give them lodging, and go there and offer peace to the home; and they should stay there until they wished to leave those parts, eating and drinking whatever was placed before them. And if anyone refused them, he said, they should exit the city or village, shaking the dust from their feet to testify that they had accepted absolutely nothing from them. And he said that Sodom and Gomorrha would have a gentler sentence than those who refused his apostles. Then Jesus warned them of the punishment and persecution they would suffer for him; and he told them to be as crafty as serpents and as innocent as doves. Finally, he encouraged them, saying that whoever was steadfast to the end would be saved, and those who received the apostles would have as fine a reward as for receiving Jesus himself or God his Father. When he had instructed and comforted them so sweetly, they went away throughout the land preaching repentance, driving out demons, anointing the sick with oil, and healing them. (1–22)

---

[90] 28:3 **they were like sheep lying and waiting along the roads** *il guyrent ausi com berbiz asteynz par les voies*: at Mt 9:36, the modern English Bibles have, e.g., "they fainted and were scattered abroad" (KJV) or "they were harassed and helpless" (NIV, NRSV); *V* "erant vexati et iacentes sicut oves non habentes pastorem." All have some version of "without a shepherd," omitted in the *Estoire*.

29. How Jesus raised the widow's son. And, with his disciples and a throng of people, Jesus went to a town called Nain.[91] And as he approached the city gate, he encountered a corpse and the people of the city following behind it. Now this was a widow's son, her only child; and the widow walked along weeping and grieving for him. And Jesus, on seeing her, felt great compassion and told her not to weep; and he went and touched the bier, and the pallbearers halted. And Jesus commanded the dead man to get up, and he rose up at once and began speaking; and Jesus took him and gave him to his mother. And all the people were amazed and praised God; and news of this[92] travelled throughout Judea and all about the kingdom. And the Baptist's followers visited John in prison and reported this and all of Jesus's other miracles to him, to establish for certain[93] that he was the Christ. (1–12)

30. How Saint John the Baptist sent word to Jesus. And John called two of his disciples and sent them to Jesus to hear and see for themselves that he was the Christ. And he told them to go to Jesus on his behalf and ask if he himself claimed to be the Christ or if they should wait for another. And when they came to Jesus, they said that John the Baptist had sent them to ask if he himself claimed to be Christ or if they should expect another. And Jesus himself healed many of their diseases and afflictions, restoring sight to numerous blind persons and expelling many demons. And he told the messengers to go and tell John what they had seen and heard:

"Tell him that the blind see and the lame walk, lepers are cleansed, the deaf hear, the dead are raised up, and the poor are appointed to preach the gospel! And blessed is he who is not dissatisfied with me."[94]

And when John's messengers had gone away, Jesus told the people about John, saying that he was not like a reed stirred by the wind, nor was he raised in riches like worldly-minded folk, nor was he only a prophet. Indeed, he was more than a prophet—he was the angel that God had promised would come before Christ to prepare the way. And he said finally that, before him, no one higher had ever been born of a mother. And, hearing that Jesus valued John so, all the

---

[91] 29:2 **Nain** *Naym*: *La Terre des Sarrazins*, fol. 199r, describes Nain as a mountaintop town. Above the town is the brook of Sidon where Jesus raised the widow's son. See further Pringle, *Churches*, 2:115–16 (Na'im).

[92] 29:9 **news of this** *ceste feme* [read *ceste fame*]: *V* "hic sermo" (Lk 7:17). The published edition of the *Estoire* needlessly corrects to *ceste novele*. See the note for 21:30.

[93] 29:11 **to establish for certain** *pur [fere] saver*

[94] 30:12 **who is not dissatisfied with me** *qe n'est mespaié de mei*: at Lk 7:23, the modern English Bibles have, e.g., "whosoever shall not be offended in me" (KJV) and "who does not fall away on account of me" (NIV). *V* "quicumque non fuerit scandalizatus in me"; PGH "pat ne ben nouȝth myspaide wip me" ("that be not displeased with me," Goates, 31).

people and the publicans who had been baptized by him praised God; but the lawyers and Pharisees not baptized by him scorned Jesus's words. Then Jesus said that they were like children who would neither laugh nor cry with their friends.

"John the Baptist," he said,[95] "neither eats bread nor drinks wine, and you say he is a drunkard; and I do eat and drink, and you call me a glutton and a drunkard,[96] the friend of publicans and sinners." (1–24)

31. How Jesus converted the Magdalene. Then a Pharisee invited Jesus to eat with him, and he entered his house and sat to eat.[97] And a woman possessed by seven demons who was known in the city as a sinner—when she heard that Jesus was eating there, she took a box of ointment and went to stand behind him, just beside his feet. And with her tears she bathed his feet, drying them with her hair, kissing them, and rubbing them with ointment. And the Pharisee, when he saw that Jesus was thus allowing the sinful woman to touch them,[98] thought to himself that if Jesus were truly a prophet, he would know how sinful she was and would not permit it. Then Jesus said that he had something to say; and the Pharisee invited him—as one would a teacher—to say it. Then Jesus told him that a creditor had two debtors:

"The one owed him five hundred pence and the other, fifty. Now neither had the means to repay him, and the creditor forgave the debt of both. Now I ask, which loved him more?"

"I think," said the Pharisee, "the one to whom he forgave more."

Then Jesus told him that he had answered correctly. And he turned to the woman and began saying to the Pharisee:[99]

"Simon, behold this woman. I entered your house and you gave me no water for my feet, but with her tears she bathed my feet and dried them with her hair. You did not kiss my mouth, but since entering here she has not stopped kissing my feet. You did not anoint my head with oil, but she anointed my feet with oint-

---

[95] 30:22 **he said** *ceo dist Dieu* [read *ceo dist il*]: Lk 7:33.

[96] 30:24 **drunkard** *deue* [read *beveour*]

[97] 31:2 **entered his house and sat to eat** *entra sa maison e s'asist a manger*: later in this chapter, the Pharisee is identified as Simon. The author of *Les sains pelerinages* (ca. 1231) places the home of Simon the Leper ("*Symon le leprous*") in Bethany (*Itinéraires à Jérusalem*, 1047). See Pringle, *Churches*, 1:122–37, at 122, 125, 136.

[98] 31:7 **that Jesus was thus allowing the sinful woman to touch them** *qu'il les suffri ensi toucher de la peccheresse*: "them" refers to Jesus's feet. The pilgrim Saewulf (1102–03) reports having seen, beneath the altar of the church of St Lazarus in Bethany, the place where Mary had washed Jesus's feet with tears and anointed his head with ointment (Pringle, *Churches*, 1:123).

[99] 31:17 **and began saying to the Pharisee** *e li comensa a dire*: AN *li* can be translated either "to her" or "to him." Despite Jesus's body language, the context makes clear that his remark is addressed to Simon the Pharisee.

ment; and for this, I tell you, she is forgiven many sins. And this is why she loves so much: for one who is forgiven less, loves less."

Then Jesus told the woman that her sins were forgiven. And the other diners began thinking:

"Who is this person to forgive sins?"

And Jesus told the woman to go in peace, for her faith had saved her. And she joined the other women whom Jesus had healed of their afflictions and who were following him and supplying his needs from their substance:[100] Joanna, the wife of Herod's steward Chuza; Susanna; and many others. And she followed Jesus through the villages and towns, wherever he preached. (1–31)

32. How Jesus chose the seventy-two[101] **disciples.** Then Jesus selected seventy-two others,[102] sending them out ahead in pairs to wherever he intended to go. And he told them to go in righteousness,[103] taking neither bag nor scrip nor shoes; but they should offer peace wherever they entered, eating and drinking what they were given, healing the sick they met, and taking no other reward. But he told them[104] that Christ was with them. And if any city refused them, he said, they should shake the dust from their feet to signify that—because the people had not received their preaching—they would not accept even their dust. Nevertheless, the apostles should tell the people that Christ was near; and they should also know that, on Judgment Day, Sodom would have a lighter punishment than their city. Jesus said:

"For whoever hears you, hears me; and whoever scorns you, scorns me; and whoever scorns me, scorns the One[105] who sent me."

Then Jesus began to condemn cities where he had performed many miracles but which refused to repent: Chorazin, Bethsaida, and Capernaum.[106] And he said, if the pagans had seen as many miracles, they would have repented; and thus the cities would have a harsher punishment than the pagans. (1–17)

---

[100] 31:29 **and supplying his needs from their substance** *e li troverent a despendre de lour chateus*: Lk 8:3.

[101] 32:1 **seventy-two** *settante dozze* [read *settante deus*]: the commissioning of the Seventy-Two (Lk 10:1–16) repeats many of the instructions issued to the Twelve in chap. 28 (Mt 10:1, 5–15; Mk 6:7–11; Lk 9:1–5).

[102] 32:1–2 **seventy-two others** *setaunte dozze autres* [read *setaunte deus autres*]

[103] 32:3 **And he told them to go in righteousness** *E lor dist qu'il alassent joustement*: there is no direct biblical source for "in righteousness" or "righteously." PGH "And he badde hem goo swipe" ("And he bade them go immediately," Goates, 33).

[104] 32:6 **he told them** *lour deit* [read *lour dist*]

[105] 32:13 **whoever scorns me, scorns the One** *qui despit moy, [despit] Celi*

[106] 32:15 **Chorazin, Bethsaida, and Capernaum** *Corozaym e Bethsaida e Chapharnaum*: the Work on Geography (1128–1137) identifies Chorazin as the place "in which the Antichrist was brought up" (Wilkinson, *Jerusalem Pilgrimage*, 192).

33. How Jesus received his disciples on their return. Soon the seventy-two disciples returned gleefully to Jesus, saying, demons had obeyed them in Jesus's name. And Jesus answered that they would have power to tread on serpents, scorpions, and all manner of demons in his name, and would not be harmed. But they should avoid vainglory for, as Jesus said:

"I saw[107] Satan fall like a thunderbolt from heaven on account of his pride. If demons obey you, take no joy in it; rather be joyful to be chosen by name for the glory of heaven."

Immediately Jesus began to rejoice in the Holy Spirit, thanking God his Father for choosing to reveal such great things to the meek and humble, not to the learned and illustrious. Then he said that all who were exhausted and burdened should come to him, and he would comfort them. Then, turning to his disciples, he told them that they were blessed to witness his works and hear his teaching; for many prophets and kings had desired this, but it had not been granted them. (1–14)

34. How Jesus answered the lawyer who asked what was the greatest commandment. Then a lawyer stood and asked Jesus what he must do to have eternal life. And Jesus asked what the Law required a man to do; and he answered, to love God with all his heart, all his soul, all his strength, and all his thought; and to love his neighbor as himself. And Jesus told him that he should do this and he would have eternal life. And then the lawyer asked who his neighbor was, and Jesus showed him that every man was. And he told him a parable of a man who in travelling from Jerusalem[108] to Jericho was captured by thieves, robbed, and mortally wounded. And a priest and a deacon[109] who found him left him lying there; but a pagan Samaritan took pity on him and carried him on his mount to an inn where he cleaned his wounds with oil and wine and cared for him all night. And the next day, he gave two deniers to the innkeeper, asking him to look after him until his return, when he would reimburse him any additional expense.[110]

Then Jesus asked the lawyer:

---

[107] 33:5–6 **for, as Jesus said: "I saw [. . .]"** *quar, [ceo dist]: "Jeo vi [. . .]"*

[108] 34:8 **from Jerusalem** *en ierusalem* [read *de Jerusalem*]

[109] 34:9 **a deacon** *un diacre*: at Lk 10:32, the modern English Bibles have "a Levite"; *V* "Levita." See also the note for 7:19.

[110] 34:13 **any additional expense** *quanqu'il [averoit] plus despendu*: Ernoul's pilgrimage account (ca. 1231) places this inn between Jerusalem and Jericho and identifies it as the former "Rouge cisterne," or Red Cistern (*Itinéraires à Jérusalem*, 70–71). Jerome called the place the "red ascent" on account of the blood shed there by the traveller's attackers. According to the pilgrim Theodoric (1169–1172), Joseph was thrown into this well by his brothers; the Templars later built a strong castle here. A map (ca. 1252) attributed to Matthew Paris marks the location of the Red Cistern (see Pringle, *Churches*, 2:345–46 [Tal'at ad-Damm]).

"Which of the three was the wounded man's neighbor, the priest, the deacon, or the Samaritan?"

And he answered:

"The one who took pity on him."

And Jesus told him to go and do likewise, that is, to treat every man as his neighbor. (1–20)

35. How Saint Martha lodged Jesus. Then Jesus came to a village and entered the house of Martha, Mary Magdalene's sister.[111] And Martha bustled about making Jesus at home and waiting on him, as she always did. But Mary left all the entertaining to her sister and went to sit at Jesus's feet to listen to what he was saying.[112] Behold, Martha came and, standing before Jesus, said:

"My Lord, haven't you noticed that my sister is letting me serve you by myself? Won't you tell her to get up and help me?"

And Jesus answered:

"Martha, Martha, you are anxious and upset about many things, but now only one thing matters. Mary has chosen the better part, and she will not be deprived of it." (1–11)

36. How Jesus taught his disciples to pray. Afterwards Jesus happened to be in prayer; and when he had finished, one of his disciples asked him to teach them to pray, just as John the Baptist had taught his disciples. And Jesus answered that in their prayer, they should conscientiously say their Our Father.[113] For, like the

---

[111] 35:2 **Mary Magdalene's sister** *la seor Marie Magdaleyne*: in a sermon in 591 (Hom. in Evang. 2.33, PL 76.1239–1246), Gregory the Great had effectively combined in a single Mary the identities of three distinct women described in the New Testament Gospels: Mary of Bethany, sister of Martha; the unnamed female sinner at the banquet of Simon the Pharisee (see chap. 32); and Mary Magdalene who, exorcised of her demons, became a close follower of Christ. Medieval preachers and authors adopted this "composite Mary" on Gregory's authority. See Katherine L. Jansen, *The Making of the Magdalen: Preaching and Popular Devotion in the Later Middle Ages* (Princeton: Princeton University Press, 2000), 28–29, 32–35, 116n.

[112] 35:3–5 **But Mary left all the entertaining to her sister [. . .] to listen to what he was saying** *Mes Marie la lessa tout a convenir e ala seoir decoste les piez Jhesu e oi ses paroles*: the author of *Ancrene Wisse* contrasts Martha's busyness and Mary's quiet receptiveness, recommending the latter model to anchoresses: "Managing a household is Martha's part; Mary's part is stillness and rest from all the world's noise, so that nothing may hinder her from hearing God's voice . . . You should sit with Mary stone-still at God's feet and listen to him alone" (*Ancrene Wisse*, ed. and trans. Robert Hasenfratz, Middle English Texts [Kalamazoo: Medieval Institute Publications, 2000], 400, 400n).

[113] 36:4 **they should conscientiously say their Our Father** *qu'il deissent en lour oreyson lour Pater nostre, e ceo ententivement*: Saewulf's pilgrimage account (1101–03) states, "A stone's throw from [the top of the Mount of Olives] our Lord wrote the Lord's Prayer

man who had gone to bed when his neighbor came begging bread for an unexpected guest—pounding on the door, crying out, depriving him and his children of rest (and although the man acted less for friendship than to extricate himself)—he would get up and give the neighbor more than he asked. Likewise, said Jesus:

"God hears him who prays conscientiously. For just as fathers—even if their children misbehave—give them good things and do not oppose them, so the Heavenly Father will indulge those who pray to him." (1–12)

37. How Jesus stood up for his disciples for gathering ears of corn on the Sabbath. About that time, on a feast day, Jesus happened to go walking through a cornfield. And his disciples, being hungry, went out ahead of him and—taking corn to rub between their hands—ate the kernels. And the Pharisees came and, reprimanding them, reported them to Jesus for having done this on the Sabbath. And Jesus asked them, had they not read how David—when there was nothing else to eat—had eaten consecrated bread reserved for the priests?

"Moreover," he said, "the priests serving in the Temple work on the Sabbath and are excused out of respect for the Temple. And one more exalted than the Temple is here; but if you understood the Scripture—which says that God favors mercy over retribution—you would not have condemned the innocent. For the Sabbath is made for man, not man for the Sabbath; and even I am the Lord of the Sabbath." (1–13)

38. How Jesus healed the palsied hand. On another Sabbath, as Jesus was preaching in a synagogue, a man whose right hand was palsied appeared before him. And the Pharisees and scribes, wishing to accuse Jesus, were watching carefully to see if he would consent to heal a man on the Sabbath; and others asked him if one should heal on the Sabbath. And Jesus commanded the man to go stand outside, and he obeyed. And Jesus asked them whether one should do good or evil on the Sabbath, and they fell silent. And Jesus told them that none of them would hesitate to haul out his sheep[114] on the Sabbath if it fell into a ditch, and surely one should more readily help a man than a sheep.

"Thus I determine," said he, "that it is lawful to do good on the Sabbath."

Then Jesus looked at them fiercely because he was sad that they were so blind. And he told the paralytic to hold out his hand; and immediately as he extended it, it was as sound as the other. (1–13)

39. How Jesus fled and healed those who followed. Then the Pharisees and Herod's followers went away to plot how they might destroy Jesus. And Jesus

---

with his own hands upon the rock, in Hebrew . . . " (Wilkinson, *Jerusalem Pilgrimage*, 107). For the church of the Lord's Prayer, see Pringle, *Churches*, 3:117–24.

[114] 38:8 **haul out his sheep** *lavast ses berbiz* [read *levast sa berbiz*]

travelled—one might say, fled—with his disciples toward the sea, and many from all the countries round about followed him. And he healed the sick, then—because of the throng—went to sit in a ship on the sea. And they stood at anchor just offshore, and he preached to the multitude. And then he asked them not to reveal where he was.[115] And wherever they found them, the demon-possessed came and fell to their knees before him, saying that he was the Son of God. And he forbade them to reveal him, threatening them sternly if they disobeyed. (1–10)

40. How Jesus healed the blind and mute demoniac and answered the scribes. Then Jesus arrived at a house, and the people followed and crowded him so that he and his disciples could not eat. And his disciples thought him mad for behaving so solicitously toward the people and healing their sick, and they went outside to take hold of him and bring him back inside. And even so, Jesus did not stop, but turned to a blind and mute demoniac,[116] driving out the demon; and at once the man began to see and speak. And the people said that it seemed clear that he was the Christ; but the Pharisees and scribes who came from Jerusalem said that he was driving out the least demons by their prince Beelzebub. And then Jesus called them together and demolished their accusation with five proofs that it could not be true. Then they asked him to show them some sign in heaven, to demonstrate his authority. And Jesus, seeing the people running to him, told them that they would have no sign but that of the prophet Jonah: for just as Jonah lived three days and three nights in the belly of the whale and was then saved—to signify that the people of Nineveh would be saved by believing in him—so Jesus would be buried in the ground and would then rise again, signifying that all who believed in him would be resurrected. Then Jesus told them that on Judgment Day, the people of Nineveh would condemn them for believing the preaching of Jonah, who worked no miracles; and yet they did not believe in him who performed so many wonders. They would also be condemned by the pagan queen of the South,[117] because she came such a great distance to hear the wisdom of Solomon; and yet, they would not believe in him who taught them God's law in their own country and more wisely than Solomon. And he told them that they would experience what had happened to the man who had a demon expelled from him, yet did not mend his ways; rather, he came and took up

---

[115] 39:7 **where he was** *ou il fust*: PGH "where pat he were" ("where he was," Goates, 38); but see Mk 3:12, "he sternly ordered them not to make him known" (NRSV).

[116] 40:6 **but turned to a [. . .] demoniac** *mes se prist a un demoniac*: AN *se prendre a* may also mean "to attack," "go against" (*ANOH*), but these are not justified by *V* (see Mt 12:22).

[117] 40:20–21 **the pagan queen of the South** *la reyne de Saba qu'estoit payene*: see the note for iii.28.

seven demons worse than the first one, which returned to possess the man with its whole entourage.

And as Jesus was saying these things with such sweetness and wisdom, a woman in the crowd cried out in a loud voice, saying:

"Blessed are the womb that bore you and the breasts you suckled!"

And Jesus answered:

"But they are blessed indeed who hear the word of God and observe it."

Behold, as Jesus was speaking so solicitously to the people, his mother came with his cousins. And she wanted to speak to him and could not reach him on account of the throng; but she sent word by a messenger that he should come to her. And Jesus answered him that, in the same way that he loved his mother and his kinsmen, so too he loved all who heard his word and observed it. (1–37)

41. How Jesus answered the Pharisee who reproached him at table. Then a Pharisee invited Jesus to eat with him, and Jesus accepted. Behold, as Jesus sat, the Pharisee deemed that he had sinned for not washing before the meal according to their custom. And then Jesus began to criticize the Pharisees for their hypocrisy and the lawyers for their bad example; and he told them that God would send them the greatest punishment ever meted out since the death of Abel. (1–6)

42. How Jesus taught his disciples to shun avarice by reason of two brothers. After this, it happened that there was an enormous throng around Jesus. And he began to caution his disciples in clear terms to avoid the hypocrisy of the Pharisees, teaching them also to be bold and resolute in the persecutions they would suffer at their hands. And one of the people came and begged Jesus to command his brother to release his share of their inheritance. And Jesus answered:

"Man, who appointed me judge or arbiter over you?"[118]

Then Jesus told his disciples to beware of avarice; for, as he said:

"No abundance can preserve a miser's life."

And, as an example, he related how one year a miserly rich man, who had abundant grain, considered where he might store it. And he decided to tear down his barns to make them bigger; and he would store all his crops there and would rest, eat, drink, and celebrate for many years. And at once God said to him:

"Fool, this night demons[119] will require your soul, and who then will have all that you have prepared?"

---

[118] 42:7 **judge or arbiter over you** *juge ou departeur sur vous*: *ANOH* does not list *departeur*. Compare *V* "iudicem aut divisorem super vos" (Lk 12:14); PGH "juge and partener ouer ȝou" ("judge and dispenser [or broker] over you," Goates, 40).

[119] 42:14 **this night demons** *ceste nuyt . . . les diables*: *V* and the modern English Bibles have vague constructions here, not "demons" (Lk 12:20); PGH is most explicit: "Fole, þis ilch nyȝth schullen fendes fechchen þi soule in to helle" ("Fool, this very night shall fiends fetch thy soul into Hell"; Goates, 41).

"So will it be," said Jesus, "with him who hoards treasure for himself and is not rich in God."

Then Jesus began to teach his disciples not to worry about their food or clothing, but to be charitable and to prepare for the Judgment. And then he went back to the people, directing them to discern the time of Christ's coming as they predicted weather by atmospheric conditions:

"If you see a cloud rise in the west," he said, "you say that rain is coming, and it rains. And if the wind turns southerly, you say it will be hot, and it gets hot. But why can you not discern the wonders you see now, when such things never occurred before? Now believe that Christ has come," he said, "or vengeance[120] will be taken on you!" (1–26)

43. How Jesus urged the people to repent by reason of the Galileans slain by Pilate. At that same time some people came to Jesus, telling him that Pilate had slain many Galileans who had gone up Mount Gerizim with a false prophet. And they had made their offerings there, and he promised to ascend to heaven before them; but Pilate arrived and killed them along with the prophet.[121] Then Jesus told them that, despite their awful deaths, the Galileans were not the most wicked in the land, but that God had allowed their deaths to incite others to mend their ways; for without this, they would all perish together, and not only they but the people of Jerusalem, too. For God had also allowed eighteen men to be killed by a tower at Siloam,[122] in Jerusalem, as a correction to all the others. Then Jesus told them a parable of a man with a barren fig tree in his vineyard who ordered his vinedresser to cut it down. And the vinedresser asked him to leave it for one more season, and he would tend it diligently. And if it bore fruit, so much the better; if not, he would cut it down the next year. (1–14)

---

[120] 42:25 **or vengeance** *e* [read *ou*] *vengeaunce*

[121] 43:2–5 **Pilate had slain many Galileans [. . .] along with the prophet** *Pilate out occis une masse des Galileis qui estoient alez o un faus prophete en le mount de Garizin. E li offrirent la lour offrendes, e il lour promist qu'il mounteroit au ciel devaunt eus. E sourvint Pilate e lé occist ensemblement o li*: the details after "Galileans" (*Galileis*) are not found in *V* or in the modern English Bibles. See Lk 13:1 and page 37. In PGH, the Galileans make their offerings to Jesus (Goates, 41–42). The incident, which is unknown outside Luke's gospel, seems to parallel Josephus's account of Pilate's slaughter of Samaritans on Mount Garizim. See *The New American Bible, New American Version* (Oxford: Oxford University Press, 2007), 1769; *The Works of Flavius Josephus*, trans. William Whiston (London: George Routledge and Sons; and New York: E.P. Dutton & Co., n.d.; archive.org), 427–28; and *Hist.evang.*, cols. 1585–86.

[122] 43:9–10 **eighteen men [. . .] killed by a tower at Siloam** *dis e wit homes [. . .] agravantez en Siloa [. . .] d'une tour*: the reference is to Lk 13:4. Siloam is a precinct of Jerusalem; Christ healed a blind man who washed at the pool of Siloam (Jn 9:7; see 59:54–60).

44. How Jesus healed the stooped woman. Afterwards, one Saturday, Jesus Christ happened to preach in a synagogue; and he healed a woman who for eighteen years had been so stooped, she could not stand upright. The synagogue ruler, despising that Jesus had healed her on the Sabbath, told the people to come to Jesus on the other six days for healing, not on the Sabbath. Then Jesus said:

"Hypocrites, which of you would not untie and water his livestock on the Sabbath? And wasn't it more imperative to unbind on the Sabbath this noble woman whom the Devil had bound for eighteen years?"

And Jesus's eloquent words made his adversaries feel very ashamed, but the people rejoiced at all the things he so gloriously accomplished. (1–10)

45. How Jesus preached in parables while sitting in the ship. Then Jesus arrived at the sea, but such a great throng formed around him that he went to sit in a ship. And he taught them in parables, telling them that he was like a man sowing seed—some of it beside the path, some on rocky ground or among thorns, and another part on good soil. And then he said that he was like the man who planted good wheat-seed in his field; and while people were sleeping, his enemy came and overplanted it with corncockle. And he said that his listeners were like corn that grows day and night until harvest-time comes, then suddenly it can no longer increase.[123] And then he said that they were also like a mustard-seed that, though quite small when sown, grows incredibly high. And then he also compared them to yeast[124] that, despite its smallness, leavens an oven-load. Then his disciples came and asked him to explain these parables. And he explained them all, saying that they were blessed and privileged to listen to his teaching, which the people were not worthy to hear. And then he told them a parable of a treasure hidden in a field, another of the fine pearl, and a third of the net.[125] And he asked them if they understood, and they said yes. And he said that for this reason, every learned scribe was like the peasant[126] who, depending on the season, brings out from his storeroom old things and new. (1–18)

---

[123] 45:7–9 **And he said [. . .] it can no longer increase** *E pus dist qu'il estoit ausi de ceus que l'oirent com del blé que crest nuyt e jour jeskes vigne a oust e ne se puet mie sudeinement multeplier*: this appears to be a version of the Parable of the Growing Seed, Mk 4:26–29.

[124] 45:10–11 **compared them to yeast** *il est[oit] ausi d'eus com del levain*

[125] 45:14–15 **a parable of a treasure [. . .] and a third of the net** *une parable du tresor muscé en chaump, e une autre de la preciouse margarite, e la tierce de la seine: abbreviatio*. For the three parables, see Mt 13:44–50. PGH names only the first two parables (Goates, 43).

[126] 45:17 **peasant** *peisaunt*: at Mt 13:52, the modern English Bibles have "householder," "master of a household," "owner of a house"; *V* "homini patri familias."

46. How Jesus came again into his country, and the people insulted him. [127] Then Jesus went into his country and taught in the synagogue. All were amazed by his teaching, saying to one another:

"Isn't this the son of Joseph the carpenter? Isn't Mary his mother? Aren't James, Joses, Simon, and Judas his brothers? And his sisters, aren't they here among us? How has he become so wise and mighty?"

And Jesus answered:

"No prophet is as honored in his country as elsewhere."

And he worked few miracles there because of their unbelief. (1–9)

47. How the Jews persecuted him for healing the paralytic on the Sabbath. After this, Jesus went to a feast in Jerusalem. Now in Jerusalem there was a cistern with five porches[128] where those afflicted with all manner of diseases lay waiting for the angel to move the water, as he often did. And whoever reached the water first after the angel stirred it, he was cured, whatever his affliction. Now there was a man who at that point had lain ill for thirty-eight years. And Jesus came there on the Sabbath and, seeing that the man had lain there so long, asked him if he wished to be healed. And he replied that there was no one to carry him to the water when it was troubled, for each time—before he could reach the water—someone else got there first. Then Jesus commanded him to get up and carry his bed to his house; and at once he was healed, and he rose up and carried his bed home. Whereupon the Jews, believing[129] the man had been healed by the water, told him he was not supposed to carry his bed on the Sabbath; and he answered that the one who had healed him had said to take away his bed. And they asked who that was, and he could not answer. Then Jesus found him at the Temple and told him to sin no more, lest worse befall him. And he went and reported to the Jews that it was Jesus who had healed him, wherefore the Jews persecuted Jesus for doing such things on the Sabbath. Then Jesus made them a long speech to show that he could very well do such things on the Sabbath. (1–19)

---

[127] 46:1 **How Jesus came again into his country, and the people insulted him** *Coment Jhesu vint autre foiz en son pais e il le despisoient*: see the note for 23:1.

[128] 47:2–3 **a cistern with five porches** *une cisterne que avoit cink porches*: Saewulf's pilgrimage account (1101–1103) calls this place the Sheep Pool, also giving its Hebrew name, Bethsaida (Wilkinson, *Jerusalem Pilgrimage*, 105). At Jn 5:2, some modern English Bibles call it Bethsaida and Bethesda, but NRSV Beth-zatha; *V* "Bethsaida," "Probatica." See the note for 21:8–9. For the chapel of the Sheep Pool, see further Pringle, *Churches*, 3:389–97.

[129] 47:12 **believing** *quil* [read *qui*] *quidoient*

Here begins the fourth meditation, for Wednesday

48. How Jesus slipped away into the wilderness when he got word that John the Baptist was beheaded. Then it came to pass that Herod was celebrating his birthday with all the prominent men[130] of Galilee, and the daughter of his wife Herodias performed acrobatic tricks[131] for the king and his guests. And the king was so pleased that he swore to give her whatever she asked, even if she required half his kingdom. Her mother advised her to ask for nothing but the head of John the Baptist; and she promptly requested the Baptist's head on a plate. And the king became sad, but on account of the celebration and the prominent guests — and not wanting to disappoint her — he had the head of John the Baptist brought to her on a plate,[132] and she gave them to her mother. Then his disciples arrived and buried his body; and they came and told Jesus. And the apostles came at the same time and reported their works and teachings to Jesus. And Jesus told them to come with him privately into the wilderness to rest a while, for it was night and they had found no time to eat on account of the crush of people. And Jesus took them all with him into a ship and crossed the water to a secluded place in the wilderness; and he went up onto a mountain and sat there with his disciples. (1–18)

49. How Jesus fed five thousand men. Behold, when Jesus had gone with his disciples into the wilderness, the people were observing which way he went; and

---

[130] **48:4 prominent men** *hauz homes*: *abbreviatio*. The modern English Bibles' wording of Mk 6:21 varies, e.g., "high officials and military commanders and the leading men" (NIV) and "lords, high captains, and chief estates of Galilee" (KJV); *V* "principibus et tribunis et primis Galilaeae."

[131] **48:4–5 the daughter of his wife Herodias performed acrobatic tricks** *la fille Erodias sa femme ore tonbba*: for *tumber*, *ANOH* has "to tumble, perform acrobatic tricks," citing the same New Testament event in a passage in W. de Wadington, *Le Manuel des pechez*, in Robert of Brunne's *Handlyng Synne*, ed. F. J. Furnivall (London: Roxburghe Club, 1862); and EETS o.s. 119, 123 (London, 1901–1903), l. 3030.

[132] **48:10–11 he had the head of John the Baptist brought to her on a plate** *fist porter la teste Johan le Baptistre en un' esquele*: John Phocas's pilgrimage account (1185) states that Herod beheaded John the Baptist in Sebaste, the city where the Forerunner had been held in prison: "This Prison is underground, and has twenty steps leading down to it. In the centre of it is an altar containing the spot where [the Forerunner] was beheaded by the guard . . . In the central upper part of the city is a mound, on which Herod's palace stood in ancient times, where the banquet took place, and the abominable girl danced . . ." (Wilkinson, *Jerusalem Pilgrimage*, 322; see also 156 and 195). *La Terre des Sarrazins*, fol. 199r, locates the palace at Macheronte, near Sebaste. Josephus and medieval texts indicate Machaerus in Transjordan. In John Phocas's account, the left hand of the Baptist and his cremains were among the relics to be venerated at Sebaste. See Pringle, *Churches*, 2:283–301, at 283, 286, 297. See also the discussion in *Hist.evang.*, col. 1574.

everyone living in that country rushed there, taking their sick with them. And Jesus came down from the mountain and took pity on them, for they were lying like lambs along the roads. And, comforting them with gentle words, he healed all the sick. And as evening drew on, his disciples came and told him to let the people get themselves something to eat while daylight remained. And Jesus answered that they should feed the people; but the disciples replied that they had nothing to offer. And when Jesus saw that many more people had come, he said to Saint Philip:

"Where can we buy bread to feed these people?"

And he asked this to test him, for he knew what he would do. Then Philip said that two hundred pennyworth of bread was insufficient to divide up, bit by tiny bit, among them. And Jesus asked how many loaves there were; and Saint Andrew said that there was a child with five barley-loaves and two fishes — next to nothing for so many people. Then Jesus commanded that the bread and fishes be brought to him and the people divided into groups of hundreds and fifties and seated on the grass; and this was done. And Jesus looked toward heaven and, giving thanks to his Father, blessed the bread and fishes, broke them, and handed them to his disciples who gave them to the people.[133] And when they had eaten their fill, Jesus commanded them to gather up the scraps; and they filled twelve baskets with the surplus. **The fifth time in the third week.**[134] And at once Jesus bade all his disciples to go to the ship and return to Bethsaida while he disengaged from the people; and the apostles went away. And when they perceived that Jesus had fed them so abundantly with so little, the people said that he was a true prophet, for they comprehended that they were five thousand[135] men plus the women and children. And then they schemed to make him king by force, but meanwhile Jesus had stolen away alone to the mountain to pray. Then it came to pass that his disciples were caught in a great gale and could not possibly cross back over. And, towards daybreak, Jesus came walking towards them on the waves, making as if to pass by them. And the disciples all saw him and were so

---

[133] 49:20 **who gave them to the people** *e il les donerent au people*: for descriptions of the location of the Feeding of the Five Thousand in medieval pilgrim texts, see Pringle, *Churches*, 2:334–39 (at-Tabgha). The site of this miracle is often called the Table of Our Lord (*Mensa* or *Tabula Domini*), but the same name is sometimes also used to refer to the place of Christ's post-Resurrection meal with his disciples. See *Hist.evang.*, col. 1576.

[134] 49:22 **The fifth time in the third week** *La quinte feytz en la tierce simaine*: the first of three chronological tags (see below, notes for 59:20 and 59:53–54). In *The Sarum Missal*, the Gospel reading for Midlent Sunday (i.e., the fourth Sunday of Lent, or Laetare) is Jn 6:1–14, the miraculous feeding of the five thousand (*The Sarum Missal*, trans. A. Harford Pearson, 2nd ed. [London: Church Printing Company, 1884; www.archive.org], 90), which the *Estoire* has just retold.

[135] 49:26 **five thousand** *sis mile* [read *cink mile*]: a scribal slip. The chapter heading has "five thousand," as do Mt 14:21, Mk 6:44, Lk 9:14 and Jn 6:10.

terrified[136] that they began to shout, yelling that it was a ghost. And immediately Jesus spoke to them, telling who he was and saying that they should not be afraid. Then Saint Peter said:

"Lord, if it be you, bid me come to you on the water."

And Jesus bade Peter come; and he sprang from the ship and walked on the waves towards Jesus. And there came a tremendous gust of wind, and Peter became afraid and immediately began sinking; and he cried to Jesus to save him. And at once Jesus extended his hand and seized Peter; and he asked him straightaway why he was afraid. And he brought Peter with him aboard the ship, and at once the wind ceased; and presently the ship came to shore at their destination. The next day the people whom Jesus had fed noticed that there was no ship[137] except the one Jesus had brought and that he had not boarded with his disciples. And the people boarded other vessels transiting there from Tiberias and came seeking Jesus at Capernaum. And when they had found him, they asked him how he had come.[138] And Jesus replied that they were not seeking him for his teachings[139] but for the meals he would provide; and he said that they should seek the food that would never spoil. And they answered that their forebears had received manna in the wilderness when Moses led them out of Egypt. And Jesus answered that Moses did not provide the manna, but God his Father. And he would do more for them if they accepted to believe in him: he would give them his own body and blood. And if they ate and drank them, they would have eternal life; but without eating his flesh and drinking his blood, they would not have everlasting life. And when he had explained this at length to them, they began to grouse and to ask each other, how could he give his flesh to eat and his blood to drink to those who believed in him? And several of his disciples forsook him and went away. Then Jesus said to his twelve apostles:

"Do you mean to depart from me?"

And Saint Peter answered:

"Lord, to whom else would we go? Your word is so true and sweet. You promise eternal life. And though we understand not what you say, we are sure you are Jesus the Son of God."

Then Jesus told them that one of the twelve was a devil; and by this he meant Judas who betrayed him. (1–64)

---

[136] 49:31–32 **were so terrified** *avoient [si] grant pour*

[137] 49:42–43 **the people whom Jesus had fed noticed that there was no ship** *s'averti le people que Jhesu out [p]eu qu'i[l] n'i out nule nef*

[138] 49:46 **how he had come** *coment il fust venu*: at Jn 6:25, *V* and the modern English Bibles have not "how" but "when"; PGH "hou it fered of hym & hou hym was bitydde" ("how he fared and what had become of him," Goates, 48).

[139] 49:46–47 **not [. . .] for his teachings** *pas pur son sermon*: at Jn 6:26, the modern English Bibles have variations of "not because you saw signs" (NRSV); *V* "non quia vidistis signa."

50. How Jesus healed all who touched him in Gennesaret. In those days Jesus went to the land of Gennesaret, and everyone there recognized him immediately. They ran to him from all over the territory, bringing their sick and begging to touch at least the hem of his cloak; and as many as touched him were healed. (1–4)

51. How Jesus answered the scribes who criticized his disciples for not washing. Then Jesus came back into Galilee, and scribes who had arrived from Jerusalem saw his disciples eat before[140] washing their hands. According to their custom, the Jews were wont to wash their hands often before eating. And they asked Jesus why his disciples did not observe the customs of their forebears; and Jesus asked them, why did they not keep the commandments of God, for God commanded us to help our father and mother. And they said that it was better to commit one's possessions to the Temple than to one's father or mother; and, in keeping their rules, they did many other things contrary to God's law.[141] Then Jesus called the people to him, telling them that man is defiled not by the food he eats but by the evil speech that issues from his mouth. Then, when Jesus arrived at his lodging, his disciples told him that his talk had shocked the Pharisees; but he said not to be concerned by it, for the Pharisees were blind men leading the blind. And Saint Peter asked him to spell out his meaning to his disciples. And Jesus answered that what goes into a man's mouth does not enter his heart and thus does not defile the soul; but through the mouth the heart spews evil thoughts, murder, adultery, fornication, theft, false witness, blasphemy, greed, malice, deceit, lasciviousness, envy, arrogance, and folly. And these things defile the soul, but eating with unwashed hands does not. (1–19)

52. How Jesus healed the Canaanite woman's daughter. Then Jesus slipped away towards Tyre and Sidon. And a pagan woman from those parts came and asked him to exorcise a demon from her daughter, and Jesus answered not a word.[142] Then his disciples came and urged him to send her away, for she was crying out after them; and Jesus said that he had been sent only to the Jews. And he stole away and entered a house; and the woman came and, falling at his feet, begged for mercy. And he told her that it was not right to take bread intended for children and give it to dogs. And she answered:

"And yet, dogs eat the crumbs that fall from the master's table and from his children's hands."

---

[140] 51:3 **disciples eat before** *deciples [manger] avaunt*

[141] 51:9 **many other things contrary to God's law** *e autres choses plusors firent il countre la lei Dieu*: severe *abbreviatio*. See Mt 15:6–11.

[142] 52:3 **Jesus answered not a word** *Jhesu ne li respoundi nul mot*: for the location as discussed in medieval pilgrim accounts, see Pringle, *Churches*, 2:317–29 (Sidon, Church of the Saviour), at 321.

Then Jesus said:

"Ha, woman, great is your faith! As you wish, so be it! For such a reply, go your way. The demon has left your daughter."

And when she arrived home, she found her daughter lying on her bed; and the demon had gone out of her. (1–15)

53. How Jesus healed the deaf-mute at the Sea of Galilee. Then Jesus arrived along the Sea of Galilee. And they brought a deaf-mute to him[143] and begged Jesus to touch him. And Jesus took hold of him and led him[144] away from the people. He put his fingers in the man's ears, touched the man's tongue with his saliva, and, looking toward heaven, sighed deeply and said:

"Be healed!"

And at once he began to speak properly and to hear. And Jesus commanded them to tell no one of this; but the more they spread the news, the more people marvelled. And Jesus went up onto a mountain and sat; and the people followed, bringing him the mute,[145] the blind, the lame, the weak, and many other infirm, and setting them at his feet. And he healed every one. (1–11)

54. How he fed four thousand men. At that time, since the people had remained there without food, Jesus called his disciples to him, saying that he felt compassion for the people who had been with him three days with nothing to eat. And he said that he did not want to send them away fasting lest they grow weak along the road, for some had come a great distance. Then his disciples said that they had nothing to feed them with, nor could they get that much bread in the wilderness. And Jesus asked them how many loaves they had. And they replied:

"Seven."

And he bade the people to go sit on the ground, and taking the bread and giving thanks to his Father, he blessed the loaves, broke them, and gave them to his disciples who distributed them among the people. And they had a few fishes, and he blessed them and had them handed out; and they ate their fill and collected seven full baskets of leftovers. Now four thousand men[146] were there, in addition to the women and children. Then Jesus sent them away. (1–14)

55. How Jesus answered the Pharisees in Magadan. Then Jesus boarded a ship and went to the vicinity of Magadan; and the Pharisees came and asked him to show them a sign in heaven. And, groaning deeply, Jesus answered that they

---

[143] 53:2 **they brought [. . .] to him** *o[n] li mena*

[144] 53:3 **took hold of him and led him** *il le prist e l'amena*: Plooij includes PGH's "name & ledde" ("took and led"; Goates, 51) among his "test-readings for the Diatessaron" (Plooij, "The Pepysian Harmony," 15). See the notes for 8:8 and 8:14.

[145] 53:10 **bringing him the mute** *porterent a* [read *ovés*] *eus les mus*

[146] 54:13 **four thousand men** *quatre [mile] homes*

knew how to read the portents of fair weather and storms,[147] but were blind to the signs of Christ's coming; and on this account they would have no sign besides the prophet Jonah's. (1–6)

56. The neglect to pack bread, and how Jesus encouraged his disciples afterwards. And when his disciples forgot to take bread along on the ship, Jesus told them to avoid the yeast of the Pharisees, Sadducees, and Herodians. And they sensed that Jesus said this because they had forgotten to bring bread with them. And Jesus rebuked them for their lack of faith, reminding them how many leftovers had been collected from only five loaves, and then from seven, and how many people had been fed. Then they saw that they had misunderstood Jesus: he was not talking about yeast. He was telling them to avoid the teaching of the Pharisees and others. (1–9)

57. How Jesus spat on a blind man's eyes to heal him. Then Jesus came to Bethsaida;[148] and they brought him a blind man and begged Jesus to touch him. And taking his hand and leading him outside the city, Jesus spat on the man's eyes, touched them, and asked if he could see at all. And he answered that he saw men like trees walking about. And once more Jesus touched his eyes,[149] and he saw everything clear as day. And Jesus told him to go home and, if he went into the city, to tell no one of this thing. (1–7)

58. How Herod feared Jesus. About that time, Herod got word of Jesus's miracles. And he was afraid, having heard that he was John the Baptist raised from the dead; and Herod himself was convinced of this, too. But others said that he was one or another of the prophets of old brought back to life; and on this account Herod yearned to meet Jesus. (1–5)

59. How Jesus fared at the feast of tabernacles where he freed the woman and gave sight to a blind man. Then the feast of tabernacles drew nigh, and Jesus was in Galilee. And his kinsmen told him that if he was performing miracles in God's name, he should arrange to go to the feast in Jerusalem so his followers might witness his works; for even his kinsmen did not believe in him. Then Jesus said: in that case, he would not go to the feast, for the time to reveal himself was not yet come; but they should go ahead since for them any day was fitting, and the world loved them and despised him for vilifying the people. Then his

---

[147] 55:4 **how to read the portents of fair weather and storms** *les signes de beau tens e de tempeste savoient il conoistre*: a continuation of the discussion at 42:19–25, in which Christ urges listeners to be alert to signs of his coming in the same way that they predict changes of weather based on current conditions.

[148] 57:2 **Bethsaida** *Betheida*

[149] 57:5 **once more Jesus touched his eyes** *autre foith [tocha] ses oyz*

kinsmen departed for the feast. And Jesus stayed until they had left, following them later in secret. And the people attending the feast were continually asking about Jesus: some said that he was a good man, others that he was misleading the people. Behold, as the feast reached its height, Jesus came into the Temple and taught the people, and they were amazed that he could know the Law without benefit of study. Then Jesus said that his teaching came not from him, but from God who had sent him. And he rebuked them for plotting to kill him and pointed out their error, for they were performing circumcisions on the Sabbath; and, they said, he had sinned by healing a man on the Sabbath. Then, some said, he was the Christ. And others expressed amazement that the chief priests did not arrest him: for they were scheming to kill him,[150] and there he was in person! And then **on the Saturday of the third week**,[151] after Jesus had stayed for some time among the people, the chief priests and the Pharisees heard that his teaching was stirring up the people. And they met together, sending soldiers to seize him and bring him to them for trial. And the soldiers arrived to arrest Jesus; but when they heard him speak, they could wish him no ill. Whereupon the soldiers reported to their lords, who asked why they had not brought Jesus in; and they answered that no one had ever spoken like Jesus.

"How's that?" they said, "So you have been deceived? Don't you see that not a single ruler or Pharisee believes in him—only the accursed people do!"

Then Nicodemus, who had met previously with Jesus and was one of them,[152] told them that the Law condemned no one without a hearing. And they asked Nicodemus angrily if Jesus were from Galilee, claiming no prophet could possibly come from there; and then they all went home. And the next morning, as Jesus sat in the Temple teaching the people, the scribes and Pharisees arrived, bringing with them a woman from among the people[153] who had been taken in adultery. And they told him of this and asked what they should do about it, for Moses had commanded that such women be stoned. And they did this so that if Jesus said to stone her, they could discredit him for harshness, and the people

---

[150] 59:19 **were scheming to kill him** *le quid[er]ent a occire*

[151] 59:20 **on the Saturday of the third week** *le samadi en la tyerce simaine*: inspired perhaps by Jn 7:37 (*V* "in novissimo autem die magno festivitatis"), this chronological tag introduces a conference of chief priests and Pharisees initiated five verses earlier, at Jn 7:32. In fact, the story of the adulterous woman, which begins at 59:32, is based on Jn 8:1–11, corresponding to the Gospel reading for the Saturday after Oculi, the third Sunday of Lent, in the Sarum Use (*The Sarum Missal*, 89). PGH omits. For the biblical sources of chap. 59, see Appendix. See also the notes for 49:22 and 59:53–54.

[152] 59:29 **had met previously with Jesus and was one of them** *estoit venu avaunt a Jhesu quil* [read *Jhesu e qui*] *fui un d'eus*: for Nicodemus's earlier meeting with Jesus, see chap. 11.

[153] 59:34 **a woman from among the people** *une feme enmi le people*: at Jn 8:3, *V* and the modern English Bibles omit "from among the people," but NRSV includes "a woman who had been caught in adultery."

who thought him so compassionate would love him less; and if he said to release her, they could accuse him of transgressing God's law.[154] Then when Jesus saw them coming, he stooped and drew on the ground lest the woman feel ashamed. And they planted themselves in front of him, demanding vehemently to know what they should do with the woman. And Jesus rose, glared at them, and said that whichever of them was without sin should cast the first stone at her. Whereupon he squatted down again to resume drawing on the ground. And immediately they began exiting one by one, the elders leading them. And when Jesus saw that they had all left, he stood back up and gently addressed the woman:

"Woman, where are your accusers? Did no one condemn you?"

"No, Lord," she said, "no one."

Then Jesus said:

"Neither do I condemn you. Go, sin no more!"

Then Jesus began proving to them that he was the Son of God and they, sons of the Devil, not the children of Abraham. And he goaded them so, they wanted to stone him; but Jesus hid himself and exited the Temple. **The fourth feast-day in the fourth week**.[155] And as he went along, he saw a man sitting who was blind from birth. And his disciples asked him which it was, for his sins or for his forebears', that the man had lost his sight. And Jesus answered:

"For neither, but to display the power of God in him."

Then he spat on the ground and, making mud with his saliva, anointed the blind man's eyes. And he told him to go wash in the pool of Siloam; and he went and washed, then returned, his sight restored. Thereupon his neighbors, who had often observed the blind beggar, no longer recognized him once he could see; but he told them how Jesus had healed him. And because he was healed on the Sabbath, the neighbors took him to the Pharisees. And they asked him what had happened, saying that Jesus was not of God because he had done this on the Sabbath. And he answered them so boldly and eloquently that they became furious and drove him away. And Jesus got news of this and sought him out. And, on finding him, Jesus inquired if he believed in the Son of God; and he asked

---

[154] 59:36–39 **And they did this [. . .] transgressing God's law** *E ce firent il pur ce que si il deist: 'Lapidez la!', il l'eussent escrié com cruel, e le people que le tynt si pitous l'ust moyns amé; e si il deist: 'Lessez la quite!', il l'eussent pris com celi que eust fet contre la lei Dieu: amplificatio.* The *Estoire* inserts a rationale found neither in *V* nor in the modern English Bibles. See Jn 8:6.

[155] 59:53–54 **The fourth feast-day in the fourth week** *La quarte fferié en la quarte simaigne*: *ANOH* defines *ferié* as "feast day" or "day of the week." In the Use of Sarum, the Gospel reading for Wednesday of the fourth week of Lent is Jn 9:1–38, the story of Christ's healing of the blind man, which begins here. See F. Dickinson, *Missale ad usum insignis et praeclarae ecclesiae Sarum* (Burntisland: Pitsligo, 1861–1883; repr. Farnborough, Hants.: Gregg, 1969), cols. 221–222. PGH omits. See also the notes for 49:22 and 59:20 above. For the biblical sources of chap. 59, see Appendix.

who that was, and Jesus said, it was he. And immediately he fell at his feet, worshipped him, and said he believed in him. Now, following their custom, the Jews had resolved that whoever confessed Jesus as the Christ should be expelled from the synagogue. Thereupon Jesus began explaining that he was the true Light of the world and the true Shepherd, and that the Pharisees and rulers were blind men, thieves, and murderers.[156] (1–73)

60. How Jesus first forewarned his apostles of his Passion. Then it came to pass that, while praying and walking down the road with his disciples, Jesus asked them who people said he was. And they answered: some supposed he was John the Baptist, and others, Elijah; and still others thought he was Jeremiah or another prophet. And he asked who they thought he was. Then Saint Peter answered, he was the Christ, the living Son of God. Then Jesus said, Peter was the rock upon which he would establish his Church; and he would give him power in heaven, on earth, and in hell. Then Jesus began explaining to his disciples that he would have to go to Jerusalem to be condemned by the elders, chief priests, and scribes and to be put to death and raised again on the third day. Then Saint Peter began criticizing him for this omen, saying that such a thing could never happen. And Jesus answered:

"Away from me, Devil! You are a burden to me; for you follow not God, but men."

And he said that whoever wished to be his disciple[157] should deny himself, take up his cross daily, and follow him. And he told them that some were there who would not die until they saw him coming in glory.[158] (1–17)

61. How Jesus was transfigured, and then healed the lunatic. A week later, Jesus took Saint Peter and Saint John[159] and slipped away to a high mountain to pray. And as he prayed, his face shone like the sun, and his clothing became as resplendently white as snow. And Moses and Elijah appeared; and they told him of the torments awaiting him in Jerusalem. Then Saint Peter said to Jesus:

"Lord, it is good that we tarry here. Pray let us make three tabernacles—one for you, one for Moses, and one for Elijah."

---

[156] 59:73 **thieves, and murderers** *larons e mustrissours* [read *larons e murdrissours*]

[157] 60:15 **whoever wished to be his disciple** *quil* [read *qui*] *le vousist seure*

[158] 60:17 **until they saw him coming in glory** *jeskes ataunt qu'il le veissent tel com il vendroit glorifier*: at Mt 16:28, *V* and the modern English Bibles have variants of "coming in his kingdom."

[159] 61:1–2 **Jesus took Saint Peter and Saint John** *prist Jhesu seint Pierre e seint Johan*: the *Estoire* omits St James who appears here in Mt 17:1, Mk 9:2, and Lk 9:28; PGH also includes James (Goates, 57). For a description of significant places on Mount Tabor, including medieval pilgrims' accounts of the site of the Transfiguration, see Pringle, *Churches*, 2:63–85, at 63–69.

But he said this out of fear, for he was at a loss for words. Behold, a bright cloud appeared behind them, and a voice spoke to them from the cloud, saying:

"This is my dear Son, with whom I am well pleased. Listen to him!"

And they fell to the ground, terrified. And Jesus raised them up, telling them to fear not; and they looked and saw none but Jesus. And as they came down, he bade them[160] tell no one what they had seen until he was risen from the dead. Then they asked if Elijah would not come before the Judgment; and Jesus answered that he would, saying that he would restore the condition of the people; but they would deal with Elijah as with John the Baptist and with him.[161] The next day, a great throng met Jesus as he came down the mountain. And he arrived to find the scribes quarreling with his disciples before the people. And as soon as they saw him, they ran toward him, greeting him with great awe; and he asked them what they were arguing about. And a man stepped forward, saying that he had brought his lunatic son to Jesus's disciples, and they could not heal him. And Jesus told him to bring his son to him; and he asked the father how long his son had been afflicted. And he said, since childhood, adding that the spirit had often thrown him into fire or water to destroy him.

"But if you can," he said, "help us!"

Jesus answered:

"If you can believe, I will be able to help you."

And the man cried out, weeping:

"Lord, I believe, only help my unbelief!"

And immediately, as the boy approached Jesus, he fell down—as he often did—and was so horribly convulsed that many said that he had died. And Jesus commanded the spirit to depart, and it left him at once; and Jesus lifted the boy up and entrusted him to his father. And when Jesus had returned to his lodging, his disciples inquired why they had failed to drive out the spirit; and Jesus answered that it was because of their little faith. And he told them that if they had complete faith, they could do all things; but that kind of spirit, he said, was exorcised only by prayer and fasting. (1–37)

62. How Jesus again warned his disciples of his Passion. Then Jesus went secretly into Galilee, and again he forewarned his disciples of his Passion and Resurrection. And he told them that when these things came to pass, to remember what he had told them before. And they became grief-stricken and sad, knowing not if he was speaking of the inevitable or only in parables; but they dared not[162] ask him his meaning. (1–6)

---

[160] 61:12–13 **And as they came down, he bade them** *E il descendi e lour comaunda* [read *E com il descendirent, il lour comaunda*]: Mt 17:9.

[161] 61:16 **they would deal [. . .] and with him** *ausi feroient il de Elie com de Johan le Baptistre e de li*: severe *abbreviatio* of Mt 17:11–13.

[162] 62:5 **they dared not** *il nosa* [read *il n'oseient*]

63. How Jesus paid the temple tax and taught his disciples about humility and charity. Afterwards Jesus arrived in Capernaum; and those who collected the tribute to the Roman emperor came and asked Saint Peter if Jesus was not paying the tax, and Peter answered that he was.[163] And presently, as Saint Peter arrived at his house, Jesus came to ask from whom kings exacted a tax, from their sons or from outsiders; and Peter answered that it was from outsiders.

"Then the sons are exempt," said Jesus. "But lest we offend them, go to the sea and cast your net. And in the mouth of the first fish to arrive, you will find a penny that will cover the two taxes. Give that for my tax and yours!"

And immediately Jesus asked[164] his disciples what they had been discussing on the way. Now on the road they had been arguing about which of them was greatest; and thereafter they came to Jesus and put the question to him. And Jesus, knowing their hearts, bade a child stand in their midst beside him. And he kissed the child, telling them that if they did not change and become as meek as a child, they would never enter the kingdom of heaven.

"For whoever humbles himself like this child, he is greatest. And whoever receives such a child in my name, receives me. And the least of you," said Jesus, "is the greatest."

Then Saint John answered, saying that they had seen a man, not a follower of Jesus, driving out devils in his name, and he forbade him. And Jesus told them not to forbid him:[165] for no one performing miracles in his name could immediately speak ill of him, and whoever was not against them was for them; and whoever scandalized a child who believed in him, it were better for him to be drowned. Then Jesus taught them to reprimand privately those who offended them, forgiving offenders who asked forgiveness; but if they refused to reform, his followers should report the offense to their prelate. And if the offenders did not obey the prelate, they should shun them from then on; and whatever the Holy Church decided in their case, he would validate.[166]

"For wherever there are two or three in my name," he said, "I am there among them."

---

[163] 63:4 **Peter answered that he was** *il dist que oyl*: the pilgrimage guide called *Les Pelerinaiges por aler en Iherusalem* (ca. 1231) states that Jesus had been imprisoned near Capernaum for failure to pay the tax, which is described as a kind of toll ("près d'iqui est la prison où Nostre Sire fu mis iusqu'à tant qu'il ot paié le treuage de son passage"), and that he gained his release by the miracle of the fish (*Itinéraires à Jérusalem*, 102).

[164] 63:10 **Jesus asked** *comaunda* [read *demaunda*] *Jhesu*

[165] 63:20–21 **and he forbade him. And Jesus told them not to forbid him** *E il li avoit defendu E ihesu lor dist quil ne li defendisent pas E il li auoit defendu E ihesu lor dist quil ne li defendisent pas* [read *e il li avoit defendu. E Jhesu lor dist quil ne li defendisent pas*]

[166] 63:27–28 **whatever [. . .] he would validate** *quantque Seint' Eglise ajugeroit, serroit estable devaunt li*: the *Estoire* loosely paraphrases Mt 18:17.

Then Saint Peter asked how many times he should forgive when asked for forgiveness—should he forgive seven times?

And Jesus answered:

"Not only seven times, but seventy times seven."

Then Jesus told them the parable of the king who called in his servant's debt when the servant refused to treat his fellow-laborer as the king had dealt with him. And Jesus said that his Father would treat them likewise if they forgave not their neighbor. (1–38)

64. How the Samaritans refused him lodging, and how the Pharisees warned him against Herod. Then Jesus went out of Galilee towards Jerusalem to submit to his Passion. And as he was passing through Samaria, he sent messengers ahead, asking the people to receive him; but they refused because he was on his way to Jerusalem. Then said Saints James and John:

"Lord, do you want fire to come down from heaven to consume them?"

And Jesus turned and rebuked them, saying that they did not know that they should behave mercifully; for he had come not to take vengeance on men but to save them. Then they went to another town. And as Jesus walked along the road, a man asked him if few would be saved. And Jesus answered, many of that people would perish, and many pagans from all corners of the world would be saved; and the first would be last, and the last, first. Then Pharisees came to Jesus and told him to go away, for Herod was seeking him to destroy him. And Jesus replied:

"Go tell that fox: I will expel demons and heal the sick today, tomorrow, and the third day! And then I will have finished, for no prophet should die outside Jerusalem." (1–16)

65. How Jesus healed the man afflicted with dropsy and preached at mealtime about meekness and charity. Then one Sabbath, it came to pass that Jesus entered the house of a chief Pharisee to eat. And a man with the dropsy stood there before him; and all were watching closely to see if Jesus would heal on the Sabbath. And Jesus asked the scribes and Pharisees if one should do good on the Sabbath, and they did not answer; and Jesus touched the man and healed him. And, he asked, which of them would not immediately haul out his ox or his ass if it fell into a ditch on the Sabbath; and they could not answer. Then Jesus taught the guests that, when invited to a feast, they should not take the most prestigious seat. And he also taught the host that whenever he gave a feast,[167] he should invite the poor, though they could hardly pay him, and God would recompense him in the next world. Then a guest said that blessed was he who would eat in the kingdom of God; and Jesus replied, explaining that as many as consented to come could eat there. And then he told a parable of a prominent man[168] who

---

[167] 65:10 **a feast** *geste* [read *feste*]
[168] 65:14 **a prominent man** *un feste* [read *un hauz home*]

prepared a big feast. But when everything was ready, all those invited sent regrets—one because he wanted to see his estate,[169] another to try out[170] some oxen, and another because he had just married. And the notable men became angry, saying that none of them should eat his food; and he invited the poor and the sick to come instead, and filled his house. (1–19)

66. How, along the road, Jesus preached against earthly pleasures. Then Jesus went on toward Jerusalem, and multitudes followed him. And he turned and told them: whoever wished to come to him and be his disciple must abandon all earthly pleasures, take his cross, and follow him. And he added that—just as one intending to build a high tower considers first how to finish it, and like a king with only ten thousand men who ponders how to resist another king's attack with twenty thousand—similarly, said Jesus:

"Whoever wants to be my disciple must first think hard, forsaking all that interferes with his love for me." (1–9)

67. How Jesus answered those who grumbled about the sinners. After this, publicans and sinners arrived and drew near to hear Jesus. And at this the Pharisees and scribes grumbled that Jesus received such people and even ate with them. Whereupon he told them three parables[171] to show that he must do this, for the shepherd rejoices more to find one stray sheep than for a hundred others. And a woman is happier to find a penny she has lost than for ten others. And gladder is a man whose son has gone abroad, wasting the father's money in loose living, when the son returns home alive—even if he comes back naked and unshod—than for his other son who has never disobeyed him. Jesus added:

"God's angels rejoice more for one repentant sinner than for a hundred righteous with no need to repent." (1–11)

68. How Jesus taught his disciples to be compassionate and reproached the Pharisees. Then Jesus taught his disciples to be merciful; and he gave them the example of a servant whose lord, after hearing that the servant had wasted his goods, wanted to strip him of the stewardship of a city he had entrusted to him. And the servant made friends as well as he could, and he discounted their debts to his master. And the lord heard of this and praised him for acting wisely, for in God's eyes, worldly people are wiser than others in dealings with their kind. Then the greedy Pharisees heard how Jesus was teaching his disciples to give

---

[169] **65:16 he wanted to see his estate** *il uoleient ueoir sa fille* [read *il voleit veoir sa ville*]: another scribal slip. At Lk 14:18, the modern English versions have not "his daughter" but "a field," "a piece of land"; *V* "villam". See the note for 96:10.

[170] **65:16 another to try out** *auquns pur ce qu'il uoleient* [read *voloit*] *esprover*

[171] **67:4 three parables** *treis parables*: *abbreviatio*. The harmonist alludes to "The Lost Sheep" (Lk 15:3–7), "The Lost Coin" (Lk 15:8–10), and "The Prodigal Son" (Lk 15:11–32).

alms and shun worldly things; and they scoffed that God should promise material comfort and earthly honor to those who observed his law. Then Jesus rebuked them for their hypocrisy, telling them that the Law's promise about earthly things held only in John the Baptist's day; for thereafter God promised heaven to his servants, and whoever coveted heaven would have to win it by force. Then Jesus showed them that even in the Old Law, God hated avarice and loved penance. And he told them the story of a rich man who dressed as fashionably and as comfortably as he could, dining luxuriously every day. And there was a leper full of sores lying at his door who craved the crumbs falling from his table, but no one gave him a thing; rather, dogs came and licked his sores. Behold, the leper died and was borne up by the angels and placed with Abraham. Afterwards, the rich man died and was consigned to hell. And he was as perverse in hell as he had been on earth. (1–21)

69. How Jesus taught his disciples to avoid scandal. Then Jesus again taught his disciples to shun scandal and to rebuke wrongdoers, forgiving those who asked forgiveness as many times as they repented. Then the apostles asked him to increase their faith; and he answered that if they believed completely, they could do all things. And he taught them especially to set little store by their works:

"Who would believe[172] that anyone would say, 'Go eat!' to a slave just returning from his labor. Rather," he said, "the slave is told to prepare his lord's food first. And after he has served his lord, the slave sits and eats; but no one ever thanks him for doing all this. In the same way," said Jesus, "when you have done all that you are ordered to do, you say: 'We are unworthy slaves. We have done what was required of us, out of duty.'" (1–11)

70. How Jesus healed the ten lepers. After this Jesus went into a city, and ten lepers approached him, crying out from a distance for mercy. And Jesus told them to go show themselves to the priests who would pronounce them clean. And as they went, they became completely clean. And as soon as he saw that he had been healed, a Samaritan among them returned, praising God. And he came, fell at Jesus's feet, and thanked him. And Jesus replied:

"Now weren't all ten healed? And where are the other nine? Has none but this foreigner returned to praise God?"

And Jesus told him to stand up and go his way, for his faith had saved him. (1–9)

71. How Jesus answered the Pharisees who asked when Christ would come. Then the Pharisees came and asked Jesus when Christ would come. And Jesus

---

[172] 69:6 **Who would believe** *qui [cr]uest*

answered that Christ's kingdom would not come by stealth, for all would know when it came.

"Even so," he said, "Christ is among you."

Then he told his disciples that the time would come when they would long to see him on earth, at least for a day, but they would not see him.[173] And yet, he said, he would come again so openly that everyone would see him; but first he must be rejected by the people and suffer various torments. Then he told them the terrifying events of his coming, teaching them to prepare for it through humility and prayer. And he told them to pray unceasingly, giving the example of a bad judge in a certain city who for a long time held up a widow's rightful claim. She begged him so for justice that he finally granted it to be rid of her.

Jesus said:

"And much more will God grant the petition of his elect if they entreat him night and day."

Then Jesus told this story of people[174] who trust in their good qualities but scorn those of others:

"A Pharisee and a publican went to pray in the Temple. The Pharisee stood thanking God that he was not like sinners, especially the publican, and listing his good deeds. The publican stood far off, refraining even from lifting his eyes to heaven; rather, he smote his breast and, like a sinner, begged God's forgiveness. I tell you," said Jesus, "the publican was heard and the Pharisee denied. For whoever exalts himself will be humbled, and whoever humbles himself will be raised up." (1–25)

72. How he answered the Pharisees who asked if a man might justifiably leave his wife. Then the Pharisees came to Jesus, asking if a man might divorce his wife on any pretext; and Jesus asked them what Moses said of this. And they answered that, according to Moses, whoever intended[175] to divorce his wife must give her the reason in writing, then let her go. And Jesus told them that it was because they were so cruel[176] that Moses had proscribed killing them. But from the time that God created man and woman, he forbade that a man leave his wife, even for his father or mother. And later on at their house, Jesus's disciples asked him about this; and he answered, a man could not leave his wife except in cases of fornication, and in such situations he could not remarry. Then his disciples said, if that was true, it was better not to marry.[177] And Jesus told them:

---

[173] 71:7 **they would not see him** *il ne le uorroient* [read *verroient*] *pas*

[174] 71:17 **story of people** *saumple a* [read *saumple de*] *une gent*

[175] 72:4 **whoever intended** *quil* [read *qui*] *vousist*

[176] 72:6 **so cruel** *pur lor [cr]uauté*

[177] 72:11 **it was better not to marry** *ne feroit pas prendre feme*: the sense is that it was better not to marry in the first place.

"Some are naturally chaste, and others have learned it; still others are chaste out of good will toward God."

And not all could be chaste; but any who could be, should be. (1–14)

73. How Jesus blessed and embraced the children. Then people arrived to present children to Jesus so that he might lay hands on them and bless them; but his disciples rebuked those bringing the children. And when Jesus saw this, he became angry; and he called to them, telling them to let[178] the children come to him.

"For theirs is the kingdom of God," he said. "And whoever is not childlike will not enter therein."

Then he hugged them, blessed them, and went away. (1–8)

74. How Jesus answered the ruler who asked how he might be saved, and his answer to Saint Peter. Behold, as Jesus walked along the way, a rich young ruler came. And he knelt before Jesus and asked what he must do to inherit eternal life. And Jesus answered, if he wanted to have eternal life, he should keep God's commandments. And he asked which ones, and Jesus named the commandments of the Old Law. And he said that he had observed them his entire life, asking what he still lacked. And Jesus looked at him lovingly and said that if he wanted to be complete, he should go and sell all he possessed, give to the poor, and follow him; and he told him that he would have all as treasure in heaven. And when the rich man heard this, he went away sadly, for he had many possessions. And Jesus told his disciples that a rich man could hardly enter heaven, and they were astonished at his words. Then he told them that those who trust in their riches could not enter heaven any more than a camel could pass through the eye of a needle. Then they were more amazed and said:

"Who then can be saved?"

Then Jesus said:

"With man, salvation is impossible, but God can justify him."

Then Saint Peter asked, what would be their reward for leaving everything to follow him? And Jesus answered that Peter would be with him and would judge all Israel on Judgment Day.

"And all who are now leaving their parents and kinsmen and property for my sake," he said, "will receive a hundredfold in this world with the persecutions they suffer; and in the next world they will have eternal life. But those who appear as last will be the very first, and those who seem first will be the very last."[179]

---

[178] 73:4 **telling them to let** *lor dist qui il* [read *qu'il*] *lessassent*

[179] 74:23–24 **But those who appear as last will be the very first, and those who seem first will be the very last** *Mes mout serrunt primers qui pierent dareyns, e mout dareyns qui perent primereyns*: with this paradox, Jesus is emphasizing a key concept of his teachings

Then Jesus told them a parable in relation to this, about a man who brought laborers into his vineyard and paid first those who had come later, giving them just as much.[180] (1–27)

75. How for the third time Jesus warned his disciples of his Passion, and how he answered Saints James and John. Afterwards, as Jesus continued toward Jerusalem, those following him were very frightened and fearful, for he was already closely watched. And he walked ahead of them and — taking the twelve apostles aside — told them that as soon as he reached Jerusalem, the Scripture and all the prophecy concerning his Passion and Resurrection would be fulfilled; and he told them everything that would happen. But they did not understand him, for he did not want to sadden them overmuch.[181] Then came the mother of Saints James and John to ask that they might sit closest to him in his kingdom, the one on his right, the other on his left. And Jesus answered that they did not know what they were asking. And he inquired, could they drink his drink and bathe in his bath? And they said yes. Then Jesus said that they would drink his drink and bathe in his bath, but that — as for sitting on his right or his left — he could not grant this for kinship,[182] but only to those whom his Father had prepared for it. Behold, the other ten apostles were disgusted that the two brothers had made this request; and Jesus called them to him, saying that they should not behave as worldly people did. For whosoever wished to be the greatest among them should be a serf to all, just as he himself had dwelt among them as their servant and came to give his very life to ransom his people. (1–19)

76. How Jesus healed a blind man at the entrance of Jericho.[183] Behold, as Jesus neared Jericho, a blind man was sitting alongside the road. And, on asking peo-

---

on humility, as seen earlier in the story of the proud Pharisee and the humble publican (71:17–25).

[180] 74:25–27 **a parable [. . .] giving them just as much** *un parable de un home que amena overours en sa vigne e paia ceus plus tost ke vindrent plus tart, e ataunt lor dona*: severe *abbreviatio* of "Laborers in the Vineyard" (Mt 20:1–16).

[181] 75:7–8 **But they did not understand him, for he did not want to sadden them overmuch** *mes il ne l'atendirent pas, quar il ne les volust pas trop contrister*: loose paraphrase of Lk 18:34. "And they understood none of these things: and this saying was hid from them, neither knew they the things which were spoken" (KJV); *V* "ipsi nihil horum intellexerunt et erat verbum istud absconditum ab eis et non intellegebant quae dicebantur."

[182] 75:14 **for kinship** *pur cosinage*: this phrase is absent in *V* and in the modern English Bibles (Mt 20:23, Mk 10:40); PGH "for no cosynage" ("for no kinship," Goates, 69).

[183] 76:1 **How Jesus healed a blind man at the entrance of Jericho** *Coment Jhesu gari un aveogle a l'entré de Jherico*: the New Testament sources of this chapter are identical to those for chap. 78 below. The phrasing of the two chapters is also sometimes nearly identical. See the note for 78:1.

ple about the throng moving past him, he was told that Jesus of Nazareth was going by. And immediately he cried out to Jesus to have mercy[184] on him; and those in front told him to be quiet, but he shouted all the more. And Jesus paused to ask him what he wanted; and he said, to see. And Jesus commanded him to see, and immediately he saw and walked on with Jesus; and the people praised God. (1–8)

77. How Jesus visited Zacchaeus's house and there told the parable of the ten talents. Then Jesus went away to Jericho. Behold, a rich man named Zacchaeus — the chief official[185] of the land — wanted to see him but, being a short man, could not on account of the throng. And Zacchaeus ran ahead and climbed a sycamore fig-tree to see him before he departed the country.[186] And Jesus, when he came abreast of him, looked up[187] and saw him. And he bade him climb down at once and give him lodging; and he came down immediately and gladly took him in. And all the on-lookers grumbled, saying that Jesus had stopped at a sinner's house. Then Zacchaeus came and, standing before Jesus, declared he would give half his possessions to the poor and with the other half repay fourfold whatever he had wrongfully taken from anyone. Then Jesus told him that his entire household was saved that day because Zacchaeus was vindicated; and he said that he had come therefore to seek and to save the lost. Then he told them a parable about ten talents entrusted by a high-born man to his servants;[188] and he commanded them to trade on them while he went to a far-off country to claim it as king. And Jesus said this because they believed he would reveal himself as a king as soon as he arrived in Jerusalem. And he gave them to understand that the Jews would not accept him, that he would therefore be destroyed, and that he would come on Judgment Day to reveal himself as king and to reward each as he deserved. (1–15)

78. How he healed two blind men in leaving Jericho.[189] Then Jesus went out of Jericho. And two blind men sitting near the road got word that Jesus was passing by, and they cried out to him for mercy. And the people told them to hush, but

---

[184] 76:4 **to have mercy** *qu'il out* [read *eust*] *mercy*

[185] 77:3 **chief official** *chef baillif*: at Lk 19:2 in the modern English Bibles, Zacchaeus is said to be a publican or tax collector; *V* "princeps publicanorum."

[186] 77:5 **before he departed the country** *avaunt qu'il alast du pais*: at Lk 19:4, the modern English Bibles speak rather of Jesus's approach; *V* "quia inde erat transiturus." In its description of Jericho, Abbot Daniel's pilgrimage account (1106–1108) states, "And here is the house of Zacchaeus and to this day there stands the stump of that tree on which he climbed to see Jesus" (Wilkinson, *Jerusalem Pilgrimage*, 138). See further Pringle, *Churches*, 1:275–76 (Jericho, church of the house of Zacchaeus), at 276.

[187] 77:6 **him, looked up** *li le regarda sus* [read *li, regarda sus*]

[188] 77:14 **a high-born man to his servants** *un hauz hom [. . .] a ses serjaunz*: *abbreviatio*. An allusion to "The Ten Talents" (Lk 19:12–24). See also the note for 93:24.

[189] 78:1 **How he healed two blind men in leaving Jericho** *Coment Jhesu gari deus aveogles a l'issue de Jherico*: see the note for 76:1.

they shouted all the more. And Jesus paused to ask what they wanted; and they said, to see. And he touched their eyes, and immediately they saw. And one of these was named Bartimaeus. (1–6)

79. How Jesus answered the Jews at the feast of the dedication of the Temple. Now when the winter feast of the dedication of the Temple arrived, Jesus entered the Temple in Jerusalem. And the Jews came to him, insisting that he tell them clearly if he was the Messiah. And Jesus answered that they could see very well by his works that he was.

"But you do not believe in me," he said, "for you are not my sheep. My sheep obey and follow me, and I give them everlasting life. And no man can take them from my Father, to whom I will give them,[190] for my Father and I are one and the same."

Then they picked up stones to stone Jesus, but he answered, saying:

"I have done you much good, why do you want to stone me?"

And they said, not for any good work, but for blasphemy, because he claimed to be one with God his Father. Then he showed them that, in his Holy Scripture, God clearly calls his elect "gods."[191] And they gave up stoning him and tried to seize him. But he slipped through their hands and crossed over the River Jordan where Saint John the Baptist had once dwelt. And he stayed[192] there with his disciples, and many came to him and believed in him. (1–17)

80. How Jesus raised Lazarus and how, on this account, the chief priests and the Pharisees plotted against him. And when Jesus had stolen away to the River Jordan, one of his friends, Lazarus—the brother of Saint Martha and Saint Mary Magdalene[193] whom Jesus especially loved—happened to fall ill in Bethany, a league from Jerusalem,[194] and was about to die. And the sisters sent word to Jesus about his friend's suffering; and Jesus answered that the suffering was to glorify God, not to augur Lazarus's imminent[195] death. Then, after remaining there two more days, Jesus told his disciples he wanted to return to Judea. And they expressed amazement since the Jews had wanted to stone him not long before. Then Jesus answered that they should not be afraid to follow him, for he could always

---

[190] 79:8 **to whom I will give them** *a qui je les bailleray*: in *V* and in the modern English Bibles, the Father has given the sheep to the Son (Jn 10:29).

[191] 79:14: **God clearly calls his elect "gods"** *Dieus apele apertement ses eliz dieus*: Ps 82:6 (NIV).

[192] 79:16 **stayed** *nient* [read *mist*]

[193] 80:3–4 **Mary Magdalene** *Marie Madaleyne*: see the note for 35:2.

[194] 80:4–5 **in Bethany, a league from Jerusalem** *en Betaigne a un liwe de Jerusalem*: for a general description of Bethany's abbey of St Lazarus, including in medieval pilgrims' accounts, see Pringle, 1:122–37.

[195] 80:7 **imminent** *aremenaunt* [read *arement*]

save them. For he was, he said, like the sun whose light keeps man from suffering hurt, at any hour of day. Then he told them that their friend Lazarus was sleeping, and that his slumber was a sign of healing. Then Jesus told them outright that Lazarus was dead, saying that he was glad not to have been there, lest their faith be tested by seeing his friend die in his presence.

"But," he said, "let us go to him!"

Then Saint Thomas said to the other disciples:

"Let us go die with our Master!"

For, as Thomas saw it, Jesus was going deliberately among his mortal enemies.[196] Then, on the fourth day after Lazarus's burial, Jesus arrived at Bethany, waited outside the city, and sent for Martha. And she came and fell at his feet, saying that if he had been there, her brother would not have died.

"But I know," she said, "that God will yet give you anything you ask."

Then Jesus said that Lazarus would rise again;[197] and she answered that she knew he would rise again at the Judgment. Then Jesus asked her if she believed he was the Resurrection and the Life; and she answered that she believed he was Jesus Christ, the Son of God. Then Jesus told Martha to fetch her sister,[198] and she went away and told her sister privately that Jesus had come and had sent for her. Then Mary set out at once; and she was followed by a multitude of Jews from Jerusalem who were there to comfort them for the death of their brother and who thought she was going to mourn at the tomb. And when Mary reached Jesus, she fell immediately at his feet, weeping; and she said that if he had been present, her brother would not have died. Seeing her tears and the Jews accompanying her, Jesus shuddered and wept. He asked where they had buried Lazarus, and they led him there.[199] Then some said that Jesus seemed to have loved Lazarus dearly; others said that it was amazing that Jesus had not been able to keep his friend alive, yet had restored sight[200] to a stranger blind since birth. Behold, Jesus, still troubled, arrived at the tomb. Now Lazarus had been laid in a cave-like tomb with a stone placed over it. Then Jesus bade them remove the stone, and Mary answered that Lazarus stank by now, for he had lain dead for four days. And Jesus said that if her faith did not fail her, she would see wonders. Then they cleared

---

[196] 80:19–20 **For, as Thomas saw it, Jesus was going deliberately among his mortal enemies** *Quar Jhesu, ce li fui vis, ala de gré entre ses morteaus enemis*: in *V* and in the modern English Bibles, the disciples issue this warning collectively (Jn 11:8).

[197] 80:24 **would rise again** *relever[oi]t*

[198] 80:27 **Then Jesus told Martha to fetch her sister** *Donc dist Jhesu qu'ele s'en alast quere sa suer*: *V* and the modern English Bibles omit this text, but see Jn 11:28.

[199] 80:34–35 **they led him there** *il le menerent cele part*: Abbot Daniel's pilgrimage account (1106–1108) states, "As you enter the gates of this little town [Bethany], on your right hand is a cave in which is the tomb of holy Lazarus; in this cell Lazarus fell ill and died" (Wilkinson, *Jerusalem Pilgrimage*, 133).

[200] 80:37 **sight** *vie* [read *veue*]

away the stone; and, raising his eyes to heaven, Jesus thanked his Father for hearing his prayer. Then he cried out in a loud voice, saying:

"Lazarus, come forth!"

And Lazarus issued forth right away, his hands and feet bound with cloth strips, and his face wrapped in a shroud. Then Jesus bade them unbind and release him. Behold, many who witnessed this believed in Jesus; and the others went to the Pharisees to report what Jesus had done. Then the chief priests held a meeting and said that if they allowed Jesus to work miracles at will, the people would believe in him, and the Romans would come and destroy them for allegedly and unilaterally taking a new lord. Then one of them, Caiaphas by name, who was high priest that year, called them ignoramuses for forgetting that it is better for one man to die for the people's sake than for all to perish.[201] Thus they plotted from that day forward to kill Jesus; and they decreed that anyone knowing Jesus's whereabouts should inform them so that they might arrest[202] him. Then Jesus stole away to Ephraim,[203] a city at the edge of the wilderness. (1–56)

Here begins the fifth meditation, for Thursday

81. How Jesus came to Jerusalem by way of Bethany and was given a magnificent procession. Then, as the Passover was approaching, the people came from the countryside to Jerusalem to prepare themselves for the feast. And as they stood in the Temple, they asked how it was that Jesus had not also come. And then, six days before the Passover, Jesus arrived at Bethany where he had raised Lazarus. And they made him a supper; and Martha served, and Lazarus was among the diners. Behold, Lazarus's sister Mary took a pound of most precious ointment and anointed Jesus's head and feet as he sat at table, and the fragrance permeated the house. Then said Judas Iscariot:

"Why waste this ointment? It could have been sold for more than four pennies and the money given to the poor!"[204]

---

[201] 80:52–53 **called them ignoramuses [. . .] than for all to perish** *il ne savoient nul bien quant il ne penserent, ce dist, que meuz lor fust que un homme fust occis pur le people que tout le people fu peri*: a paraphrase of the speech of Caiaphas (Jn 11:49–50).

[202] 80:55 **arrest** *p[r]endre*

[203] 80:56 **Then Jesus stole away to Ephraim, a city** *Donc s'en ala Jhesu en tapinage en une cité que out noun Effram*: called Saint Helyes in the twelfth century, the place was associated with the prophet Elijah who had been given food and water there by an angel. See Pringle, *Churches*, 2:339–44 (at-Taiyiba).

[204] 81:12 **and the money given to the poor** *e estre donez as povres*: the *Estoire* omits "the money," inserted here for clarity.

And he laughed contemptuously at the woman.²⁰⁵ And he said this not because he was generous, but because he was a thief; and he held the money bag with all that was put in it. Then Jesus said that she had done this to honor his burial; and he praised her, for the poor she would always have, but not his body.

"And she is doing what she can," he said, "therefore her deed will be told in the Gospel throughout the world in memory of her."

Then many people heard that Jesus was there, and they came not only for Jesus but also to see Lazarus whom he had raised from the dead. Then the chief priests resolved to kill Lazarus, for on account of him many believed in Jesus. The next day, as Jesus approached Jerusalem and arrived at Bethphage, he told two of his disciples to go on ahead to the city and fetch for him a she-ass and her colt.²⁰⁶ And if anyone refused them, they should say their lord needed the animals, and they would be released to them. And they went and found everything just as Jesus had said. And when people asked why they wanted the animals, they answered as Jesus had directed them, and they let them go. And they led the asses to Jesus and, putting their garments on the colt, set Jesus upon it. And some spread their garments in the street, and others leaves and branches. And as Jesus started down the Mount of Olives, the multitude began praising God for the miracles they had seen Jesus perform. And they began to sing and shout, confessing him as the Messiah, their legitimate king from the line of David, as promised by God. Behold, when they heard that Jesus was coming to Jerusalem, the throng of people attending the feast went out to meet him; they took branches in their hands, singing and praising God, just as those coming behind Jesus were doing. And when the Pharisees saw people celebrating Jesus and singing his praises—and that he allowed it—they came and told him to have them stop it.²⁰⁷ And Jesus answered that if they were silent, the stones would cry out. Behold, as Jesus drew near the city and looked out over it, he began to weep. And he said that if Jerusalem knew what he knew, it too would weep; for it would be surrounded and utterly destroyed because it had been unaware of the time of God's presence there. And as Jesus entered the city, the entire population became agitated, asking who he was. And people said that he was Jesus, the prophet from Nazareth; and then those who had seen Jesus raise Lazarus said that he was de-

---

²⁰⁵ 81:13 **And he laughed contemptuously at the woman** *E eschiua sus la dame par desdeing* [read *E escharnist la dame par desdeing*]: at Mk 14:5, the modern English Bibles state variously, e.g., "And they murmured against her" (KJV), "and they were angry with her" (NJB); *V* "et fremebant in eam."

²⁰⁶ 81:23–24 **a she-ass and her colt** *un' anesse e son poleyn*: a painted stone formerly belonging to a small Crusader-era church at Bethphage (Bethpage) was discovered in 1877. The scenes on the stone's four faces depict Jesus's meeting with Mary and Martha (?), the raising of Lazarus, the disciples taking the she-ass and foal, and Christ's entry into Jerusalem. See Pringle, *Churches*, 1:157–59.

²⁰⁷ 81:37–38 **to have them stop it** *qu'il les desturba[st]*

serving of great honor. And the Pharisees said enviously among themselves that they had resisted him needlessly and without effect:

"For behold," they said, "all the people are following him." (1–47)

82. How Jesus behaved in the Temple on Palm Sunday and how he answered the chief priests and scribes who challenged him[208] about the children. And Jesus rode through the city to the Temple where he found merchants selling offerings. And he drove them all out, upsetting the money changers' tables and overturning the dove-vendors' chairs. And he told them, God ordained his Temple as a house of prayer, and they had made it a den of thieves. And he did not even allow anyone to bring through the Temple any vessels not consecrated by sacrifice.[209] And, seeing this, the rulers of the people, the scribes, and the chief priests sought a way to arrest and convict him, but they dared not on account of the people who loved him dearly and heard him so willingly. Behold, the blind and the lame came to him, and he healed them. And the city's children ran ahead of him, singing as though before their legitimate king and true Messiah of the line of David. Then the high priests and the Pharisees came and told him that they thought he should not allow this, lest he become puffed up. And he answered that, as they well knew, David the prophet said that[210] God would exalt his Messiah from the mouths of children to confound his enemies. And then Jesus fasted in the Temple until evening. And then he looked around for anyone who would offer him lodging; and when no one volunteered, he retired with his apostles to Lazarus's house in Bethany and taught them about the Christian faith.[211] (1–19)

83. How Jesus cursed the fig tree in returning the next day to Jerusalem. The next morning, Jesus returned to Jerusalem. And as he came along the road, he became hungry. And he went to a fig tree, looking for fruit; but when he arrived there, he found nothing but leaves. And immediately he cursed the fig tree, saying that it would never bear fruit. And in that moment it dried up, withering down to its roots; and the disciples were utterly amazed. And the next day, as they walked back towards Jerusalem, Saint Peter pointed out how shriveled the fig-tree was. And Jesus told them that if they had complete faith and love, not only would they do likewise to a fig-tree, they would also move mountains. (1–9)

---

[208] 82:2 **challenged him** *sopposerent* [read *l'opposerent*]

[209] 82:7 **through the Temple any vessels not consecrated by sacrifice** *nul vessel parmi le temple qui ne fust seintefiez as sacrifices*: at Mk 11:16, the phrase "not consecrated by sacrifice" is absent in *V* and in the modern English Bibles.

[210] 82:15 **David the prophet said that** *David le profete [. . .] [dist] que*

[211] 82:17–19 **And then he looked around [. . .] about the Christian faith** *E donqes regarda il entour luy si nul le vousist prier a herberger. E quant nul ne le fist, donqes s'en parti il ové ses apostres en Betaigne chief Lazere e lor aprist la crestienté*: *amplificatio*. See pages 38–39.

84. How Jesus sat observing the Temple and answered those who challenged his authority. Then, arriving in Jerusalem, Jesus sat and observed the Temple[212] with its merchandise and all manner of other worldly things; and he sat and taught the people. And the chief priests, the scribes, and elders came to him, asking who had given him authority to do such things as he did in the Temple. And Jesus replied that if they would answer his question, he would answer theirs and tell them who had given him authority:

"Tell me if John the Baptist was of God, or not."

And they thought:

"If we say that he was sent by God, Jesus will ask us why[213] we did not believe in him. And if we say he was not of God, the people will stone us."

And they answered that they didn't know. Then Jesus told them that neither would he say who had given him such power, until they answered his question.[214] (1–13)

85. How Jesus confounded the scribes and Pharisees with three parables. Then Jesus told them three parables[215] showing that their very answer condemned them. The first was of a man with two sons: and the first consented to obey his father and obeyed him not; and the other refused to do anything, but did it anyway.[216] Jesus told them another parable of a man who planted a vineyard; and he rented it to some people who killed all those sent by the lord to collect fruit, even the lord's own son. Then he told them how he was like the stone cast out into the road by the masons building Solomon's temple.[217] And then, when they were ready to lay the last stone, they placed it at the head of a corner to finish off two walls; and it fit so beautifully that all were amazed. Then Jesus told them the

---

[212] 84:2 **observed the Temple** *regarda e le temple* [read *regarda le temple*]

[213] 84:10 **why** *pur[quei]*

[214] 84:13 **until they answered his question** *qu'il li respoundirent a sa demaunde*: this phrase lacks in *V* and in the modern English Bibles (Mt 21:27; see Mk 11:33, Lk 20:8).

[215] 85:2 **three parables** *treis parables*: *abbreviatio*: the three parables are "The Two Sons" (Mt 21:28–30), "The Vineyard" (Mt 21:33–39), and "The Marriage Feast" (Mt 22:1–14; see Lk 14:16–24). A quotation of "The Rejected Stone" (Ps 118:22) is inserted after the second parable. See the note for 85:7–8.

[216] 85:4–5 **but did it anyway** *e nespurquant le fist*: in *V* and in the modern English Bibles, the second son is presented first (Mt 21:28–30).

[217] 85:7–8 **he was like the stone cast out into the road by the masons building Solomon's temple** *il estoit figurez par une pierre que touz les masons qui firent le temple Salamon engetoient en voie*: literally, "he was prefigured by a stone cast out into the road by all the masons building Solomon's temple." Jesus is alluding to the Messianic prophecy of the Rejected Stone in Ps 118:22: "The stone which the builders refused is become the head stone of the corner" (KJV). Christ's fulfillment of the ancient prophecy is proclaimed repeatedly in the New Testament (see, e.g., Mt 21:42, Mk 12:10, Lk 20:17, Acts 4:11, Eph 2:20, and 1 Pt 2:7). See *Hist.evang.*, col. 1605.

The Anglo-Norman Gospel Harmony

third parable of a king who[218] held a wedding celebration for his son; and those he had invited to the wedding rebelled, killing his servants when they came to summon them. And when the chief priests, the scribes, and the Pharisees perceived that the parables were about them, they wanted to arrest Jesus but dared not for the people; for all the people thought him a true prophet, and they listened to him willingly from dawn to dusk. (1–16)

86. How Jesus answered the Pharisees and the Herodians about the tribute. Then the Pharisees went and plotted with Herod's soldiers[219] to arrest Jesus as a felon and a traitor if he said not to pay tribute[220] to the Romans. And if he said to pay it, they would denounce him and embroil him with the people. Presently they came and sent their followers to him — these were disciples unknown to the bailiffs.[221] And right away they began flattering him, saying that they were well aware that he spoke the truth to all men, and asking him to state whether they should pay tribute to Caesar, or not. And Jesus, knowing their intent immediately, told them to produce the coin required for the tribute; and they showed him a penny. And he asked whose likeness it was, and whose inscription; and they said, Caesar's. And he told them to render unto Caesar what was his, and to God what was his. And they went away confounded. (1–12)

87. How Jesus answered the Sadducees. That same day the Sadducees came to Jesus — those who say there is no resurrection of the body. And they questioned him about a woman who had taken seven brothers as husbands, asking: by the Old Law, whose wife would she be at the resurrection?[222] Then Jesus told them that they were mistaken and had misunderstood the Scriptures: for in the next world they would not have wives as on earth, but would be like the angels of God. Then, using the Law, he explained to them that the resurrection[223] would occur, for God claimed to be the God of Abraham, Isaac, and Jacob.

---

[218] 85:11 **parable of a king who** *parable [de un roi] que*

[219] 86:2 **plotted with Herod's soldiers** *se conseillerent as chivalers Herodes*: for *chevaler*, see page 45. In *V*, the Pharisees send Herod's followers, the Herodians, to Jesus (Mt 22:15–16; see Mk 12:13). For *se conseiller*, ANOH has "to take counsel together, confer," but the context makes clear that the Pharisees are seeking to entrap Jesus.

[220] 86:3 **if he said not to pay tribute** *si il deist que um dust* [read *que um ne dust*] *doner truage*. This rejected reading, which is not noted in the published critical edition of *Estoire*, follows PGH (Goates, 80). There is no specific model for this phrase in *V*. See pages 35–37.

[221] 86:5–6 **unknown to the bailiffs** *ne li estoient pas* [read *ne estoient pas*] *acointé ové les bailifs*: this phrase lacks in Mt 22:16, Mk 12:13, and Lk 20:20.

[222] 87:4 **the resurrection** *la resureccion generale*: Mt 22:28; see Mk 12:23, Lk 20:33.

[223] 87:7 **the resurrection** *generale resureccion*: Mt 22:31; see Mk 12:25, Lk 20:35.

"Thus it seems they are yet alive, for he could not be the God of the dead."[224] (1–9)

88. How Jesus answered the lawyer about the Law's greatest commandment. When Jesus had answered the Sadducees so well that they had no more questions, a lawyer got up and—to test Jesus—asked him what[225] were the Law's highest commandments. And Jesus answered:

"Love God with all one's heart, all one's life, all one's thought, and all one's might"; and "love one's neighbor as oneself" was, he said, the second.

And all the Law and the prophets hung on these two commandments. Then the Pharisee said that, truly, he had spoken well; and Jesus answered that because he had consented to the truth, he was not[226] far from the kingdom of God. (1–9)

89. How Jesus asked the Pharisees whose son the Messiah would be. Then, when all the Pharisees had gathered in the Temple, Jesus asked them from which line the Messiah would come; and they answered, from David's. Then he asked them how it could be that in his psalms, David called the Messiah his Lord, if the Messiah had not appeared before David. And none of them could answer, nor did any dare question him again from that day forward. (1–6)

90. How he taught the people and his disciples about the Pharisees' hypocrisy. Then Jesus said to the people and his disciples:

"Do as the scribes and Pharisees direct you, not as they do."

And he said that they were hypocrites in several ways: they were harsh with others and easy on themselves, they sought to be held in honor, and they prospected for gifts from widows and for offerings from the humble. And he likened them to tombs dressed up on the outside and stinking within. And he told them, their wickedness was as good as hereditary, for their ancestors had killed God's prophets, and they would do likewise to the prophets and teachers he would send them. And Jesus said therefore that, from that time forward, he would take vengeance on them for all the blood they had spilled since Abel's day. Then, lamenting over the city, Jesus said:

"Jerusalem, you who kill prophets and who stone those sent to you, I have often wished to gather your people as the hen gathers her chicks under her wings,

---

[224] 87:9 **he could not be the God of the dead** *Dieus de ceus que ne purroient il pas etre* [read *Dieus de ceus que sont mort ne purroit il pas etre*]

[225] 88:2–3 **no more questions, a lawyer got up and—to test Jesus—asked him what** *plus que demaunder que* [read *plus que demaunder, leva sus un mestre e pur assaier Jhesu li demaunda que*]

[226] 88:8–9 **Jesus answered [. . .] he was not** *Jhesu lor dist qu'il n'estoient pas* [read *Jhesu li dist qu'il n'estoit pas*]

but you would not. Now then, henceforth you will be desolate: for however much you believe in me, I tell you, you will not see me again after this Passover." (1–16)

91. How Jesus praised the poor widow's offering. And as Jesus sat and watched the people bringing their offerings, many rich men came and gave abundantly. And a destitute widow came and put in a farthing.[227] And Jesus called for his disciples and told them that the poor widow had given more than all the others: for the others had given much because they had much, but she had given everything she had, her entire substance. (1–6)

92. How Jesus answered when pagans asked to speak with him about the voice from heaven. Behold, certain pagans[228] attending the feast approached Saint Philip, saying that they greatly desired to see Jesus. And Saint Philip reported this to Saint Andrew, whereupon they went together to tell Jesus. And Jesus answered that the time had come for him to be glorified by pagans.[229] For he was like wheat, he said, which—once it is sown—does not multiply until it has lain dormant:

"But once it has lain almost dead in the earth, then it multiplies well, bearing much fruit. And as it is with me, so too with my own: whoever loves his life in this world against my will, he will lose it; and whoever hates his life for my sake, he will find it. Whoever is my servant, let him follow me! And wherever I am, there will my servants be also. Whoever serves me, my Father will glorify him."

Then Jesus said that he was very troubled; and he asked his Father to spare him from that time forward.[230] And he said:

"Father, glorify your name!"

Then came a voice from heaven, saying:

"I have glorified it, and shall glorify it again."

Then some said that this was thunder; others, that an angel had spoken with Jesus. Then Jesus said that the voice was not meant for him, but for them. And he said that if he were crucified, he would draw everyone to him. Then the people answered: the Law said, Christ would live forever; and they asked, how

---

[227] 91:3 **And a destitute widow came and put in a farthing** *[E] vint une trespovre veove que [offri] un feodering.*

[228] 92:2 **pagans** *paiens*: at Jn 12:20, the modern English Bibles have "Greeks"; *V* "gentiles."

[229] 92:5 **by pagans** *des paiens*: at Jn 12:23, this tag lacks in *V* and in the modern English Bibles.

[230] 92:14–15 **and he asked his Father to spare him from that time forward** *e pria son Pere qu'il [l]e sauvast de cel' oure en avaunt*: in *V* and in the modern English Bibles, Jesus states this rhetorically (Jn 12:27).

could he speak of his crucifixion if he were the Christ? Then Jesus told them that presently they had little understanding, but should walk according to their light. Then many of the chief rulers believed in Jesus; but they dared not believe openly because of the Pharisees, lest they be expelled from the synagogue, for they loved men's praise more than God's. Then Jesus said:

"Whoever believes in me believes also in the One who sent me. And whoever scorns me, I will not judge him yet, but my teaching will condemn him at the Judgment."

And when Jesus had said this, he went and hid himself from them. (1–31)

93. How Jesus warned his disciples privately of the destruction of the Temple and taught them in four parables how to prepare for the Judgment. And as Jesus went out of the Temple, his disciples came and pointed out to him how strong and magnificent the Temple was. But he told them that it would be destroyed so completely that not one stone would remain upon another. And then as Jesus sat on the Mount of Olives across from the Temple, Saints Peter, James, John, and Andrew asked: when would this occur and what signs would portend the destruction and Judgment? Then Jesus told them that many false prophets would come, and pestilence, famine, earthquakes, and storms; and he would be betrayed, arrested, and killed, and Christianity preached throughout the world. Then he told them the signs that would foreshadow the Judgment. And he said:

"The sun[231] will become dark, the moon will withdraw its light, and the stars will appear to fall from heaven; and the powers of heaven will be stirred up,[232] and the earth's inhabitants will wither in fear[233] at the swelling of the sea and the waves. And then the sign of the Cross[234] will appear in the firmament. Then will they see me come from heaven with great might and glory. And then I will send my angels with great fanfare and great acclamation, and they will gather up the elect from the entire world. Thus, when you see these things beginning," he said, "be glad, for then your salvation is at hand. But the angels know neither the day nor the hour; rather, the people will be caught off guard, as in Noah's

---

[231] 93:11–12 **And he said: "The sun** *E dist quele solaill* [read *E dist: 'Le solaill*]

[232] 93:13 **the powers of heaven will be stirred up** *les vertues del ciel serront muez*: at Mt 24:29, the modern English Bibles have "the powers of the heavens shall be shaken" (KJV), "the heavenly bodies will be shaken" (NIV), "the powers of heaven shall be moved" (Douai-Rheims). In this apocalyptic passage, Jesus is describing in vivid terms the signs that will foreshadow the Judgment and the consummation of the divine plan.

[233] 93:14 **and the earth's inhabitants will wither in fear** *e la gent en terre seccheront de poour*: at Lk 21:26, it is possible that the original text of the *Estoire* had *si cherront*, "will faint" (PGH "falle adoun," "fall down"), but figurative *seccheront* also conveys the meaning well; *V* "arescentibus hominibus prae timore."

[234] 93:15 **the sign of the Cross** *le signe de la Croiz*: the modern English Bibles follow *V*, "the sign of the Son of Man" (Mt 24:30); PGH "þe croice" ("the cross"; Goates, 84).

day. And so, do not burden your hearts with gluttony, drunkenness, or anxiety about worldly things, but watch and listen continually so as to be worthy to stand before me."

Then Jesus told them four parables.[235] The first was about servants who stayed awake waiting for their lord, in case he returned late. The second, about a man who, fearing a thief, planned how he would keep careful watch. The third, about ten virgins who were to go out to meet a groom and his bride, but five were shut out because they were unprepared when the groom arrived. The fourth, about a man who made a long pilgrimage and entrusted his property to his servants—to one, five besants; to another, two; to the third, a single besant. And on his return, he rewarded especially the two who had doubled his money; but the third he had thrown in prison for bringing no increase. Then Jesus pictured Judgment Day for them, saying that when he came in majesty to the Judgment, all nations would then be assembled before him. And he would receive them just as the shepherd does his sheep and goats, putting the sheep on his right and the goats on his left. And those on the right, on account of their acts of mercy towards his followers, he would call to his Father's kingdom. And those on the left, because they did not act mercifully towards his followers, he would drive with the demons into eternal punishment. (1–39)

94. How, on the Wednesday, Judas plotted his betrayal before the council.

When Jesus had explained all these things to his disciples, he told them that at the Passover—which would be on the third day following—he would be handed over to be crucified. Then the chief priests and the elders of the people assembled in the court of the high priest, Caiaphas by name; for Jesus had said the previous Tuesday, they would not see him again unless they believed in him. And so, he had gone away, and they considered how they might betray Jesus and kill him. Then they said that this should not be done while the feast was underway, lest the people grumble about it or forbid it. Then Judas, hearing that they had gathered, went to ask what they would give him to deliver Jesus to them privately; and they offered thirty pennies, and he accepted. And from that time on, Judas watched how he might betray Jesus and hand him over to them without involving the people; for during the three days before this, Jesus had been teaching the people all day in the Temple, from morning to evening. And he went by night to Bethany—to the Mount of Olives—and still the people sought him mornings in the Temple, to hear him. And so, Jesus lay low on the Wednesday and the Thursday. (1–17)

---

[235] 93:24 **four parables** *quatre parables*: *abbreviatio*. The parables are "The Servants Waiting for their Master" (Lk 12:35–48), "The Householder" (Mt 24:48), "The Ten Virgins" (Mt 25:1–12), and "The Talents" (Mt 1:14–30). See also the note for 77:14.

Here begins the sixth meditation, for Friday

95. How Jesus bore his Passion, from compline until matins. And on Thursday evening, the feast of the Passover began, and each household had to sacrifice a lamb. Then the disciples came to Jesus, asking where he wished to celebrate the Passover and where they should prepare the lamb. And Jesus told Saint Peter and Saint John to go into the city and follow a man they would meet who was carrying a pot of water. And where the man entered, they should ask for a place for Jesus and his disciples, and he would grant their request on the spot. And they went and found things just as Jesus had said. And they prepared the lamb in a great upper room, all ready and equipped, that the host provided them.[236] When evening fell, Jesus came with his disciples and sat for supper; and he said that he had greatly desired to sup with them[237] and to hold this Passover before his suffering. Then, as he was eating, he took the wine-cup and gave thanks to his Father; and he drank and gave it to them, telling them to divide it among themselves. Then he said that one of them would betray him; and each began to ask if he himself were the one. And Jesus answered that he was the one[238] who ate from his platter; and he said, it were better for him never to have been born. Then Jesus shared his body and his blood with them,[239] and he told them to consecrate bread and wine in remembrance of him. Then they began to quarrel about which of them was greater. And Jesus said that with them, worldly conventions would not apply: for the eldest, he said, would be as the youngest, and the sovereign a servant, just as he had been like their servant while in their company. And just as they had accompanied him through his temptations, he said, so would they be with him in his Father's kingdom. Then Jesus told Saint Peter that Satan had asked God his Father's permission to tempt him — to shake him as vigorously as wheat in a winnow — and Jesus had even prayed especially for Peter lest his faith fail.

---

[236] 95:9–10 **in a great upper room [. . .] that the host provided them** *en un grant soler que l'oste lor livera*: John of Würzburg's pilgrimage narrative (ca. 1170) specifies that the Supper took place in the "large and spacious" upper room, but that "Our Lord [used] the lower floor of the house to give an example of humility, in washing the disciples' feet" (Wilkinson, *Jerusalem Pilgrimage*, 254). The Last Supper and other key events of the final days of Christ's earthly ministry are traditionally located to the site of the church of St Mary of Mount Sion. See Pringle, *Churches*, 3:261–87, and the note for 113:18.

[237] 95:12 **sup with them** *soper [o] eus*

[238] 95:16 **he was the one** *que [si estoit] un d'eus*

[239] 95:17–18 **Then Jesus shared his body and his blood with them** *Pus les cumina Jhesu de son cors et de son sank*: at the Last Supper, as the time of Jesus's Passion approaches and his earthly ministry draws to a close, he institutes the Christian sacrament of the Eucharist in which the bread symbolizes his body, and the wine, his blood.

"And you," said Jesus, "once you return, strengthen your brothers."[240]

Then Saint Peter said that he was prepared to go with him to prison and to death; and Jesus answered, that very night the cock would not crow before Peter had denied him three times. Then Jesus asked them if they had lacked anything when he sent them out without bag or scrip or shoes;[241] and they said, nothing. And he told them, whoever had a bag or scrip now should sell it and buy a sword. And whoever had none should sell his coat; for the Scripture concerning the Passion, he said, must be fulfilled. And they answered that they had two swords there; and he said that two was enough. Then Jesus rose and, removing his clothing, girded himself with a towel; and he poured water into a basin and began to wash their feet and dry them. But when Jesus came to Saint Peter, the apostle told Jesus that he would never wash his feet; and Jesus said that unless he washed them, Peter would have no part with him. Then Saint Peter said that he should wash not only his feet, but also his hands and his head.[242] Then Jesus answered:

"Whoever has bathed needs only to wash his feet; but you are clean, yet not all."

Then, when Jesus had washed his feet, he collected his clothing and went back and dined. And he told them that he had done this to set an example of how they should treat one another. Then Jesus became troubled and said that one of them would betray him; and each looked at the other, imagining which it might be. Behold, Saint John the Evangelist was then reclining in Jesus's bosom, and Saint Peter motioned to him to ask Jesus who it was. And then, leaning on Jesus's breast, John asked him who it was; and Jesus said, the one to whom he would give a sop of bread. And he took a sop and gave it to Judas, and immediately Satan entered into him. And Jesus told him to do quickly what he would do,[243] and no one knew why he said it. Some believed that, because Judas had money, Jesus was telling him to buy what they would need at the feast, and that he give something to the poor. As soon as Judas had received the morsel, he immediately left

---

[240] 95:28 **once you return, strengthen your brothers** *auqune foiz vous returnez e confortez voz freres*: at Lk 22:32 in the modern English Bibles, the equivalent of *auqune foiz vous returnez* is variously, e.g., "when thou art converted" (KJV), "when you have turned back" (NIV), and "once you have recovered" (NJB); *V* "et tu aliquando conversus."

[241] 95:32 **without bag or scrip or shoes** *sanz sachel e saunz escrippe e saunz chauceure*: for the commissioning of the Twelve, see chap. 28.

[242] 95:41 **his hands and his head** *sé mayns e sa teste*: in its translation of Jn 13:9, PGH includes the variant "al þe body" ("[his] whole body"), which Petersen calls a survival from the Diatessaron of Tatian (*Tatian's Diatessaron*, 170). The *Estoire* omits this particular phrase; likewise, *V* and the modern English Bibles.

[243] 95:52 **to do quickly what he would do** *feist [tost] ce q'il fist*: Jn 13:27.

the company. Then Jesus said that he was glorified, and that this would shortly be revealed.[244]

"And just as I told the Jews that they could neither seek nor follow me, so too, my sons, say I now to you. But I give you a new commandment, that you love one another; love each other as I have loved you. By this men will know[245] that you are my disciples, if you love one another."

Then Saint Peter asked where he would go; and Jesus replied, they could not follow him then, but would follow later. Then Saint Peter asked why he could not follow him right away, saying that he would lay down his life for him. And Jesus replied that Peter would deny him three times before the cock crowed.[246] Then Jesus began to encourage them, and he answered then whatever questions they wanted to ask. And he warned them of the persecutions they would suffer for his sake, but he promised to come again to them. And he promised them the Holy Spirit, which would give them[247] power, knowledge, and comfort in all the things they would need. Then Jesus told them that the hour had come when they would vanish, leaving him all alone.[248] Then he lifted his eyes to heaven and recommended them to God his Father. And he prayed for them and for all who—through their preaching about him—would believe that all were one in him, that they be led to him in glory and see and know him eternally. (1–74)

96. How Jesus fared from matins until prime. When they had given thanks, they went out, departing the city for the Mount of Olives. And Jesus told them that they would all abandon him[249] that very night, for so was it written in the prophecy. But after he was raised from the dead, he said, he would go ahead of them into Galilee, and they would see him there. Then Saint Peter answered that he would never desert him, even if the others did so. And Jesus reminded him that he would deny him three times that night before the cock crowed twice.[250] And Peter answered that he would not, even if he had to die with him; and the others said the same. Then came Jesus with his disciples towards the brook of Cedron to

---

[244] 95:56–57 **Then Jesus said [. . .] shortly be revealed** *Donc dist Jhesu qu'il estoit honorez, e ce pareit par tens*: *abbreviatio*. The *Estoire* summarizes Jn 13:32.

[245] 95:60 **By this men will know** *En ce il conoistront la gent* [read *En ce conoistront la gent*]

[246] 95:65 **Peter would deny him three times before the cock crowed** *il le renoieroit treis foiz avaunt que le cok chantast*: *repetitio* of material presented in 95:30–31.

[247] 95:69 **which would give them** *qil lor dorroit* [read *qi lor dorroit*]

[248] 95:70–71 **when they would vanish, leaving him all alone** *quil les lerroit tout soul e senfueroit* [read *qu'il le lerroient tout soul e s'enfueroient*]. See the note for 96:3.

[249] 96:3 **they would all abandon him** *les guerpiroit il touz* [read *le guerpiroient il touz*]: Mt 26:31. *Repetitio*. See the previous note.

[250] 96:7 **he would deny him three times before the cock crowed twice** *il le renoieroit treis foiz la nuyt avaunt ke le koc chantast deus foiz*: *repetitio*. See 95:30–31 and 95:64–65.

a hamlet named Gethsemane.[251] And there he entered a garden where he often met with his disciples, and Judas knew well the custom and the place. Then Jesus told his disciples to wait there while he prayed; and he took Saints Peter, James, and John and went away. And he became sorrowful and fearful; and he told them that he was sad unto death and that they should wait there, watch with him, and pray, lest they be tempted. And suddenly and hastily[252] he went away from them about a stone's throw, fell to his knees, and begged his Father, if it was his will, to spare him the Passion. Behold, an angel came from heaven to comfort him, but in his agony he continued to pray; and his sweat fell to the ground like drops of blood. And when he came back to his disciples, he found them asleep for sorrow; and he told them to watch and pray lest they fall into temptation. And then he went back again and asked his Father to do his will. And when he returned, he found them sleeping again, and they knew not how to answer him. And he left them then and went back to pray as before. And then he came back and told them, they had already slept enough by then, and to rise and come with him. And he told them that a traitor was near. Behold, Judas appeared with a troop of pagan soldiers and men-at-arms[253] that the chief priests, the scribes, and the Pharisees had given him, equipping them with weapons, lanterns, and torches in order to arrest Jesus. And Judas told them to arrest the one he would kiss. And then Jesus stepped forward and asked whom they were seeking; and they said, Jesus of Nazareth. And he said that he was Jesus, as he had told them, and if they were seeking him, they should let the others go. Now Judas was with them, and he came to Jesus and kissed him. And Jesus said to him:

"Friend, why have you come? Are you betraying me, Judas, with a kiss?"

Then came the constable with the soldiers and the Jews' men-at-arms, and they seized and held Jesus; and the disciples asked if they should strike them with their swords. And Saint Peter drew his sword and struck a servant of the high priest, Malchus by name, severing his right ear. And Jesus told them to wait a while; and he told Saint Peter to put away his sword, for whoever dealt another sword-blow would die.

---

[251] 96:10 **a hamlet named Gethsemane** *une vile que out noun Jessemany*: for *vile*, *ANOH* has "town," "township," "city," and PGH "toun" ("town," Goates, 90); *V* "villam" (Mt 26:36), "praedium" (Mk 14:32). See the note for 65:16.

[252] 96:15 **suddenly and hastily** *sodeinement e hastivement*: this phrase is absent in *V* and in the modern English Bibles. See Mt 26:36–46, Mk 14:32–42, Lk 22:39–46, and Jn 18:1–2.

[253] 96:25–26 **with a troop of pagan soldiers and men-at-arms** *o un' eschele de chivalers paiens e o serjaunz*: at Jn 18:3, the modern English Bibles' wording is somewhat divergent, e.g., "a band of men and officers" (KJV) and "a detachment of soldiers and some officials" (NIV).

"Do you not think," he said, "that I could ask my Father, and he would immediately send me more than twelve legions of angels? But the Scriptures must be fulfilled."

Then, touching the servant's ear, Jesus healed him. Then the soldiers and men-at-arms bound Jesus,[254] and all the disciples fled. But a young man was following Jesus, wearing only a linen cloth; and they took hold of him, but he abandoned the cloth and fled.[255] Then Jesus rebuked them for coming armed and by night to arrest him, as they would a thief. And then they took Jesus to the house of Annas whose daughter the high priest Caiaphas had married[256] that year; and Saint Peter and Saint John followed at a distance to see what would happen. And when they arrived at Annas's house, Saint John entered as a household friend would do; but Saint Peter stood far off. Then Saint John asked the doorkeeper to let Saint Peter come in.[257] Behold, the servants made a fire in the courtyard and were sitting by it to warm themselves, for it was cold; and Saint Peter came and sat with them by the fire. And the doorkeeper came and remarked to Peter that he had been with Jesus; but he denied it[258] before everyone, saying that he did not know him. And he rose to leave the courtyard, and the cock crowed. And another maidservant came and, seeing him, said to bystanders that he had been with Jesus. And a servant came and said to him that he had been a disciple of Jesus; and the others said, that was quite true. But he began to swear that he had not been Jesus's follower. And a while later another insisted that Peter was Jesus's disciple — that Peter was a Galilaean confirmed it, he said; and the others remarked that his speech proved it. Then the cousin of the man whose ear Peter had cut off said to him that he had seen him in the garden when Jesus was arrested. Then Peter began cursing the followers of Jesus and swearing that he had never met him. Behold, as he uttered the words, the cock crowed. And Jesus turned toward Peter and looked at him; and Peter remembered that Jesus had told him that this would come to pass. And the others left him; and he went out of the courtyard at

---

[254] 96:43–44 **the soldiers and men-at-arms bound Jesus** *lierent les chivalers e les serjaunz Jhesu*: in Belard of Ascoli's pilgrimage account (ca. 1155), Christ was captured in a crypt dug into the rock of the Mount of Olives: "At [the crypt's] entrance there appears the shape of three fingers of his sacred hand, imprinted in the rock of the crypt, which, so it is said, he made when he was captured" (Wilkinson, *Jerusalem Pilgrimage*, 229–30). For the cave church in Gethsemane, see Pringle, *Churches*, 3:98–103.

[255] 96:44–46 **a young man [. . .] and fled** *un juvenceal le sui afublé de un drap linge senglement; e il le tindrent, e il lessa le drap e s'enfui: abbreviatio*. See Mk 14:51–52.

[256] 96:48 **Annas whose daughter the high priest Caiaphas had married** *Anné qui fille Cayphés l'evesque out esposé*: the *Estoire* and PGH interchange the names Annas and Caiaphas (see Goates, 132). Caiaphas had married Annas's daughter; *V* "Annam . . . erat enim socer Caiaphae" (Jn 18:13).

[257] 96:51–52 **to let St Peter come in** *qu'ele lessa[st] entrer seint Pere*

[258] 96:55 **he denied it** *il lesdenia* [read *il le denia*]

once and wept bitterly.[259] Behold, as Jesus stood before Annas, the latter[260] questioned him about his followers and his teaching. And Jesus answered that there was nothing deceitful or secretive about his teaching; rather, he taught the people openly in the Temple. One of Annas's servants struck him and asked him if he should speak so to the high priest. And Jesus replied that if he had spoken amiss, that his mistake be pointed out;[261] but if he had not spoken wrongly, that he not beat him. Then they sought false testimony against Jesus, that they might put him to death: and some came saying that he had claimed he would destroy God's Temple and rebuild it in three days; and others testified differently and did not agree. And many other false witnesses appeared, but they could not make their stories match. Then the high priest stood and asked Jesus why he did not answer. Then he entreated Jesus, for God's sake, to tell them if he was the Christ, the Son of God. And Jesus answered that he was, and that they would see him come in God's majesty to judge the world. Then the high priest rent his clothes, saying that Jesus had blasphemed against God; and he said that he required no more testimonies, for he had heard them all. And he asked them what they thought; and they said that Jesus deserved death. Then those holding Jesus began spitting in his face and mocking him; and they blindfolded him and struck him on the neck beneath the ear.[262] And they said that if he were the Christ, let him guess who had hit him; and they spoke many other shameful things to him. (1–87)

97. How Jesus fared from prime until the third hour. Then Annas sent Jesus bound to the high priest, Caiaphas. And all the chief priests, the scribes, and the elders of the people met first thing in the morning to discuss how they might put

---

[259] 96:68 **and wept bitterly** *e plorra mout amerement*: Saewulf's pilgrimage account (1101–03) states, "after he had denied the Lord, [Peter] hid in a very deep cave, which is still to be seen there . . . " Called Gallicantus [=cock-crow], this place is "under the wall of the city, on the slope of Mount Sion" (Wilkinson, *Jerusalem Pilgrimage*, 108). Jerusalem's church of St. Peter-in-Gallicantu was in fact a must-see for medieval pilgrims. The church, which was erected over the cave of Peter's tearful remorse, had survived the Crusader siege of 1099. In ruins by 1323, the structure had disappeared by 1335, although pilgrims still visited the grotto. The tradition later affixed itself successively to a stele and to two other caves in Jerusalem, but then unmoored itself from any specific place (Halbwachs, *La Topographie légendaire*, 72–73). See the discussion by Pringle, *Churches*, 3:346–49.

[260] 96:68 **the latter** *e il* [read *cil*]

[261] 96:72–73 **Jesus replied that if he had spoken amiss, that his mistake be pointed out** *Jhesu li dist [que si il eust mesdist], qu'il li deist de quei*

[262] 96:85–86 **on the neck beneath the ear** *desouz l'oie en col*: this detail lacks in the modern English Bibles.

him to death. And they led him before the council[263] and demanded that he tell them if he was the Christ. And Jesus answered:

"If I tell you that I am the Christ, you will not believe it. And if I ask you a question, you will neither answer me nor set me free. Henceforth,"[264] he said, "I will be at the right hand of God."

"So, are you the Son of God?" they asked.

Jesus replied:

"So say you."

"Why should we want more witnesses?" they asked. "We have heard his own words for ourselves."

Then they all rose, bound Jesus, led him to Pilate—a governor under Caesar who was a judge and a pagan—and delivered Jesus to him. But, wishing to remain clean, they did not enter Pilate's house; this was so that, in the evening, they might eat the paschal lamb. Then Pilate came out and asked, what were their charges against Jesus? And they said that they had found him deceiving the people, forbidding the payment of tribute to Caesar, and claiming to be Christ and King. Then Pilate said that they should judge him themselves according to their Law, and they answered that they could not put any man to death without Pilate. Then, entering the hall where he handed down judgments, Pilate summoned Jesus. And Judas, when he saw that the Jews had sentenced Jesus to death, brought back the thirty pennies that the chief priests had given him, offered them, and said he had sinned by betraying such a worthy man. And they told him to settle for himself what he had done, it mattered little to them. And he cast down the silver before them in the Temple and went off and hanged himself; and his belly burst, spilling his entrails. Then, taking the pennies, the high priests said they should not be put with the other offerings; rather, by common accord, they bought a potter's field as a burial place for foreigners.[265] This was just as the prophet had said. (1–31)

98. How Jesus fared from the third hour until midday. Then Jesus stood before Pilate, who asked him if he was King of the Jews. And Jesus answered that his kingdom was not of this world, but that he had come to bear witness to the truth; whereupon Pilate asked him what truth was. And immediately Pilate turned and

---

[263] 97:4 **they led him before the council** *E le menerent en concil*: the NIV calls this council the Sanhedrin. See Mk 15:1; *V* "universo concilio."

[264] 97:7 **Henceforth** *des[ore]més*

[265] 97:30 **a potter's field as a burial place for foreigners** *le chaump de un potier pur sevelir la les estraunges*: *Les chemins et les pèlerinages de la Terre Sainte* (before 1265) relates that near the pool of Siloam in Jerusalem is a field called Acheldema [="the field of blood"], "the place that was purchased for thirty pennies ['deniers'] for the burial of outsiders" (*Itinéraires à Jérusalem*, 195). See Acts 1:19; see also the discussion of the burial chapel of St Mary in Akeldama in Pringle, 3:222–28.

went out to the Jews, telling them that he found no cause to condemn Jesus; and again they accused Jesus of many things. But Jesus answered neither them nor Pilate, who marveled greatly at this. And then they said that he had stirred up the people from Galilee to Jerusalem. And when Pilate heard that Jesus was from Galilee, he sent him to Herod, the ruler of Galilee who was then in Jerusalem. And when Herod saw Jesus, he was very pleased, for he had been eager to witness some of his miracles. And he asked him about many things, but Jesus answered not a word. Then Herod and his soldiers scorned him, and Herod dressed him in a white garment like a fool[266] and remanded him to Pilate. And so Herod and Pilate were reconciled, for they had been enemies before this. Then Pilate gathered the chief priests, the rulers, and the people and told them that—since neither he nor Herod found any cause to condemn Jesus—he would chastise him[267] and let him go. Behold, the people came to Pilate requesting that he release a condemned prisoner to them, as he did each year in honor of the feast. And he asked which they preferred, Jesus or Barabbas, a thief imprisoned for his acts of treason and larceny[268] in the city; and at the urging of the chief priests and the scribes, the people chose Barabbas. Then Pilate asked them, what should he do with Jesus, for he found no cause to condemn him. And they all cried out, shouting and clamoring unceasingly that he crucify him. Then Pilate took Jesus and had him scourged. And the soldiers dressed him in purple, putting a fine cloak on him; and they placed a garland of thorns instead of a crown on his head, and a reed in his hand. And they knelt before him, hailing him as their king; and they spat in his face and struck him beneath his ear; and they grabbed the reed and dealt blows to his head. Then Pilate brought Jesus, in cloak and crown, out to the Jews and said to them:

"Behold your king!"

Then they all shouted in unison for Pilate to crucify him. And he told them that they should take him and crucify him, for he found no cause for it. Then they insisted that, according to their Law, he should be put to death for calling himself the Son of God. And when Pilate heard this, he was more afraid. And he went in again to Jesus and asked him whence he had come, and Jesus answered not.

---

[266] 98:12–13 **dressed him in a white garment like a fool** *le vesti d'un drap blanc com fol*: *V* and the modern English Bibles omit the detail, "like a fool" (Lk 23:11). The curious expression occurs twice in this context in the AN *Complaint of Our Lady* (COL / GN, 89) and again in *Mirour* (64; see Forshaw ed., 88, 89). PGH "and cladde hym in a white cloþ as he hadde ben a foole" ("and clad him in a white cloth as if he had been a fool," Goates, 95). *Hist.evang.* speaks rather of mockery or derision: "Et in signum illusionis induit eum alba veste" (col. 1627).

[267] 98:16 **he would chastise him** *il l'enchaceroit*: at Lk 23:16, the modern English Bibles have "chastise," "punish," "flog"; *V* "emendatum ergo illum."

[268] 98:20 **treason and larceny** *traison e larcine*: at Mk 15:7, *V* and the modern English Bibles use "insurrection" and "murder" instead (see Lk 23:19).

"What," said Pilate, "you refuse to speak to me? Don't you know that I have authority to set you free or to crucify you?"

Then Jesus told Pilate that he had no power but what he received from above, whereupon Pilate wanted to release him. But the Jews told Pilate that if he freed him, he would be no friend of Caesar, for Jesus had claimed to be king over against Caesar. Then Pilate led Jesus outside and sat in the sight of all to judge him.[269] And he said to the Jews:

"Behold your king!"

Then they all cried out for Pilate to crucify him. And he told them that he was about to[270] crucify their king; and they replied that they had no king but Caesar. Behold, as Pilate sat, his wife sent word directing him to have nothing to do with Jesus; for that very day she had been tormented by a vision because of him. Whereupon Pilate took water and, washing his hands before the multitude, said:

"I am innocent of this just man.[271] See to the matter yourselves."

And they all answered:

"Let his blood be on us and on our children!"

Then Pilate released Barabbas to them; and, having flogged Jesus, he handed him over to them to crucify at will. And the pagan soldiers took Jesus and led him into the court; and they mustered the entire troop of some five hundred soldiers in front of him, outfitting him like a king as before. And they derided him, kneeling before him and mockingly doing homage as to a king; and they spat in his face and struck his head with the reed. Then they stripped Jesus of the purple[272] and dressed him again in his own clothing. And they put his cross upon his shoulders and led him out of the city with two other condemned prisoners. Behold, as they were walking, an outsider named Simon passed by; and they compelled him to carry the cross behind Jesus.[273] Now a great multitude followed Jesus, especially women who were weeping and wailing for him. And Jesus

---

[269] 98:41–42 **sat in the sight of all to judge him** *sist en un lu commun pur juger le*: *abbreviatio*. At Jn 19:13, *V* "et sedit pro tribunali in locum qui dicitur Lithostrotus hebraice autem Gabbatha"; and the modern English Bibles have, e.g., "sat on the judge's bench at a place called The Stone Pavement, or in Hebrew Gabbatha" (NRSV). See *Hist.evang.*, col. 1627. See also Pringle, *Churches*, 3:91, 93, 94, 366.

[270] 98:44–45 **he told them that he was about to** *il lor disoit si il* [read *disoit qu'il*] *devoit*

[271] 98:50 **I am innocent of this just man** *Je su net de ceo dreiturel*: with this remark, and by washing his hands, Pilate seeks to absolve himself for releasing the blameless Jesus to the crowd. He knows that, once Jesus has left his custody, the mob will have Jesus crucified.

[272] 98:59 **purple** *propre* [read *purpre*]

[273] 98:61–62 **behind Jesus** *aprés Jhesu*: *Hist.evang.* identifies the crucifer as Simon of Cyrene, the father of two of Jesus's disciples, Alexander and Rufus (col. 1629).

turned and bade them not to weep for him but rather for the retribution that the people merited, and which would befall them. (1–65)

99. How Jesus fared from midday until the ninth hour. When they came to Mount Calvary,[274] they stripped Jesus, put him on the cross, and nailed him to it; and he begged his Father to forgive them. And when they offered him wine mixed with myrhh and vinegar, he tasted it but would not drink. Then they hanged one thief on Jesus's right and the other on his left. But Pilate had a board inscribed in Hebrew, Greek, and Latin placed upon Jesus's cross, signifying that he was Jesus of Nazareth, King of the Jews. As the place was close by the city, many Jews read the inscription and told Pilate, he should put[275] that Jesus had claimed to be King of the Jews, not that he was in fact; but Pilate replied, what he had written would stand. Then the soldiers took Jesus's garments, divided them in four parts, and cast lots for them. For his tunic, though, they said that because it was seamless, they should not tear it[276] but cast lots for it, the winner taking all. Then they sat to watch him. Behold, his mother, Saint John, Mary Cleopas, and Mary Magdalene went and stood beside Jesus's cross. Now when Jesus saw his mother and his beloved disciple standing there, he said to his mother:

"Woman, sweet disciple, behold your son!"[277] Then he said to the apostle: "Behold your mother!"

And from that time on the apostle considered her his mother and looked after her as a mother. Afterwards the people stood waiting for what would happen to him.[278] And some passed before Jesus, waggling their heads at him, reviling him, and telling him to save himself and come down[279] from the cross if he was the Son of God; and they berated him for claiming he could destroy the Temple and rebuild it in three days. And the rulers and the chief priests with the scribes

---

[274] 99:1–2 **When they came to Mount Calvary** *Quant il vindrent al mount de Calvarie*: John of Würzburg's pilgrimage narrative (ca. 1170) gives details of Christ's Crucifixion not found in the gospel account: "the stone on which the Cross had been fixed, in the very part which had been touched by his blood, was cracked in the middle. Through this crack his blood flowed down to a place below, where certain people say that Adam had been buried, and he was thus baptized in the Blood of Christ." John locates the Place of the Skull "to the right of the entrance of the great church" (Wilkinson, *Jerusalem Pilgrimage*, 258–59).

[275] 99:8 **Pilate, he should put** *pilate quist meist* [read *Pilate qu'il i meist*]

[276] 99:12 **they should not tear it** *il ne la vo[le]i[en]t decirer*

[277] 99:16 **Woman, sweet disciple, behold your son!** *Douz deciple, feme, veez la vostre fiz!*: following *V*, the modern English Bibles have variants of "Woman, behold thy son!" (Jn 19:26), omitting "sweet disciple"; PGH "Wommman, loo! Ɣere þi son" ("Woman, behold! There thy son"; Goates, 98).

[278] 99:19–20 **what would happen to him** *que nauendroit* [read *que li avendroit*]

[279] 99:21 **and come down** *e descendi[st]*

and elders also mocked him among themselves; and they said that he had saved others but could not save himself.

"If he is Christ, King of Israel," they said, "let him come down now from the cross, and we will believe in him! He trusted in God, now let God save him if he will, for he claimed to be his Son!"

Even the soldiers mocked him, saying that if he were King of the Jews, he should save himself. And likewise, one of the thieves said to Jesus that if he were the Christ, he should save himself and them. But the other thief rebuked him, saying: did he not fear God? And he said that they had deserved a shameful death, but Jesus had done nothing wrong; thus he asked Jesus to remember him when he came into his kingdom. And Jesus replied, truly, that very day he would be with him in Paradise. Behold, the sun withdrew its light from noon until mid-afternoon, and darkness fell over all the earth. (1–36)

100. How Jesus fared from the ninth hour until vesper. About mid-afternoon Jesus called out in a loud voice, crying, "Eli, Eli!" and saying this psalm from the psalter:

"God, my God, look upon me!"[280]

Then some of the bystanders said, he was calling Elijah. Then when he had fulfilled all the Scriptures about his Passion except the one foretelling that they would give him vinegar to drink, Jesus said that he was thirsty. And immediately someone ran and, taking a sponge, soaked it in vinegar, bound it with hyssop to a reed,[281] and held it to Jesus's mouth. But the others told the man to wait to see for sure whether Elijah would come to save him. Then Jesus, on tasting the vinegar, said it was all finished. And he cried out again in a loud voice, saying:

"Father, into your hands I commend my spirit!"

And in so saying, he bowed his head and gave up the ghost. Behold, at that very moment[282] the curtain hanging before the altar in the Temple was rent in two;

---

[280] 100:2–3 **and saying this psalm from the psalter: "God, my God, look upon me!"** *e dist cel saume du sauter: Deus, Deus meus, respice in me*: at Mt 27:46 and Mk 15:34, instead of this exact quotation from Ps 21:2, *V* and the modern English Bibles have variations of "My God, my God, why have you forsaken me?" (NIV), which omits the part of the Psalm verse that has 'look upon me' and then goes on. In the ME *Estorie*, while Christ is dying, Satan sits on the cross to try to detect sin in him. See Millward, ed., *La Estorie del Evangelie*, 52, 189. Similarly, in *Hist.evang.*, col. 1630.

[281] 100:8–9 **taking a sponge [. . .] to a reed** *prist une esponge e moilla en eisil e lia de ysope a un rosel*: at Jn 19:29, the modern English Bibles have, e.g., "put the sponge on a stalk of the hyssop plant" (NIV) and "put a sponge . . . on a branch of hyssop" (NRSV).

[282] 100:13–14 **at that very moment** *meime l'oure*: the "interpolation of a chronological reference" at Mt 27:51 is "in agreement with numerous Diatessaronic witnesses both East and West" (Petersen, *Tatian's Diatessaron*, 170); PGH "wiþ þat" ("with that, immediately"; Goates, 100).

and the earth shook, rocks were riven, and tombs opened up.[283] Then said the commander of a hundred soldiers who was standing guard over Jesus nearby:

"In truth, he was righteous and the Son of God."

And the centurion with all his soldiers was very afraid, for they saw clearly that Jesus had died willingly. And the multitude standing there, looking up, and witnessing all these wonders beat their breasts out of guilt and returned to the city. Now all Jesus's friends and the women who had followed and served him from Galilee to Jerusalem stood far off, witnessing all these things. (1–22)

101. How Jesus was taken away after his death. Then the Jews came to Pilate because they did not want the crucified hanging so near the city on the Sabbath of Passover; and they asked him to have their thigh-bones broken and their bodies taken down. Then soldiers came and fractured the thigh bones of the thieves hanging with Jesus, but they did not break Jesus's thighs since he was already quite dead. But one of the soldiers pierced Jesus's side with a lance, and immediately blood and water flowed out, as the Scripture says. Then, since it was already evening, there came a rich noble with ten soldiers under his command, a good and just man[284] who—as a disciple of Jesus—had never consented to the Jews' plan or actions; but he came secretly, out of fear. And he went in boldly and urgently to Pilate on account of the Sabbath and asked him for Jesus's body. Now Pilate was surprised that Jesus should have died so quickly, and he sent for the centurion guarding Jesus to ask whether he was dead; and he answered, yes, without a doubt. Then Pilate committed Jesus's body to Joseph, who then came to take it down. Behold, Nicodemus the scribe appeared—he who had earlier come to Jesus by night[285]—bringing about a hundred pounds of myrrh mixed with aloes. And Joseph had a fine, clean, and new linen cloth bought; and he removed Jesus's body,[286] wrapping it in balm with that cloth and others, following the Jews' burial customs. Now he was in a garden close by the place where Jesus had been crucified, and in this garden was a tomb newly hollowed out in the rock. No one had ever been buried in it, for Joseph had had it made for his

---

[283] 100:15 **and tombs opened up** *e les sepulcres overirent*: see the note for 102:6–7.

[284] 101:8–9 **a rich noble with ten soldiers under his command, a good and just man** *un noble e riche baron bon e dreiturel qui out dis chivalers a sa banere*: at Lk 23:50, the modern English Bibles omit "with ten soldiers under his command" (see Mt 27:57), but *V* has "decurio." Joseph (of Arimathea) is named later in this chapter.

[285] 101:15–16 **he who had earlier come to Jesus by night** *qu'estoit avant venuz de nuyt a Jhesu*: a flashback. See chap. 11 for Nicodemus's conversation with Jesus.

[286] 101:17–18 **and he removed Jesus's body** *e osta le cors Jhesu*: in the Work on Geography (1128–37), Joseph uses pincers to remove Jesus's body from the cross (Wilkinson, *Jerusalem Pilgrimage*, 205). The body of Joseph of Arimathea was translated from Rantis to Bethlehem ca. 1130, where by that time the pincers were also displayed (Pringle, *Churches*, 1:155).

own use. And so, on account of the Sabbath, and because the tomb was so close at hand, they laid Jesus's body there and rolled a great stone before the door of the sepulcher. Now even though it was quite late, the women had followed and had seen everything relating to his burial; but then they went back into the city. And for as long as they dared to work in anticipation of the Sabbath,[287] they went and bought balm[288] and prepared their ointments, intending to come and anoint Jesus's body; but on the Sabbath they did nothing. Behold, the next day the chief priests and the Pharisees came to Pilate, saying: they remembered that Jesus had said he would rise from the dead on the third day. And they entreated Pilate to have the tomb guarded until the third day lest his disciples come, steal his body, and tell the people that he had risen. And Pilate answered that they should take care of this; and he told them to go themselves and guard it as best they could.[289] And they went then, posted watchmen at the sepulcher, and marked the stone lying at the door. (1–35)

Here begins the seventh meditation, for Saturday

102. How Jesus rose from the dead and raised several other saints. The day after the Sabbath, as soon as one could work, the Marys went and bought balm so as to come and anoint Jesus's body.[290] And, bringing their ointments, they drew near the sepulcher very early in the morning. Behold, Jesus was already risen from the dead; and he had also raised several dead saints, and they came into the city and appeared to many.[291] And then there came a tremendous earthquake, for an an-

---

[287] 101:26 **for as long as they dared to work in anticipation of the Sabbath** *tant com eles oserent overer pur le sabat*: elaboration of Lk 23:56.

[288] 101:27 **balm** *aromatz*: the modern English Bibles have "(sweet) spices" (Mk 16:1; see Lk 23:56, 24:1; Jn 19:40). The women's purchase of balm is repeated in similar terms at 102:3–4.

[289] 101:33 **as best they could** *au meuz qu'il [p]eusent*

[290] 102:3–4 **bought balm so as to come and anoint Jesus's body** *achaterent aromatz pur venir e enoindre le cors Jhesu: repetitio*. This purchase was already noted toward the end of chap. 101.

[291] 102:6–7 **and he had also raised [. . .] appeared to many** *eout les seinz questoient conuz plusors* [read *e out des seinz qu'estoient amortiz plusors resuscité que vindrent en la cité e apparurent a plusors*]: Mt 27:52–53. The text in PGH, "þe dede men arisen out of her graues" ("[He] the dead men raised up out of their graves"; Goates, 100), links the ME text to Tatian's Diatessaron (see Petersen, *Tatian's Diatessaron*, 170). The resurrection of the dead, which is mentioned in the AN and ME versions of Complaint of Our Lady (Marx and Drennan, eds., *The ME Prose Complaint of Our Lady and Gospel of Nicodemus*, 106), is greatly expanded in versions of the *Gospel of Nicodemus* in the apocryphal story, called the Descensus or Harrowing of Hell, of Simeon's resurrected sons (38, 131–35); see also 100:15 and Smith, *Art, Identity and Devotion*, 219–21.

gel descended from heaven, removed the stone from the sepulcher, and sat upon the stone. Now his countenance was as lightning and his garments white as snow. And when the watchmen saw the angel, they were terrified; and they fell to the earth like dead men. Now as they walked toward the sepulcher, the women had been discussing how they might move the stone from the door. Behold, as they looked in that direction, they saw that the stone had been removed. (1–13)

103. How Jesus appeared to the Magdalene. And when she saw that the stone had been removed, the Magdalene ran back and told Saints Peter and John that Jesus's body had been carried off. Then they rose and ran to the sepulcher. And Saint John came first to the tomb but did not enter; but he stooped and saw only the linen cloths in which Jesus had been wrapped lying there. And when Saint Peter arrived, he stooped to enter and saw — rolled up and lying to one side — the linen cloths with the shroud that had enveloped Jesus's head. Then Saint John entered and — seeing all these things also — believed the body had been carried off; for they did not know the Scripture, that Jesus must rise from the dead; and so they returned home. Behold, the other women approached the sepulcher and, on entering the garden, saw an angel clothed in fine white linen sitting to the right of the tomb; and they were very afraid. And the angel told them not to fear but to know that, in truth, Jesus was risen, just as he had promised them; and he commanded them to go tell Saint Peter and the other disciples that Jesus was risen. And two angels appeared to them and, standing by them, recalled to them that Jesus had warned that he must suffer the Passion on the cross, die, and rise up on the third day; and then they well remembered Jesus's words and hung their heads.[292] And they went out with great fear and gladness to announce the good news to the apostles. And while the angels were appearing thus, the Magdalene was elsewhere; but then she came to the sepulcher and stood and wept. And she stooped and, looking into the tomb, saw two angels in white garments, one angel seated at the head, the other at the foot. And they asked her, why was she crying? And she answered that her Lord had been carried away, and she knew not where they had put him. Behold, the angels rose to greet Jesus who had come to stand behind the Magdalene.[293] And she turned and, seeing Jesus, took him for

---

[292] 103:17–18 **and then they well remembered Jesus's words and hung their heads** *e donc lor sovint bien des diz Jhesu, e abeserent la chere*: conflation of Lk 24:5 and 24:8.

[293] 103:24–25 **Behold, the angels rose to greet Jesus who had come to stand behind the Magdalene** *Este vous leverent les angles countre Jhesu qui vint e estuit derere la Magdaleyne*: at Jn 20:11–14 and in the other gospel sources of this chapter, the modern English Bibles lack this line. See pages 32–33. Saewulf's pilgrimage account (1101–03) locates this encounter near Calvary in a place called Compas, "where our Lord Jesus Christ with his own hand marked and measured the centre of the earth . . . " (Wilkinson, *Jerusalem Pilgrimage*, 103). For the Compass, see further Pringle, *Churches*, 3:14, 26, 30.

the gardener. Then Jesus asked her, why was she crying and whom was she seeking? And she answered:

"My lord, you have taken him away. Tell me where you have put him, and I will take him and carry him away!"

With that, she turned again towards the angels as though to seek solace.[294]

And Jesus called her, saying:

"Mary!"

And she, recognizing his voice,[295] turned and fell at his feet, saying:

"Ah, fair Teacher!"

Then Jesus told her to go and tell her brothers that he would ascend to his Father and theirs, to his God and theirs. (1–36)

104. How Jesus appeared[296] to the other women. Behold, as the other women walked back toward the apostles to report what the angels had said, the[297] Magdalene came along with them. And Jesus appeared and greeted them, and they fell at his feet. And they praised him, held him, and kissed his feet. Then Jesus told them not to be afraid,[298] but to go and tell his brothers to precede him into Galilee, and they would see him there. (1–6)

105. How the soldiers were bribed. And as the women were going back to the apostles, some of the watchmen from the sepulcher came into the city and told the chief priests all they had seen. And the chief priests met immediately with the elders[299] to determine how they might disparage Jesus's Resurrection. And they paid the soldiers handsomely to say that, while they were sleeping, Jesus's disciples had come and carried off his body; and they promised to intercede for the soldiers with Pilate, even if he got angry with them. And the soldiers took the money and said as they had been told; and such was the story they told the people from that day forward. (1–9)

---

[294] 103:30 **With that, she turned again towards the angels as though to seek solace** *A ce se turna ele vers les angles ausi com queraunt confort*: see the previous note and pages 32–33.

[295] 103:33 **recognizing his voice** *ele conuyst sa voiz*: this interpolation at Jn 20:16 echoes "Eastern and Western Diatessaronic witnesses" (Petersen, *Tatian's Diatessaron*, 170). PGH "sche knew hym by his voice" ("she knew [or recognized] him by his voice"; Goates, 103). See pages 32–33.

[296] 104:1 **appeared** *apoust* [read *apparust*]

[297] 104:2 **said, the** *dist E la* [read *dist, la*]

[298] 104:4–5 **Then Jesus told them not to be afraid** *Donc lor dist Jhesu qu'eles n'eussent poour*: Mt 28:10. Christ's command not to touch him (Jn 20:17), an injunction found in *V* and in the modern English Bibles, lacks here.

[299] 105:3–4 **immediately with the elders** *tantost [o] les eynez*

106. How the women announced Jesus's resurrection to the apostles. When the women came to the apostles and reported witnessing angels who had told them that Jesus was risen, the apostles asked just what they had seen. And because they testified variously what they had seen—some one angel, others two, some angels standing, others angels sitting—the apostles did not believe them, rather they dismissed their stories as nonsense.[300] Then came the Magdalene with the other Marys who had seen Jesus; and, finding the apostles weeping and wailing, she gave them Jesus's message.[301] (1–8)

107. How Jesus appeared to Saint Peter.[302] And Saint Peter, when he heard that they had seen Jesus, rose up and ran toward the sepulcher. Behold, Jesus came and appeared to him. And Peter went back and told the other apostles and those with them that he had seen Jesus and that he was truly risen from the dead. (1–4)

108. How Jesus appeared to Cleopas and his companion. Now in the morning—the very day after the women had come to the apostles to report seeing the angels, and after Saints Peter and John had returned from the sepulcher—it happened that two of Jesus's disciples[303] left Jerusalem for a village one and a half leagues distant, Emmaus[304] by name; and they walked along, discussing all the

---

[300] 106:5–6 **they dismissed their stories as nonsense** *enz tindrent lor paroles a truiffles*: *Hist.evang.* discusses the controversy regarding the number of angels at the tomb (col. 1636, Additio 2).

[301] 106:6–8 **Then came the Magdalene [. . .] she gave them Jesus's message** *Donc vint la Magdaleyne o les autres Maries q'avoient veu Jhesu e trova les apostres ploranz e weimentanz, e lor dist ce que Jhesu lor out maundé*: this unusual sentence appears to be a conflation of Mk 16:10, Lk 24:9, and Jn 20:18.

[302] 107:1 **How Jesus appeared to Saint Peter** *Coment Jhesu apparust a seint Pierre*: in the *capitula*, the titles of 107 and 108 are interverted. See the note for vii:5.

[303] 108:4 **two of Jesus's disciples** *deus des deciples Jhesu*: one of these was Cleopas. Abbot Daniel's pilgrimage narrative identifies the other disciple as Luke (Wilkinson, *Jerusalem Pilgrimage*, 151).

[304] 108:5 **Emmaus** *Emaus*: early Christian pilgrims and writers identified this place-name with Nicopolis, twenty-two miles west of Jerusalem, also locating Cleopas's home here (Maraval, *Lieux saints et pèlerinages d'Orient*, 298). In the Rothelin Continuation of William of Tyre's *Historia Hierosolymitana*, Emmaus is the site of a fountain and castle located three leagues west of Jerusalem (*Crusader Syria in the Thirteenth Century*, trans. Janet Shirley, Crusade Texts in Translation 5 [Aldershot and Brookfield, VT: Ashgate, 1999], 21). During the twelfth century, at least two places in Palestine claimed to be the site of Christ's post-Resurrection appearance at Emmaus. The earlier tradition, sited at Nicopolis ('Amwas), competed with Abu Ghosh (Qaryat al-'Inab, *castellum Emaus*), which boasted both a health-giving spring and closer proximity to Jerusalem. See further Pringle, *Churches*, 1:7–17 (Abu Ghosh), at 7–8; and 1:52–59 ('Amwas), at 52–53.

things that had befallen Jesus. Behold, as they were walking along, talking and lamenting, Jesus overtook them and continued on the road with them; but they did not recognize him. And he asked what they were discussing as they walked, and why they were so downcast. Then the one named Cleopas answered, marvelling that the newcomer alone was oblivious of what had occurred at the late feast in Jerusalem; and Jesus asked them what this was about. They said, about Jesus of Nazareth who was so worthy and so mighty in word and deed before God and all the people, and how the chief priests and their rulers had condemned and crucified him.

"But we trust that he was the Messiah, and now today is the third day since this occurred. But some of the women among us have explained to us that they visited his sepulcher this morning but found not his body; they claim they saw angels instead, and they tell us he is alive! And some of our own went there and confirmed what the women were saying, yet did not find him!"

Then Jesus said:

"O, you idiots, you laggards, slow to believe what the prophets say! Was it not necessary that Christ suffer the Passion and enter thus into his glory?"

And then, using the Law and the prophets, he began explaining that such things must come to pass. Then later, as they approached Emmaus, he said that he would spend the night farther down the road. But they pressed him to stay with them, saying that evening was nigh; and he entered the city with them. Behold, when he sat with them to eat, he took bread, blessed it, and gave it to them; and immediately they recognized him, and he vanished from their sight. And they said to each other:[305]

"Did not our hearts burn within us while he spoke with us on the road, opening the Scriptures for us?"

And they arose immediately[306] and returned to Jerusalem; and they found the eleven apostles with their companions, who said that Jesus was truly risen and had appeared to Saint Peter. And they related their experience on the road and how they had recognized Jesus when he broke bread, but Saint Thomas and some of the others did not believe it. And with that, Saint Thomas went out, but the others sat discussing these things. (1–37)

109. How Jesus appeared to ten apostles that very day. Behold, at eventide, when the disciples had latched the doors of their meeting-room for fear of the Jews, and as they sat[307] discussing how some had seen Jesus, he came, stood before them, and said:

---

[305] 108:28–29 **And they said to each other** *[E] disoit l'un a l'autre*

[306] 108:32 **And they arose immediately** *E il leverent sus meiloure pas*: *ANOH* does not include *meiloure pas*, but the notion of haste is clear; at Lk 24:33, *V* "et surgentes eadem hora." PGH "And als swipe hij arise vp" ("And immediately they arose," Goates, 106).

[307] 109:2–3 **of the Jews, and as they sat** *des Juis [e] sistrent*

"Peace be with you! It is I, be not afraid!"

But they were terrified, believing they saw a spirit. And Jesus very gently comforted them, showing them his hands, his feet, and his side; and he told them to touch him and see that, unlike spirits, he was of flesh and bone. But they still could not believe that he was Jesus on account of their great wonder and joy. Then he asked for something to eat, and they gave him a bit of grilled fish and a honeycomb. And he took it, ate it before them, and gave back the surplus. Then he repeated:

"Peace be with you! As my Father sent me, so send I you."

When he had said this, he breathed,[308] saying:

"Receive the Holy Spirit! The sins you forgive are forgiven."

Then he reminded them of his word to them in Galilee, that to fulfill the prophecies he must endure the Passion and rise again. Then he gave them insight into the Scriptures, saying to teach repentance in his name throughout the world, but especially in Jerusalem, that people might repent by example of his Passion, and that the disciples would bear witness[309] to his works, his Passion, and his Resurrection. But meanwhile, they should remain quietly in the city until he sent them the Holy Spirit from heaven, which would empower them to do this.[310] Now Saint Thomas was not present when Jesus appeared; and when he joined them, they told him how Jesus had appeared, as has been related above. And Thomas answered that he would never believe he was Jesus, even if he saw him, but he inspected the wounds in his palms, putting his fingers in the nail-holes, and feeling with his own hand the wound in Jesus's side. (1–27)

110. How Jesus appeared to Saint Thomas and others on the eighth day. Behold, on the eighth day, the apostles were sequestered again in the same place for fear of the Jews; and Thomas was with them. And Jesus appeared, stood among them, and said:

"Peace be with you!"

Then he told Saint Thomas to put his finger in the nail-holes and his hand in his side, and to doubt no more. And when Thomas had done this, he said:

"You are my Lord and my God!"

"Truly, Thomas," said Jesus, "you believe because you have felt this, but blessed are those who never felt it and believed nonetheless."

---

[308] 109:14 **he breathed** *donc alena il*: the published critical edition of *Estoire* incorrectly transcribes *aleva*, "exulted." At Jn 20:22, *V* has "hoc cum dixisset insuflavit et dicit eis," and the modern English Bibles have "he breathed on them." PGH "po aliȝtted pe Holy Gost wiþ jnnen hem" ("then the Holy Ghost came to rest within them," Goates, 107).

[309] 109:20 **the disciples would bear witness** *il serroi[en]t tesmoigne*

[310] 109:22–23 **which would empower them to do this** *qu'il lour dorroit pouer de ceo fere*: the modern English Bibles omit this detail (Lk 24:49?).

Jesus performed many other miracles in his disciples' presence that are not recorded in the Gospels; thus he once appeared to more than five hundred men at one time. (1–13)

111. How Jesus appeared to the eleven apostles on the mountain in Galilee. Then Jesus told the eleven apostles to go to a mountain in Galilee where he once taught, and he would join them there. Behold, when they arrived, Jesus appeared to them; and on seeing him, some worshipped him, but others doubted. Then Jesus drew near to them, saying all power in heaven and earth was given to him. And he commanded them to preach throughout the world, to all nations, baptizing in the name of the Father, the Son, and the Holy Spirit, and instructing them to observe everything he had taught them. And he promised to be with them always, until the end of the world. (1–9)

112. How Jesus appeared at the Sea of Tiberias.[311] Then, at the Sea of Tiberias, Jesus appeared in this manner to Saints Peter, Thomas, Nathanael, James and his brother John, and to two other disciples. They went fishing and worked all night, but caught nothing. The next morning, Jesus stood on the shore asking if they had any fish. And they said no. Now they did not know that he was Jesus. Then he told them to cast the net on the right side of the ship, and they would find fish. And they did so, and immediately the net was so full, they could not draw it up. Then Saint John said to Saint Peter that it was Jesus. And Saint Peter, who was naked, immediately donned his garment; then, tucking it up,[312] he plunged into the sea, swimming for shore. And the others remained on the ship, making for land; and they dragged the net with the fish, for they were only about two hundred cubits from shore. And on reaching land, they saw fish roasting on a fire of coals, and bread lying beside it. Then Jesus told them to bring some of the fish they had just caught. And Saint Peter went and drew the net—it was full of fish, one hundred fifty-three of them—to shore; and yet, despite the fishes' number and size, the net did not break. Then Jesus called them to eat, and they sat. And Jesus came and gave them bread and fish; nor did any one of them ask who he was, for they well knew that he was their Lord Jesus. And when they had eaten,[313] Jesus asked Saint Peter if he loved him more than the others did. And

---

[311] 112:1 **How Jesus appeared at the Sea of Tiberias** *Coment Jhesu apparust a la mer de Thabayre*: this title is omitted in the *capitula*.

[312] 112:9 **tucking it up** *se escourta*: at Jn 21:7, *V* and the modern English Bibles omit this detail.

[313] 112:18–19 **when they had eaten** *quant il avoient mangé*: the Rothelin Continuation of William of Tyre's *Historia Hierosolymitana* adds colorful details to the familiar story, in a text dating from ca. 1229: "By the Sea of Galilee Our Lord ate with his apostles after his resurrection. He ate the backs of fishes, leaving their backbones stripped bare, but the rest of each fish remained whole. Then he threw them into the water and the fishes

Peter answered that he knew well that he loved him. And Jesus told him to feed his sheep. And Jesus again asked Peter if he loved him; and he answered that he knew well that he loved him. And Jesus told him to feed his sheep. And a third time, he asked him if he loved him. And Peter was astonished[314] that he should ask a third time if he loved him. And he answered that Jesus knew all things, and he knew well that he loved him. Then Jesus told him to feed his sheep. And he told him that when he was younger, he girded himself and went where he pleased; but in old age, he would extend his hands and another would gird him, leading him where he did not wish to go. And he said this to convey that Peter would be stretched and tortured on the cross for God's glory. And having said this, Jesus arose and went away, telling Saint Peter to follow him; and Saint Peter arose and followed. And Peter chanced to turn and see Saint John trailing him, and he asked Jesus what Saint John should do. And Jesus said that he wanted John to remain so until his return.

"What does it matter to you?" he said. "Follow me!"

Then the other disciples began to say among themselves that Saint John would not die. And yet, Jesus did not say that John would not die, only that he should remain until his return. (1–37)

113. How Jesus twice appeared on Ascension Day. Then the disciples returned to Jerusalem. And on the fortieth day after Jesus's Resurrection, they gathered in the upper room where he had given his Supper. As they sat to eat, Jesus appeared to them, sat, and ate with them. And he rebuked them for doubting those who had seen him arisen from the dead. And he told them to go preaching the Gospel to all people. And he told them that those who believed and were baptized would be saved, but those who believed not would be condemned. And believers, he said, would drive out demons in his name and speak languages they had never learned; they would take up serpents and not be hurt; and, though they drank deadly poison, it would not harm them; and if they laid hands on the sick, they would be healed. Then Jesus told them to wait in Jerusalem for the comfort his Father had promised: for John the Baptist[315] baptized with water, he said, but one day very soon they would be baptized with the Holy Spirit.[316] Then Jesus told

---

at once came to life again and swam off with the others, but all without backs except for the stripped backbones. These fish are as large as or larger than freshwater thornbacks or mullets in France" (*Crusader Syria in the Thirteenth Century*, 27). See the note for 24:16.

[314] 112:23 **astonished** *esbai*: at Jn 21:17, the modern English Bibles have "grieved" and "hurt"; *V* "contristatus"; PGH "abayst" ("broken," Goates, 110).

[315] 113:12 **for John the Baptist** *Quar Johan le Baptistre*: beginning here, the *Estoire* leaves off following the Gospels and turns to the Acts of the Apostles.

[316] 113:13 **they would be baptized with the Holy Spirit** *il serroient baptizez en Seint Esperit*: the four sentences following (through "Jesus appeared to them," 113:20) have no equivalent in the modern English Bibles. See page 39. In its section on the Acts of the

them to gather all the followers dwelling in the houses round about, men and women alike, and to go out[317] to meet him on the Mount of Olives. For the eleven apostles were staying in the same spacious upper room where Jesus had given the Last Supper, and the other disciples and the women lived in houses nearby, in a district of the city called Mount Sion.[318] And Jesus's disciples assembled at once, men and women alike, and went forth from the city to the Mount of Olives in Bethany; and presently Jesus appeared to them. And they asked him if he would restore the kingdom of Jerusalem[319] by removing the foreign king and Caesar's steward Pilate and reigning himself[320] as king, or by installing another from the line of David. Then Jesus answered that it was not their place to know the time that God had appointed at his will.

"But," he said, "you will receive the power of the Holy Spirit which will come upon you. And before this, you will be witnesses to my words, my deeds, and my Resurrection—in Jerusalem, in Judea, in Samaria, and to the end of the earth."

And having said this, Jesus lifted up his hands and blessed them.[321] And as he was blessing them, he rose from the earth before their eyes and went away

---

Apostles, the *Historica scholastica* uses similar language: "Omnes, tam Apostoli quam alii discipuli, necnon mulieres, habitabant in illa parte Hierusalem quae dicebatur Mello, scilicet in monte Sion, ubi David construxerat sibi palatium, et ibi erat coenaculum illud grande stratum, in quo praecepit Dominus sibi parare Pascha. Et in coenaculo illo tunc habitabant undecim apostoli. Caeteri autem discipuli, et mulieres habitabant circumquaque per diversa hospitia" (col. 1645).

[317] 113:14–15 **men and women alike, and to go out** *homes e femes, [e] alassent*: this phrase acknowledging the women among Christ's followers has no basis in Scripture. The phrase "men and women" recurs at 113:19. See pages 23, 39.

[318] 113:18 **a district of the city called Mount Sion** *cele partie de la cité qu'estoit apelé mount Sion*: the Second Guide (ca. 1170) locates many post-Resurrection events here: "On Mount Sion is the place where the Holy Spirit appeared upon the Apostles in tongues of flame, and enlightened their hearts. There the Washing of the Feet of the Disciples took place, and the same table is there on which the Supper was held. This place is in front of the doors of that which is called 'The Holy Spirit'. To the south is the place called 'Galilee' . . . On the opposite side, to the north, is the place where Saint Mary died to this world" (Wilkinson, *Jerusalem Pilgrimage*, 239–40). See the note for 95:9–10.

[319] 113:20–21 **if he would restore the kingdom of Jerusalem** *si il voloit donques restorer le regne de Jerusalem*: this sentence follows Acts 1:6 to this point; the rest of the sentence has no equivalent in the modern English Bibles.

[320] 113:22 **Caesar's steward Pilate and reigning himself** *le seneschal Cesar, Pilate, e regner i[l] meimes*: for *seneschal*, see page 46 and the note for 3:3.

[321] 113:29 **Jesus lifted up his hands and blessed them** *leva il sus ses mayns e les benoit*: according to the Icelandic Guide (ca. 1150), a church on Mount Olivet houses "the stone which the Lord stepped on when he ascended to the heavens, and one can see the imprint of his left foot, fourteen inches long, as if he has stepped barefoot into clay" (Wilkinson, *Jerusalem Pilgrimage*, 221–22; see also 231). Christ's "last step" and the impression of his

towards heaven; and they stood and looked after him, but a cloud came and obstructed their view. Behold, as they stood peering toward heaven after him, two angels in white apparel came and appeared beside them and asked why they were gazing toward heaven. And they told them[322] that just as he had risen to heaven, so would he also return, descending from heaven at the Judgment. Then they worshipped[323] and believed that Jesus had gone to the right hand of his Father. And they returned joyfully to Jerusalem and entered the upper room where the apostles were staying. And there, with Jesus's mother and the other women and his cousins, they prayed unceasingly until about the third hour on the tenth day[324] when the Holy Spirit visited them, giving them knowledge, eloquence, and boldness to preach the Christian faith. And then they went to the Temple, remaining there continually and praising God until they were expelled from among the people of Judea.[325] Then in the tenth year after the Ascension, when Saint James had been beheaded and Saint Peter imprisoned,[326] they all went throughout the world, each in his own direction, preaching to pagans and Jews. And Jesus's spirit guided and encouraged them, corroborating his words through miracles. (1–46)

---

footprint on the stone are depicted in Matthew Paris's *Chronica majora* (Cambridge, Corpus Christi College MS 16, fol. 146r); see Connolly, *The Maps of Matthew Paris*, fig. 38. The Dominicans gave this marble stone to Henry III in 1249, and the king in turn presented it to Westminster (135). Pringle, *Churches*, 3:72–88, at 75, includes in his description of the church of the Ascension a report by Nicolas of Poggibonsi, written a century later (1346–1350), which indicates that a marble slab, now with "two footprints, resembling the forms of two bare feet," was still present in the church.

[322] 113:34 **And they told them** *E lor disoi[en]t*
[323] 113:35–36 **Then they worshipped** *Donc [a]orerent il*
[324] 113:39 **until [. . .] the tenth day** *jusqes le dime jour*: at Acts 2:1, the modern English Bibles have "Pentecost"; *V* "dies pentecostes".
[325] 113:42–43 **until they were expelled from among the people of Judea** *jusques il furent enchacez hors de gent de Judee*: the harmonist refers broadly to the persecution of the apostles and of Stephen, Paul, Barnabas, and others. Acts 11:19 is perhaps the key verse (see also Acts 13:50, 14:2, 19 etc.).
[326] 113:43–44 **when Saint James had been beheaded and Saint Peter imprisoned** *quant seint Jake estoit decolé e seint Piere enprisoné*: Acts 12:2, 4.

Notes to the Translation

The footnotes to the translated text in the previous section call attention to significant textual emendations in the published critical edition of the *Estoire*. To keep the notes to a useful length, minor errors in spelling and scribal slips in Liber niger are generally not indicated, including 1) missing initial letters in chapter titles and 2) marginal chapter titles augmented by one or more words from the *capitula* at the beginning of the *Estoire*.

Special attention is also given to differences between the *Estoire* and both the Pepysian Gospel Harmony (PGH) and modern English translations of the Gospels, including noteworthy omissions, paraphrases, or elaboration where these occur. Such comparisons further define the character of the Anglo-Norman Gospel Harmony and may reveal passages deserving further study with reference to the early Diatessarons.

Key phrases from the *Anglo-Norman Gospel Harmony* are shown in **bold**; words and phrases from the *Estoire*, in *italics*. Numerical references to specific chapters and lines of the *Anglo-Norman Gospel Harmony* also point, with general accuracy of line number, to the corresponding words or phrases of the *Estoire*.

The Bible versions consulted are KJV = King James, NIV = New International—UK, NJB = New Jerusalem Bible, NRSV = New Revised Standard Version, and V = Vulgate. The first four versions are collectively termed the "modern English Bibles." For descriptions of places mentioned in the *Estoire*, the notes refer occasionally to *La Terre des Sarrazins* (Dean §332), a brief on Muslim princes and lands prepared for Pope Innocent III (r. 1198–1216). The manuscript consulted is Oxford, Bodleian Library, Bodleian 761 (2535), ff. 195b-200b.

Appendices

1. Biblical Sources of Chapters

This table of biblical sources of the Anglo-Norman Gospel Harmony's chapters follows the analytical summary supplied by Goates (114–22). I enclose in parentheses any corresponding passages not apparently used in a given chapter, placing in square brackets corresponding passages used previously in the text. In the following, Mt = Matthew, Mk = Mark, Lk = Luke, Jn = John, and § indicates the beginning of a new pericope within a chapter. Pericopes from New Testament books other than the Gospels are underlined.

The first meditation
1. Jn 1:1–18
2. Lk 1:5–56 § Mt 1:18–21, 24 § Lk 1:57–68, 80
3. Lk 2:1–21 § Mt 2:1–12
4. Lk 2:22–39
5. Mt 2:13–23; Lk 2:40
6. Lk 2:41–52

The second meditation
7. Mt 3:1–17; Mk 1:1–11; Lk 3:1–23; Jn 1:19–28
8. Mt 4:1–11; Mk 1:12–13; Lk 4:1–13
9. Jn 1:29–51
10. Jn 2:1–11
11. Jn 2:12–3:21
12. Jn 3:22–36

The third meditation
13. (Mt 14:1–4); (Mk 6:17–20); Lk 3:19–20 § Mt 4:12; (Mk 1:14); (Lk 4:14–15) § Jn 4:1–42 § Jn 4:43–45
14. Jn 4:46–54
15. (Mt 4:18–22); (Mk 1:16–20); Lk 5:1–11
16. Lk 4:16–30
17. Mt 4:13–22; (Mk 1:16–20); [Lk 5:1–11]
18. Mk 1:23–28; (Lk 4:33–37) § (Mt 8:14–17); Mk 1:29–34; (Lk 4:38–41) § Mt 4:23–25; Mk 1:35–39; Lk 4:42–44
19. Lk 9:59–62 § Mt 8:18–27; Mk 4:35–41; Lk 8:22–25 § Mt 8:28–34; Mk 5:1–20; Lk 8:26–40
20. Mt 9:2–8; Mk 2:1–12; Lk 5:17–26 § Mt 9:9–13; Mk 2:13–17; Lk 5:27–32 § Mt 9:14–17; Mk 2:18–22; Lk 5:33–39
21. Mt 9:1, 18–26; Mk 5:21–43; Lk 8:40–56
22. Mt 9:27–34
23. (Mt 13:54–58); Mk 6:1–5
24. Mt 4:23–25 § (Mk 3:13–19); Lk 6:12–16 § Mt 5:1–8:1; (Lk 6:20–49)
25. [Mt 5:1–7:27]; (Lk 6:20–49)
26. Mt 8:1–4; Mk 1:40–45; Lk 5:12–16
27. Mt 8:5–13; Lk 7:1–10
28. Mt 9:35–36, 10:1–11:1; Mk 6:7–13; Lk 9:1–6, 10:2–16
29. Lk 7:11–18
30. (Mt 11:2–19); Lk 7:19–34
31. Lk 7:36–8:3
32. [Mt 10:8, 15]; Mt 11:20–24; [Mk 6:11–12]; [Lk 10:1–16]
33. Mt 11:25–30; Lk 10:17–24
34. Lk 10:25–37
35. Lk 10:38–42
36. Lk 11:1–13
37. Mt 12:1–8; Mk 2:23–28; Lk 6:1–5
38. Mt 12:9–13; Mk 3:1–5; Lk 6:6–10
39. Mt 12:14–21; Mk 3:6–12; Lk 6:11
40. Mt 12:22–50; Mk 3:20–35; Lk 8:19–21, 11:14–32
41. Lk 11:37–52
42. Lk 12:1–59
43. Lk 13:1–9
44. Lk 13:10–17
45. Mt 13:153; (Mk 4:1–34); Lk 8:4–18, 13:18–21
46. Mt 13:54–58; (Mk 6:1–5)
47. Jn 5:1–47

The fourth meditation
48. Mt 14:6–13; Mk 6:21–32; Lk 9:10; Jn 6:3
49. Mt 14:13–33; Mk 6:30–52; Lk 9:11–17; Jn 6:4–71

50. Mt 14:34–36; Mk 6:53–56
51. Mt 15:1–20; Mk 7:1–23
52. Mt 15:21–28; Mk 7:24–30
53. Mt 15:29–31; Mk 7:31–37
54. Mt 15:32–39a; Mk 8:1–10a
55. Mt 15:39b-16:4; (Mk 8:10b-12)
56. Mt 16:5–12; Mk 8:13–21
57. Mk 8:22–26
58. Mt 14:1–2; (Mk 6:14–16); Lk 9:7–10a)
59. Jn 7:1–10:21 § Mt 23:1–39; Mk 12:38–40; Lk 20:45–47
60. Mt 16:13–28; Mk 8:27–9:1; Lk 9:18–27
61. Mt 17:1–21; Mk 9:2–29; Lk 9:28–42
62. Mt 17:22–23; Mk 9:30–32; Lk 9:43–45
63. Mt 17:24–27 § Mt 18:1–5; Mk 9:33–37; Lk 9:46–48 § Mt 18:5–6; Mk 9:38–41; Lk 9:49–50 § Mt 18:15–35; Lk 17:3–4
64. (Mt 19:1–2); (Mk 10:1); Lk 9:51–56 § Lk 13:22–33
65. Lk 14:1–6 § Lk 14:7–24
66. Lk 14:25–33
67. Lk 15:1–32
68. Lk 16:1–25
69. Lk 17:1–10
70. Lk 17:12–19
71. Lk 17:20–37 § Lk 18:1–8a § Lk 18:9–14
72. Mt 19:3–12; Mk 10:2–12
73. Mt 19:13–15; Mk 10:13–16; Lk 18:15–17
74. Mt 19:16–30; Mk 10:17–31; Lk 18:18–30 § Mt 20:1–16
75. (Mt 20:17–19); Mk 10:32–34; Lk 18:31–34 § Mt 20:20–28; Mk 10:35–45
76. (Mt 20:29–34); (Mk 10:46–52); Lk 18:36–43
77. Lk 19:1–10 § Lk 19:11–27
78. Mt 20:29–34; Mk 10:46, 47–52; (Lk 18:36–43)
79. Jn 10:22–42
80. Jn 11:1–56

The fifth meditation

81. Mt 26:6–13; Mk 14:3–9; Jn 12:2–8 § Jn 12:9–11 § Mt 21:1–9; Mk 11:1–10; Lk 19:29–38; Jn 12:12, 13, (14–19) § Lk 19:39–44 § Mt 21:10, 11 § Jn 12:17, 19

82. Mt 21:12, 13; Mk 11:15–18; (Lk 19:45–48) § Mt 21:14–17; Mk 11:11
83. Mt 21:18–21; (Mk 11:12–23); Mk 11:20, 21
84. Mt 21:23–27; Mk 11:27–33; Lk 20:1–8
85. Mt 21:28–32 § Mt 21:33–39; Mk 12:1–8; Lk 20:9–15a; § Mt 21:42; Mk 12:10, 11; Lk 20:17 § Mt 22:1–6 § Mt 21:45, 46 § Lk 21:37, 38
86. Mt 22:15–22; (Mk 12:13–17); (Lk 20:20–26)
87. Mt 22:23–32; (Mk 12:18–27); (Lk 20:27–38)
88. Mt 22:34–40; Mk 12:28–34
89. Mt 22:41–46; Mk 12:35–37; Lk 20:41–44
90. Mt 23:1–39; Mk 12:38–40; Lk 20:46, 47
91. Mk 12:41–44; (Lk 21:1–4)
92. Jn 12:20–50
93. Mt 24:1–51; Mk 13:1–37; Lk 21:5–36 § Mt 25:1–46
94. Mt 26:1–5 § Mt 26:14–16; Mk 14:10, 11; Lk 22:3–6 § Lk 21:37, 38

The sixth meditation

95. Mt 26:17–19; Mk 14:12–16; Lk 22:7–13 § Mt 26:20–25; Mk 14:17–21; Lk 22:14–23 § Mt 26:26–28; Mk 14:22–24; Lk 22:19, 20 § Lk 22:24–38 § Jn 13:4–15 § Jn 13:21–38 § Jn 14–17
96. Mt 26:30–35; Mk 14:26–31 § Mt 26:36–46; Mk 14:32–42; Lk 22:40–46; Jn 18:1, 2 § Mt 26:47–56; Mk 14:43–52; Lk 22:47–53; Jn 18:3–12 § Mt 26:57; Mk 14:53; Lk 22:54; Jn 18:13 § Mt 26:58, 69–75; Mk 14:54, 66–72; Lk 22:54–62; Jn 18:15–27 § Mt 26:59–68; Mk 14:55–65; Lk 22:63–65
97. Mt 27:1, 2; Mk 15:1; Lk 22:66–71, 23:1; Jn 18:28 § Lk 23:2; Jn 18:28b-33a § Mt 27:3–10; Acts 1:18b
98. Mt 27:11–14; Mk 15:2–5; Lk 23:3–7; Jn 18:33b-38 § Lk 23:8–12 § Mt 27:15–18, 20–23; Mk 15:6–14;

Lk 23:13–23; Jn 18:39, 40 § Mt 27:27–30; (Mk 15:16–19); Jn 19:2, 3, 4–15 § Mt 27:19 § Mt 27:24–26; (Mk 15:15); (Lk 23:24, 25) § Mt 27:27–30; Mk 15:16–19; (Jn 19:2–3) § Mt 27:31, 32; Mk 15:20, 21; Lk 23:26–32; Jn 19:16, 17
99. Mt 27:33–45; Mk 15:22–33; Lk 23:33–45a; Jn 19:17b-27
100. Mt 27:46–50; (Mk 15:34–37); Lk 23:46; Jn 19:28–30 § Mt 27:51–56; Mk 15:38–41; Lk 23:45b, 47–49
101. Jn 19:31–37 § Mt 27:57–60; Mk 15:42–46; Lk 23:50–54; Jn 19:38–42 § Lk 23:55, 56 § Mt 27:62–66

The seventh meditation
102. Mk 16:1 § Mt 28:1 § Mt 27:52, 53 § Mt 28:2–4 § Mk 16:3, 4
103. Jn 20:1–10 § Mt 28:5–7; Mk 16:5–7 § Lk 24:4–8; § Mt 28:8; (Mk 16:8) § (Mk 16:9); Jn 20:11–17
104. Mt 28:9, 10
105. Mt 28:11–15
106. Mt 28:2; Mk 16:10; Lk 24:4, 9, 11
107. Lk 24:12, 34
108. (Mk 16:12, 13a); Lk 24:13–35 § Mk 16:13b
109. (Mk 16:14); Lk 24:36–49; Jn 20:19–25
110. Jn 20:26–30 § I Cor 15:6
111. Mt 28:16–20; Mk 16:15
112. Jn 21:1–23
113. Mk 16:14–18 § Acts 1:4, 5 § Acts 1:6–8 § Lk 24:50; Acts 1:9–11 § Mk 16:19; Lk 24:52; Acts 1:13, 14 § Acts 2:1, 3–4, 15 § Lk 24:53 § Mk 16:20

2. Extracts of Original Text

Following are passages from the *Estoire* and the Pepysian Gospel Harmony (PGH) shown in parallel for convenience of comparison. Chapter and line numbers for the *Estoire* refer to the published critical edition, page numbers in PGH to Goates's edition. I am grateful to Shearle Furnish, Youngstown State University, for modern English translations of the passages from PGH; these are shown in the right-hand column below.

Gifts from the East
(Mt 2:1–12)

Estoire, 3:22–37	PGH (Goates, 5–6)	Translation of PGH
Este vous le douzzime jour vindrent treis {fol. 37r} philosofes de l'orient a Jerusalem e demaunderent ou fust le Rey des Gyus que né estoit, qui esteile il aveyent veu en l'orient; e disoient qu'il estoient venuz pur aourer le. Quant le rei Herodes oi ceo, si estoit mout troublé, e tote la cité ausi. E fist assembler touz les plus hauz prestres e les mestres de la ley e demaunda ou Crist	After, vpon þe twelfþe day, so comen þere þre kynges fram þe est in to Jerusalem & askeden where was þe kyng of Jewes þat was ybore, whas sterre þay hadden yseye in þe est. And hij seiden hij were ycomen hym to honoure. Þo þe kyng Heroudes herd þat, he wex al ameued, & all þat weren in þat cite. And so sone assembleden alle þe hei3est prestes and maistres of þe lawe, and askeden	Afterward, upon the twelfth day, there came unto Jerusalem three kings from the east and asked where was that newborn king of the Jews, whose star they had observed in the east. And they said they came to honor him. When the king Herod heard that, he grew agitated, and all who were in the city. Soon all the highest priests and masters of the Law assembled, and asked

deust nestre. E il respundirent que en Bedleem, quar ensi out Dieu premis par le prophete. Dunk apela Herodes les philosofes priveement e enquist quant il ussent primes veu l'esteile, e les enveya a Bedleem e lur dist qu'il enqueisent ententivement de l'enfaunt, e quant il l'eusent trové que il li maundassent, e il le vendreit aorer. E quant il avoient oi le rei, il s'en alerent vers Bedleem. Este vous l'esteile qu'il avoient veu en l'orient lour apparust e ala devaunt eus jusques ele vint e restut desus la ou l'enfaunt esteit. E il, quant il la virent, si en avoient tresgraunt joie, e entrerent la maison e troverent l'enfaunt ové sa mere. E cheirent a terre e aorerent l'enfaunt; e ovrerent lour tresors e li offrirent or, encens e mirre. E cum il penserent returner a Herodes, la nuyt en avision vint l'aungle e lur dist qu'il ne returnassent point par li. E il par autre voie returnerent en lour pais.

where Crist scholde be borne. & hij ansuereden, "In Bedleem Jude," for whi God hadd so hiȝtte þoruȝ þe prophetes. Þo cleped Heroudes þe þre kynges priuelich & asked hem whan hij seiȝen first þe sterre, & sent hem in to Bedleem & bad hem þat hij schulde enquere ententiflich of þe childe, and whan þat hij hadden hym founden þat hij scholde sende hym bode, & he wolde come & hym honure. And whan þai hadden herd þe kyng speke hij wenten hem forþ toward Bedleem. And also suiþe þe sterre þat hij hadden er yseye in þe est schewed hym, & ȝede euer toforen hem til þat þei comen þere þe childe was borne, and ouer hym wiþstode. And hij þat were so ledde wiþ þe sterre hadden gret ioye, and entred in to þe hous & founden þe childe & his moder & fellen to þe erþe and honoured þe childe, and vndeden her tresoure and offred hym gold & ensense and mirre. And als hij þouȝtten tourne aȝein to Heroudes, aniȝth so com þe angel to hem in a visioun & seide þat hij ne schulde nouȝth wende aȝein by hym. & hij by oþer weye retourned in to her countre.

where Christ should be born and they answered, "In Bethlehem of Judea," because God had declared so through his prophets. Then Herod called the three kings privately and asked them when they first saw the star and charged them forth into Bethlehem and bade them that they should inquire particularly of the child, and when they found him they should send him notice, and he would come to honor him. And when they heard the king speak they left toward Bethlehem. And as they did the star appeared that they had seen before in the east, and went ever before them until they came to where the child was born, and stood over him. And they who were led by the star felt great joy, and entered into the house and found the child and his mother and fell to earth and honored the child, and unpacked their treasure and offered him gold and incense and myrrh. And as they determined to return to Herod, by night there came to them the angel in a vision and said that they should not go again to him. And they returned by another way into their own country.

Jesus walks on the water
(Mt 14:22–26, 28–33; Mk 6:45–46, 48–52; Jn 6:14–19, 21)

Estoire, 49:18–34

E tauntost comaunda Jhesu ses deciples qu'il alassent trestouz a la nef e retornassent a {fol. 47v} Bethsaida tant com il se deliverast du people, e il s'en alerent. E le people, quant il s'avertirent que Jhesu les out peu si plentivousement de si pou, disoient qu'il estoit ver-

PGH (Goates, 47–48)

And þo comaunded Jesus his deciples þat þai ȝeden alle aȝein in to þe schippe, and þat hij returneden aȝein to Bethsayda til þat he hadde deliuered hym of þe folk. And hij þo wenten hem forþ as Jesus hem comaunded. And alle þe folk, whan hij seiȝen þat Jesus

Translation of PGH

And then Jesus commanded his disciples to go again into the ship, and to return to Bethsaida until he had delivered himself of the folk. And so they went forth as Jesus commanded. And all the folk, when they saw that Jesus had fed them so plentifully with

rai prophete, quar il virent bien qu'il estoient †cink mile hommes estre les femes e les enfaunz. E il donque se purparlerent qu'il le ferroient rey a force, mes Jhesu fuy taunt dementers en la montaigne soul pur orer. Ore avint que ses deciples estoient suspris de tresgrant tempeste e ne poeient passer en nule manere. E Jhesu, quant vint vers le jour, s'en vint alaunt sur les undes vers eus e fist semblaunt cum si il les voleit passer. E il le sourvirent touz e avoient si grant pour qu'il comencerent a crier, e disoient que ce estoit fantesme. E Jhesu tantost parla o eus e lour dist qu'il estoit e qu'il ne ussent pour. Donc dist seint Pierre: "Sire, si vous l'estes, comaundez qe je vigne a vous sur le ewe." E Jhesu li dist qu'il venist, e il saili hors de la nef e ala sus les undes vers Jhesu. E vint une treforte bueffe du vent, e il se dota e tauntost comensa a plunger; e il cria a Jhesu qu'il le sauvast. E Jhesu tendi tantost sa meyn e l'aert, e li demanda tantost purquei il avoit pour. E le mena ou li en la nef, e tauntost cessa tote la tempeste. E la nef estoit tantost a la terre, la ou il voloient aler.

hem hadde fedde so plenty[u] ouslich wiþ so litel þing, hij seiden certeynlich þat he was verray prophete. For whi þei seiȝen wel þat þere were fyue þousande men, wiþ outen children & wiþ outen wymmen. And þo þai speken amonges hem þat hij wolden alle maken hym her kyng wiþ strenkþe. & þer whiles was Jesus vpon þe mountayne for to honouren. And so bifel þat his deciples weren so bistadde wiþ tempest þat hij myȝtten nouȝth passen in none manere. And whan it com towardes þe day vpon þat ny[ȝt]h, so com Jesus towardes hem vpon þe wawes. And he made semblaunt as he wolde haue passed hem. And þo hij seiȝen hym hij hadden alle so gret dredde þat hij quakeden and seiden þat it was nouȝth bot fanteme. And Jesus spak to hem also swiþe, and badde hem haue no drede, for it was hymself. And þan ansuered seint Peter and seide: "Sir, ȝif it be ȝe, comaundeþ þat ich com to ȝou vpon þe water." And Jesus hym badde he schulde come. And seint Peter styrtte out of þe schippe, and ȝede vpon þe water to Jesu. And so com a gret wyndes blast, & seint Peter was sore adradde & bigan to synke adoun. And he bigan to crie aloude to Jesu þat he schulde hym sauen. And Jesus also swiþe bede hym take his honde & helde hym þerby, & asked hym why þat he was so sore adradd: & he ledde hym wiþ hym to þe schippe. And þe tempeste bigan also suiþe forto sesen, & þe schippe was also suiþe þere hij wolden ben.

such a little thing, they said certainly he was a true prophet. Because they saw certainly that there were 5000 men, not counting children and women. And then they determined that they would force him to be their king. Meanwhile Jesus was upon the mountain to pray. And so it befell that his disciples were so beset by a storm that they could not at all complete their crossing. And as the day approached, there came Jesus toward them upon the waves. And he appeared as if he would pass them by. And when they saw him they were so frightened that they quaked and declared that it was a phantom. And Jesus spoke to them immediately, and bade them have no dread, for it was he himself. And then answered Saint Peter and said, "Lord, if it be you, command that I come to you upon the water." And Jesus bade him he should come. And Saint Peter left the ship and walked upon the water to Jesus. Then came a great blast of wind, and Saint Peter was greatly afraid and began to sink. And he began to cry aloud to Jesus that he should save him. And Jesus immediately bade him take his hand and held him thereby and asked him why he was so frightened and led him with him to the ship. Immediately the storm began to wane and the ship was suddenly at its destination.

Jesus raises Lazarus
(Jn 11:32–46)

Estoire, 80:25–39

E quant Marie vint a Jhesu, tantost chei a ses piez plorante e dist si il eust esté la, son frere n'eust pas esté mort. Jhesu, quant il la vist plorer e les Juis qu'estoient venuz ové li, comensa a fremir. E lerma e demaunda ou il l'eusent seveli, e il le menerent cele part. Donc distrent les uns qu'il paruit qu'il l'out mout amé; e les autres disoient que mervailles estoit qu'il ne poeit tenir la vie son ami, qu'a uns estraunges qu'estoit nez aveogles dona la veue. Este vous donc Jhesu fremissaunt vint a monement. Ore estoit il mis en une fosse, e une pierre estoit mise desus. Donc comaunda Jhesu qu'il remuassent la pierre, e respoundi Marthe qu'il puoit ja, quar il out jeu quatre jours. E Jhesu li dist que si sa foi ne li fausist, ele verroit mervailles. Donc remuerent il la pierre, e Jhesu leva ses eoz vers le ciel e mercia son Piere q'il out oi sa proiere. E pus o haute voiz cria e dist: 'Lazere, venez hors!' E tantost {fol. 54r} s'en issi liez piez e mains de bendes, e sa face estoit liez de un suaire. Donc comanda Jhesu qu'il le deliassent e lessasent aler. Este vous que mout que ce virent crustrent en Jhesu, e les autres alerent as phariseus e lor counterent ce qe Jhesu out fet.

PGH (Goates, 73–74)

And whan Marie com to Jesu, als suiþe sche fel adoun to his feete wepeande and cryeande hym mercy, and seide: "Sir, ȝif þou haddest ben here, my broþer ne hadde nouȝt ben ded." And Jhesus, whan he seiȝ hire wepen and þe Jewes þat weren ycomen wiþ hire, he bigan to quaken & to wepen, and asked hem where þai hadden hym yburyed. And hij ladden hym þider. And þan seiden summe þat it semed wel þat Jesus hym hadde mychel loued. And oþer þat þere weren, seiden þat it was wonder þat he ne myȝth nouȝth helden his frendes lyf, als wel as he myth ȝiuen an vncouþ man his siȝth of eiȝe. And Jesus þo al tremblyng com to þe monument. Nou was Laȝar leide in a graue, and a ston abouen hym. And þo comaunded Jesus þat men schulden remue þe ston. And Martha seide þat þe body stank, for he hadde leyen foure dayes in þe erþe. And Jesus hire ansuered þat bot hire trewþe failed hir, sche schulde se merueile. And þo lyften hij vp þe ston. & Jesus loked towardes þe heuene and þanked his fader þat he hadde herde his bisechynge; and þan he cried aloude: "Laȝar, arise, & come out hider." And he aros vp als swiþe, his honden and his feete ybounden wiþ bondes, and his visage was bounden wiþ a su[d]arie. And þo comanded Jesus þat hij schulden vnbynden hym, and þat hij schulden leten hym gon. And þo many þat seiȝen it leueden in Jesu. And þe oþer ȝeden to þe Phariseus, and tolden hem hou Jesus hadde done.

Translation of PGH

And when Mary came to Jesus, immediately she fell to his feet weeping and crying him mercy, and said: "Lord, if you had been here, my brother would not have died." And Jesus, when he saw her weep and the Jews that had come with her, he began to tremble and to weep, and asked them where they had buried him. And they led him there. And then said some that it seemed clear that he loved him much. And others there said that it was a wonder that he could not hold his friend's life just as well as might give a stranger his eyesight. And then Jesus all trembling came to the monument. Now was Lazarus laid in a grave, and a stone above him. And then Jesus commanded that men should remove the stone. And Martha said that the body stank, for he had lain four days in the earth. And Jesus answered that unless her faith failed her, she should see a marvel. And then they lifted up the stone. And Jesus looked to heaven and thanked his father that he had heard his petition; and then he cried aloud: "Lazarus, arise, and come out here." And immediately he arose, his hands and feet bound with bands, and his face was bound with a handkerchief. And then Jesus commanded that they should free him and let him go. And then many who saw it believed in Jesus. And others went to the Pharisees, and told them how Jesus had wrought.

Magdalene at the tomb
(Jn 20:11–17, Lk 24:3–8)

Estoire, 103:16–27

E tant com ces angles aparurent issi, estoit la Magdaleine {fol. 61r} autre part, e pus vint au sepulcre e estut e plora. E s'enclina e esgarda en sepulcre e vist deus angles en blanche vesture seaunz un a chief e un autre a piez. E il li demaunderent purquei ele plorast, e ele respoundi que son Seignur estoit emporté e ele ne sout ou il estoit mis. Este vous leverent les angles countre Jhesu qui vint e estuit derere la Magdaleyne. E ele se returna e vist Jhesu e quida qu'il fust cortiller. Donc li demanda Jhesu purquei ele plorast e qui ele queist, e ele respoundi: 'Sire, vous l'avez emporté. Dites moi ou vous l'avez mis, e je le prendrai e l'emporterai!' A ce se turna ele vers les angles ausi com queraunt confort. E Jhesu l'apela e dist: 'Marie.' E ele conuyst sa voiz e se returna e chei a ses piez e dist: 'A, beau Mestre!' Donc li dist Jhesu qu'ele alast e deist a ses freres q'il mountereit a son Pierre e a lor Pere, a son Dieu e a lor Dieu.

PGH (Goates, 103–104)

And þerwhiles þat þe aungel schewed hem þise þinges, so was þe Maudeleyn by þat oþer half, and com to þe sepulchre and stoode & weep. And þo sche bihelde, and sei3 tweie aungels in white cloþing, þat on sittande at þe heued, & þat oþer at þe feete. & hij askeden hir whi þat sche wepe. And sche ansuered & seide, for þat hire lorde was borne away and sche nyste nere where þat he was leide. And wiþ þat þe aungels arisen a3eins Jesu, þat com & stoode bihynde þe Maudeleyn. And sche wiþturned hire, and wende he hadde ybe a gardynere. And þo asked Jesus hir whi sche wepe, & what sche sou3th. "Sir," sche seide, "3if þat þou haste borne hym away, where þou haste hym ileide telle þou me; and ich hym schal take wel stille, and beren away wel pryuelich." And wiþ þat sche turned hire towardes þe aungels as forto haue summe confort. And Jesus cleped hire "Marie." And þan sche knew hym by his voice, and turned hire and fel adoun to his feete and seide, "Ha! Swete sir." And þo bad Jesus hir þat sche schulde goo and suggen to hire breþeren þat he schulde stei3e vp to his fader and to her fader, and to his God & to her God also.

Translation of PGH

While the angel showed them these things, the Magdalene was to the side, and came to the sepulcher and stood and wept. And then she beheld, and saw two angels in white clothing, the one sitting at the head, and the other at the feet. And they asked her why she wept. And she answered and said, because her lord was borne away and she knew not where he was laid. And with that the angels rose to face Jesus, who came and stood behind the Magdalene. And she turned and took him to be a gardener. And then Jesus asked her why she wept, and what she sought. "Lord," she said, "If you have borne him away, tell me where you have laid him; and I shall take him quietly to bear away secretly." And with that she turned back to the angels for comfort. And Jesus called her, "Mary." And then she knew him by his voice, and turned and fell down at his feet and said, "Ah, Sweet Lord." And then Jesus bade her go and announce to her brothers that he should ascend to his father and to their father, and to his God and to their God also.

Pentecost
(Lk 24:52–53, Mk 16:20, Jn 21:25)

Estoire, 113:26–38

{fol. 63r} Este vous com il esteurent e agarderent aprés li vers le ciel, vindrent deus angles en blanche vesture e appareurent decoste eus e demaunderent purquei il eussent abousté vers le ciel. E lor disoient que ausi com il estoit mountez eu ciel, autresi vendroit il autre foiz descendaunt du ciel au Jugement. Donc †aorerent il e creurent que Jhesu estoit alez a destre son Pere. E returnerent en Jerusalem o grant joie e entrerent le soler ou les apostres meintrent. E la estoient continuelment en oreison o la mere Jhesu e o les autres dames e o ses cosins jusqes le dime jour que le Seint Esperit lor vint entour oure de tyerce, que lor dona savoir e langage e hardiesce a precher la crestieneté. E donques alerent il au temple e estoient toute foiz en temple loant Dieu jusques il furent enchacez hors de gent de Judee. En le dime an aprés l'Asencion, quant seint Jake estoit decolé e seint Piere enprisoné, donc alerent il chescun sa part par le mounde e precherent as paiens e as Juis, e l'esperit Jhesu les guia e les conforta e conferma le sermon par miracle.

PGH (Goates, 112–13)

And als hij stoden lokande on heiȝ, so comen two aungels in white wede and stoden bysyden hem, and asked hem whi hij stoden so and lokeden on heiȝ towardes þe heuene. And he seide hem, als he was ystowen vp to heuene, also schulde he comen anoþer tyme descendende to þe juggement. And þo hij þonkeden God, and wysten wel þat Jesus was went and satte on his faders riȝht honde. And þo hij retourneden him aȝein in to Jerusalem wiþ gret joye, and entreden in to þe soleer þere þe apostles woneden. And þere þai weren stedfastlich in orisouns wiþ Marie, Jesus moder, and wiþ oþer lauedies and Jesus cosynes, euere tyl þat day þat þe Holy Gost com to hem at þe tyme of vnderne, and aliȝth wiþinnen hem, and ȝaf hem wytt, and wisdom, and connyng of langages, and hardynesse to prechen þe cristendom ouer al. And þo wenten hij in to þe temple, and stoden euere þonkynge God tyl þat hij were dryuen out wiþ Jewes of Judee. And þe tueluethe ȝere after þe ascencioun of Jesu Crist, whan seint James was byheueded and seint Peter yprisouned, þo wenten hij vchon his waye ouer al þe werlde, and precheden to paienes and to Jewes. And þe Holy Gost hem wissed, & tauȝtte, and confermed her sarmoun þorouȝ miracles þat Jesus dude for hem.

Translation of PGH

And as they stood looking on high, there came two angels in white clothing and stood beside them, and asked them why they stood so and looked on high toward the heavens. And they told them, just as he was ascended to heaven, just so would he come at another time to descend in judgment. And then they thanked God, and understood well that Jesus was gone to sit at his father's right hand. And then they returned once more into Jerusalem with great joy, and entered into the upper room where the apostles dwelt. And there they were steadfast in worship with Mary, Jesus' mother, and with other ladies and Jesus' kin, until the day that the Holy Ghost came to them in the third hour, and came to rest within them, and gave them knowledge, and wisdom, and understanding of languages, and above all the hardiness to preach Christianity. And then they went into the Temple, and stood there thanking God until they were driven out by the Jews of Judea. And the twelfth year after the ascension of Jesus Christ, when Saint James was beheaded and Saint Peter imprisoned, then went they each one his own way over all the world, and preached to pagans and to Jews. And the Holy Ghost guided and taught them, and confirmed their message by miracles that Jesus performed for them.

List of Proper Names

This index shows all occurrences of all proper names. For names like Jesus or God that appear very frequently, however, only the first twenty occurrences are shown. Proper names have sometimes been substituted in the translated text for the corresponding subject or object pronouns. Numbers refer to chapter and line in this translation. For names straddling two lines, the first line number is shown. An asterisk (*) indicates that the proper name occurs more than once in the line. A line number marked with a dagger (†) refers to a proper name that has been emended in the published critical edition of the *Estoire*.

The following reference works have been consulted in the preparation of this index: *The New International Dictionary of Biblical Archaeology*, ed. Edward M. Blaiklock and R. K. Harrison (Grand Rapids, MI: Zondervan, 1983); *The Anchor Bible Dictionary*, ed. David Noel Freedman et al., 6 vols. (New York; London: Doubleday, 1992); and *The Oxford Guide to People and Places of the Bible*, ed. Bruce M. Metzger and Michael D. Coogan (New York: Oxford University Press, 2001).

Aaron 2:3, brother of Moses, forebear of John the Baptist
Abel 41:6, 90:11, son of Adam and Eve
Abraham (Saint) 1:11, 59:52, 68:19, 87:8, the patriarch
Aelred P:15, Abbot Aelred of Rievaulx
Andrew (Saint) 9:13, 17:5, 49:15, 92:4, 93:7, the apostle, brother of Simon Peter
Anna 4:13, 4:15, a widow and prophetess
Annas 96:48, 96:50, 96:68, 96:71, 97:1, a high priest
Baptist 29:10, John the Baptist; *see also* John[2] (the Baptist)
Barabbas 98:19, 98:21, 98:53, a prisoner released by Pilate
Bartimaeus 78:6, a blind man healed by Jesus
Beelzebub iii.28, 22:10, 40:9, or Beelzebul, a name for Satan
Bethphage 81:22, or Bephage, a village near Bethany
Bethany v:2, 80:4, 80:20, 81:2, 81:6, 82:19, 94:15, 113:20, a village near Jerusalem
Bethlehem 3:5, 3:6, 3:14, 3:21, 3:32, 3:34, 3:37, 5:7, 5:11, home of David and town of Jesus's birth
Bethsaida iv:12, 9:17, 32:15, 49:23, †57:2, a city on the Sea of Galilee
Boanerges 24:6, Sons of Thunder, a name for James and John
Caesar[1] Augustus 3:1, Roman emperor at the time of Jesus's birth
Caesar[2] 86:8, *86:11, 97:14, 97:19, 98:40, 98:41, 98:46, 113:22, Tiberius Caesar, Roman emperor (14–37 C.E.)

Caiaphas 80:51, 94:5, 96:48, 97:2, a high priest
Calvary, Mount 99:2, or Golgotha, place of Jesus's Crucifixion
Cana iii:3, 14:1, a village of Galilee
Canaanite iv:7, 52:1
Canterbury P:6, English town and seat of an archbishop
Capernaum iii:5, iii:8, iii:14, iii:15, iv:4, iv:18, 11:2, 14:3, 14:4, 14:8, 17:2, 18:1, 20:2, 26:2, 27:1, 32:15, 49:45, 63:2, a city on the Sea of Galilee
Cedron 96:9, or Kidron, a brook between Jerusalem and the Mount of Olives
Chorazin 32:15, or Korazin, a town in Galilee
Christ A:7, v:11, 3:13, 3:32, 7:19, 7:20, 7:23, 7:24, 9:6, 9:14, 9:18, 11:10, 12:8, 13:36, 13:37, 13:41, 16:3, 17:3, 18:6, 22:2 etc., Christ, the Messiah; *see also* Jesus, King of Israel, King (of the Jews), Lamb of God, Light of the world etc.
Chuza 31:30, husband of Joanna and steward of Herod Antipas
Clement[1] P:5, P:12, Clement, prior of Llanthony
Clement[2], Saint, P:17, Saint Clement of Rome
Cleopas vii:6, 108:1, 108:9, a follower of Jesus; *see also* Mary Cleopas
David (Saint), (King) 1:11, 3:6, 8:16, 37:6, 81:32, 82:12, 82:15, 89:3, 89:4, 89:5, 113:23, the prophet, psalmist, and patriarch
Devil 8:3, 8:5, 8:8, 8:10, 8:14, 8:19, 44:8, 59:52, 60:13; *see also* Satan
East 3:27, 3:29, 3:38
Egypt 5:2, 5:4, 5:10, 49:49, a country
Eli *100:2, from Jesus's cry from the cross, "Eloi, Eloi, lema sabachthani" (Mk 15:34)
Elijah 2:13, 7:21, 7:24, 16:12, 60:4, 61:4, 61:7, 61:14, 61:16, 100:5, 100:10, a Hebrew prophet and forerunner of Christ
Elisha 16:14, a Hebrew prophet and Elijah's successor
Elizabeth (Saint) 2:3, 2:25, 2:41, *2:48, 2:61, mother of John the Baptist and wife of Zechariah
Emmaus 108:5, 108:24, a village near Jerusalem
Ephraim 80:56, a town
Father 1:3, 1:6, 6:14, 6:17, 7:37, 8:18, 11:8, 12:11, 28:20, 33:9, 49:19, 49:50, 54:10, 63:37, 75:14, *79:8, 79:13, 80:42, 92:12 etc., a name for God; Heavenly Father 36:9; *see also* God, Lord[1], One
Gabriel 2:18, 2:28, the archangel
Galilee iii:1, vii:9, 2:28, 2:47, 5:13, 10:1, 13:2, 13:11, 13:51, 14:2, 18:21, 19:3, 19:40, 24:2, 48:4, 51:2, 59:3, 59:31, 62:2, 64:2 etc., the province; Galilee, Sea of, iv:9, 53:1, 53:2; Galilean(s) iii:33, 43:1, 43:3, 43:6, 96:61, a Galilaean, (Galilaeans); *see also* Tiberias, Sea of
Gennesaret iv:6, 50:1, 50:2, a region
Gergesa 19:3, a seaside village
Gerizim, Mount 13:32, 43:3, site of Abraham's first altar (Gen 12:6), holy mountain of the Samaritans
Gethsemane 96:10, hamlet on the slope of the Mount of Olives
God 1:2, 1:3, 1:5, 1:6, 1:8, 2:2, 2:7, 2:15, 2:19, 2:26, 2:30, 2:33, 2:42, 2:44, 2:46, 2:51, 2:57, 2:72, 3:17, 3:19 etc.; *see also* Father, Lord[1], One, Son of God
Gomorrhah 28:15, a city destroyed by God (Gen 19:24)
Herod[1] (King) iv:13, iv:21, 2:1, 3:30, 3:33, 3:36, 3:42, 4:1, 5:3, *5:5, 5:9, 5:12, Herod the Great, king of Judea

List of Proper Names 153

Herod² (King) 13:3, 13:4, 13:7, 31:30, 39:2, 48:3, *58:1, 58:3, 58:5, 64:2, 64:13, 86:2, 98:9, 98:10, *98:12, 98:13, 98:16, Herod Antipas, son of Herod the Great and tetrarch and ruler of Galilee and Perea; *see also* Herodians
Herodians v:8, 56:3, 86:1, followers of Herod Antipas
Herodias 48:5, wife first of Herod (Philip), then of her uncle Herod Antipas
Holy Spirit P:24, 2:14, 2:39, 2:49, 2:58, 2:69, 2:73, 2:74, 4:7, 4:8, 7:4, 7:28, 7:36, 8:2, 9:5, 9:6, 11:22, 12:12, 33:9, 95:69 etc.
Holy Trinity 8:1
Isaac 87:8, the patriarch, son of Abraham and father of Jacob
Isaiah 7:23, 16:3, the prophet
Israel 2:35, 2:70, 16:13, 16:15, 22:9, 74:20, a land and kingdom; King of Israel 9:24, 99:26, name for Christ; *see also* Jesus
Jacob 13:21, 87:8, son of Isaac; his twelve sons form the Twelve Tribes of Israel
Jairus iii:9, 21:2, a ruler
James¹, Saint iv:34, †15:10, 17:7, 18:9, 21:25, 24:6, 64:5, 75:2, 75:8, 93:6, 96:12, 112:2, 113:43, the apostle, son of Zebedee, and brother of John the Evangelist
James² 46:5, James, brother of Jesus
Jeremiah 60:4, a priest and prophet
Jericho iv:35, iv:36, 34:8, 76:1, 76:2, 77:2, 78:1, 78:2, a town east of Jerusalem
Jerusalem A:6, A.8, ii:3, iv:14, v:2, v:5, 2:2, 3:28, 3:30, 4:4, 4:6, 6:2, 6:6, 7:4, 7:19, 8:14, 11:1, 11:3, 13:32, 13:54 etc.
Jesus, Jesus Christ, Lord Jesus (Christ) P:1, P:2, P:8, P:16, P:17, P:20, A:1, A:5, A:6, i:1, ii:1, ii:2, ii:4, iii:1, iii:18, iii:38, iv:2, *iv:13, *v:12, *vi:3 etc.; *see also* Christ, King of Israel, King (of the Jews), Lamb of God, Light of the world, Lord², Master, Messiah, Savior of the world, Shepherd, Son of God, Teacher etc.
Jew(s) iii:36, iv:37, 7:15, 7:19, 9:20, 11:11, 11:18, 12:3, *13:16, 27:3, 27:6, 27:15, 27:17, 28:5, 47:1, 47:12, *47:17, 51:4, 52:5 etc.; *see also* King (of the Jews)
Joanna 31:29, wife of Chuza and follower of Christ
John¹ (the Evangelist), (Saint) 15:10, 17:8, 18:9, *21:25, 24:6, 61:2, 63:19, 64:5, 75:2, 75:9, 93:7, 95:6, 95:48, 95:50, 96:13, 96:49, 96:50, 96:51, 99:13, 103:2 etc., the apostle, son of Zebedee, and brother of James
John² (the Baptist), (Saint) *A:3, A:5, A:6, ii:3, iii:2, iii:17, iv:3, 2:11, 2:27, 2:64, 2:67, 7:2, 7:4, 7:8, 7:14, 7:18, *7:31, 7:32, 7:34 etc., prophet and forerunner of Christ; *see also* Baptist
John³ 9:16, identified as the father of Simon Peter
Jonah iii.28, 40:13, 40:14, 40:19, 55:6, the prophet
Jordan (River) 7:6, 7:30, 12:5, 79:15, 80:2
Joseph¹ 2:29, 2:54, 2:60, 3:4, 3:21, 4:4, 4:10, 4:16, 4:23, 5:1, 5:3, 5:10, 5:11, 5:13, 6:2, 7:40, 16:7, 46:4, Joseph, husband of Mary
Joseph² 101:14, 101:17, 101:21, Joseph of Arimathaea, a disciple of Jesus
Joses 46:5, identified as a brother of Jesus
Judas¹ (Iscariot) v:15, 49:64, 81:10, 94:1, 94:9, 94:12, 95:51, 95:53, 95:55, 96:11, 96:25, 96:28, 96:31, 96:33, 97:23, the apostle and betrayer of Jesus
Judas² 46:5, identified as a brother of Jesus
Judea iii:1, 2:47, 2:71, 5:12, 12:2, 12:5, 13:2, 13:10, 14:3, 29:9, 80:8, 113:27, 113:43, a land, Judah

King (of the Jews) 3:28, 97:20, 98:2, 99:7, 99:9, 99:26, a name for Christ; *see also* Jesus, Israel

Lamb of God 9:3, 9:10, a name for Christ; *see also* Jesus

Law (of Moses), Old Law iii:22, 1:5, 4:3, 6:8, 21:6, 24:19, 25:6, 26:9, 34:3, 59:13, 59:30, 68:11, 68:14, 74:6, 87:4, 87:7, 88:1, 88:3, 88:7, 92:22 etc., divine commandments as written by Moses in the Torah, the first five books of the Hebrew Bible; New Law 24:8, Christ's renewal of Mosaic Law through his moral and ethical teachings

Lazarus iv:38, 80:1, 80:3, 80:7, 80:12, 80:14, 80:20, 80:24, 80:35, 80:40, 80:38, 80:40, 80:44, 80:45, 81:7, 81:8, 81:20, 81:44, 82:18, resident of Bethany, brother of Mary and Martha, and follower of Jesus

Light of the world 59:71, a name for Christ

Llanthony P:6, an Augustinian house; *see also* Clement[1]

Lord[1] (God) 2:16, 2:52, 2:69, 2:70, 4:12, a name for God

Lord[2] (Jesus Christ) P:2, P:20, A:1, i:1, ii:1, ii:4, iii:1, vii:2, 1:1, 37:12, 49:35, 49:60, 61:6, 61:29, 64:6, 89:4, 103:23, 110:8, 112:18, a name for Christ; *see also* Jesus

Magadan iv:10, 55:1, 55:2, a place

Magdalene *see* Mary (Magdalene)

Malchus †96:37, a servant of the high priest

Martha (Saint) iii:23, 35:1, *35:2, 35:5, *35:9, 80:3, 80:21, 80:27, 81:7, resident of Bethany, sister of Mary and Lazarus, and follower of Jesus

Mary[1] 2:29, 2:31, 2:36, 2:43, 2:46, 2:48, 2:50, 2:51, 2:53, 2:58, 3:4, 3:7, 3:21, 3:24, 4:2, 4:4, 4:10, 4:16, 4:18, 4:23, 6:2, 23:4, 46:4, mother of Jesus

Mary[2] (Magdalene) (Saint) iii:18, vii:3, 31:1, 35:2, 35:3, 35:10, 80:3, 80:29, 80:31, 80:39, 81:8, 99:14, 103:1, 103:2, 103:19, 103:25, 103:32, 104:3, 106:6, resident of Bethany, sister of Martha and Lazarus, and follower of Jesus; also called Mary Magdalene or the Magdalene; see the note for 35:2.

Mary[3] Cleopas 99:13, a follower of Jesus; probably the wife of Cleopas

Marys, the, 102:3, 106:7

Master 80:18, a name for Christ; *see also* Jesus

Matthew (Levy), (Saint) iii:8, 20:1, 20:18, the apostle

Messiah iv.28, 4:6, 4:8, 4:16, 7:5, 79:4, 81:32, 82:12, 82:15, 89:1, 89:3, 89:4, 89:5, 108:15; *see also* Jesus

Moses 4:3, 11:23, 49:49, 49:50, 59:36, 61:4, 61:7, 72:3, 72:4, 72:6, the prophet and lawgiver; *see also* Law (of Moses)

Naaman 16:15, identified as a leper in Syria

Nain 29:2, a town

Nathanael (Saint) 9:17, 9:21, 9:22, 112:2, the apostle

Nazareth iii:3, 2:28, 2:54, 3:5, 4:24, 5:14, 6:17, 7:30, *16:1, 17:2, 23:2, 76:3, 81:44, 96:30, 99:7, 108:12, the village of Jesus's childhood and youth

Nicodemus 11:19, 59:29, 59:31, 101:15, a Pharisee and follower of Jesus

Nineveh 40:15, 40:18, a city where Jonah preached

Noah 93:20, the prophet and ark-builder

Olives, Mount of 81:30, 93:6, 94:15, 96:2, 113:15, 113:19, a mount outside Jerusalem; Olivet

One, the, 2:13, 7:7, 12:4, 32:13, 92:28, a name for God

Paradise 99:35

Passover ii:3, 6:2, 11:1, 11:3, 11:16, 13:53, 81:3, 81:6, 90:16, 94:3, 95:3, 95:5, 95:12, 101:3, a spring pilgrimage festival commemorating the liberation of the Jews from bondage in Egypt

Peter (Saint) P:16, iii:3, iii:4, iii:5, iv:19, iv:32, vii:5, 9:16, 15:1, 17:1, *18:9, 18:17, 21:12, 21:25, 49:34, 49:36, 49:37, 49:39, 49:40, 49:59, 51:14 etc., the apostle; *see also* Simon[1] (Peter)

Pharisee(s) iii:26, iii:30, iv:10, iv:21, iv:26, iv:28, iv:30, iv:38, v:7, v:8, v:10, v:12, 7:9, 7:19, 11:18, 13:10, 20:3, 20:21, 20:26, 22:9 etc., a Jewish sect depicted as legalistic tormentors of Jesus

Philip (Saint) 9:16, 9:17, 9:22, 49:10, 49:12, *92:3, the apostle

Pilate iii:34, 43:1, 43:2, 43:5, 97:14, 97:16, 97:17, 97:20, 97:22, 98:2, *98:4, 98:7, 98:8, 98:13, *98:14, 98:17, 98:21, 98:23, 98:28 etc., Pontius Pilate, Roman governor of Judea

Romans 7:3, 80:50, 86:3, Romans; the Roman people

Sabbath, *iii:25, iii:37, 37:1, 37:5, 37:8, *37:12, 37:13, 38:1, 38:4, 38:5, 38:7, 38:8, 38:10, 44:4, 44:5, *44:7, 47:1, 47:7, 47:13, 47:19 etc., the Jews' weekly day of rest

Sadducees v:8, 56:3, *87:1, 88:2, a Jewish sect said to reject the resurrection of the body and depicted as adversaries of Jesus

Samaria 64:3, 113:27, a region

Samaritan[1] 34:10, 34:16, the (Good) Samaritan

Samaritan(s)[2] iv:20, 13:11, 13:14, 13:16, 13:38, 13:45, 64:1, 70:5, person or people of Samaria

Sarepta, or Zarephath, 16:14, a coastal city between Tyre and Sidon

Satan 8:12, 33:6, 95:24, 95:51; *see also* Devil

Savior of the world 13:50, a name for Christ; *see also* Jesus

Shepherd 59:72, a name for Christ

Sidon 52:2, a coastal city near Tyre

Siloam 43:10, 59:59, pool and tower in Jerusalem

Simeon 4:6, 4:7, 4:8, 4:11, 4:18, identified as a just and devout man in Jerusalem

Simon[1] (Peter) 9:13, 9:14, 9:15, 15:4, 15:6, 15:7, 15:10, 15:12, 15:13, 15:14, 17:4, the apostle and brother of Andrew; *see also* Peter (Saint)

Simon[2] 46:5, identified as a brother of Jesus

Simon[3] 98:61, a foreign man compelled to carry Jesus's cross

Simon[4] 31:18, a Pharisee who invites Jesus to dinner

Sion, Mount 113:18, identified as a district of Jerusalem

Sodom 28:14, 32:10, a city

Solomon 40:22, 40:23, 85:8, sage and king of Israel

Son (of God) 1:9, 2:35, 2:40, 2:45, 7:38, 8:5, 8:15, 9:7, 9:24, 11:26, 11:27, 11:30, 18:15, 39:8, 49:62, 59:51, 59:67, 60:6, 61:10, 80:27 etc., a name for Christ; *see also* Jesus

South, queen of the, 40:21, or queen of Sheba

Susanna 31:30, a disciple of Jesus

Sychar 13:12, a village of Samaria

Syria 16:15, a country

Tabor, Mount, iii:12, 24:4, identified as the mountain of the Beatitudes

Teacher 9:24, 103:34, a name for Christ; *see also* Jesus

Temple iv:37, v:3, v:5, v:14, 2:6, 2:7, 2:23, 2:24, 4:2, 4:9, 4:14, 4:23, 6:17, 8:15, 11:6, 11:13, 11:14, 11:16, 37:8, 37:9, 37:10 etc., a monumental religious complex in Jerusalem and the foremost center for Jewish worship

Thomas[1] (Saint) vii:8, 80:17, 80:19, 108:35, 108:36, 109:23, 109:25, 110:1, 110:3, 110:6, 110:7, 110:9, 112:2, the apostle
Thomas[2], Saint, the martyr, P:7, Saint Thomas Becket
Tiberias 49:44, a seaside town; Tiberias, Sea of iii:6, vii:10, 15:1, 17:4, 19:1, 19:3, *112:1; *see also* Galilee, Sea of
Tyre 52:2, a coastal city near Sidon
Zacchaeus iv:35, 77:1, 77:2, 77:4, 77:9, 77:12, an official in Jericho
Zebedee 15:10, 17:8, father of the apostles James and John
Zechariah 2:3, 2:4, 2:5, 2:6, 2:8, 2:9, 2:11, 2:17, 2:19, 2:20, 2:22, 2:47, 2:63, 2:64, 2:65, 2:66, 2:68, priest, husband of Elizabeth, and father of John the Baptist